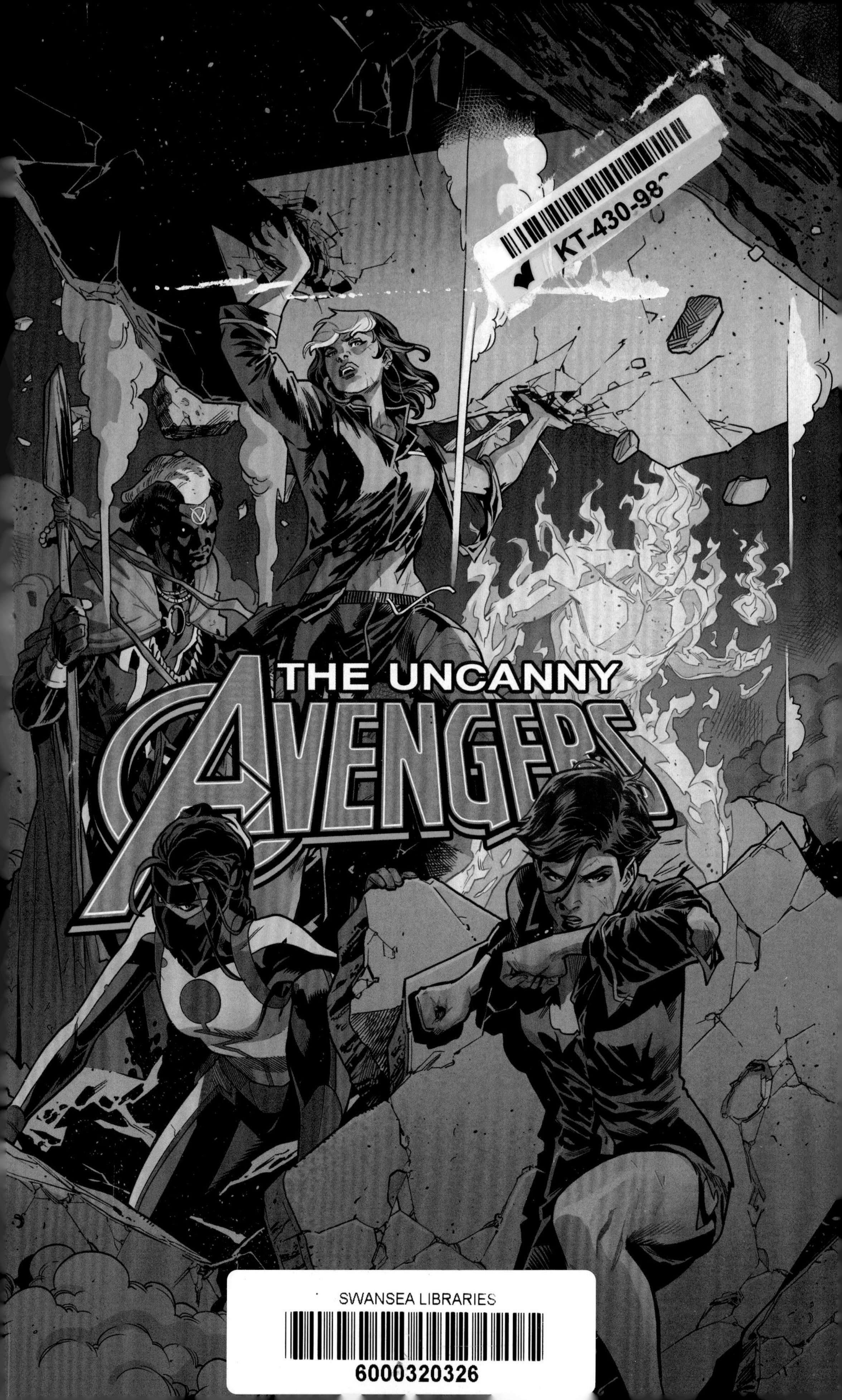
THE UNCANNY
AVENGERS

THE WORLD IS STILL RECOVERING FROM THE HYDRA TAKEOVER ORCHESTRATED BY AN EVIL VERSION OF STEVE ROGERS--AND SO IS THE UNITY SQUAD. WHEN MOST OF THE TEAM WAS TRAPPED INSIDE THE DARKFORCE DIMENSION, ONLY QUICKSILVER WAS ABLE TO RESPOND TO THE INITIAL BATTLE AGAINST HYDRA IN WASHINGTON, D.C.--ARRIVING JUST IN TIME TO SEE A POWERFUL DEMON TAKE HOLD OF HIS SISTER, THE SCARLET WITCH.

THE POSSESSED WANDA FOUGHT RUTHLESSLY FOR CAPTAIN AMERICA'S CAUSE DURING HYDRA'S REIGN, BUT NOW THAT THE EMPIRE HAS FALLEN, LIFE HAS BEGUN TO RETURN TO NORMAL. CAN THE SAME BE SAID FOR THE MAXIMOFFS?

UNCANNY AVENGERS: UNITY VOL. 5 — STARS AND GARTERS. Contains material originally published in magazine form as UNCANNY AVENGERS #26-30. First printing 2018. ISBN 978-1-302-90645-0. Published by MARVEL WORLDWIDE, INC., a subsidiary of MARVEL ENTERTAINMENT, LLC. OFFICE OF PUBLICATION: 135 West 50th Street, New York, NY 10020. Copyright © 2018 MARVEL No similarity between any of the names, characters, persons, and/or institutions in this magazine with those of any living or dead person or institution is intended, and any such similarity which may exist is purely coincidental. **Printed in Canada.** DAN BUCKLEY, President, Marvel Entertainment; JOE QUESADA, Chief Creative Officer; TOM BREVOORT, SVP of Publishing; DAVID BOGART, SVP of Business Affairs & Operations, Publishing & Partnership; DAVID GABRIEL, SVP of Sales & Marketing, Publishing; JEFF YOUNGQUIST, VP of Production & Special Projects; DAN CARR, Executive Director of Publishing Technology; ALEX MORALES, Director of Publishing Operations; SUSAN CRESPI, Production Manager; STAN LEE, Chairman Emeritus. For information regarding advertising in Marvel Comics or on Marvel.com, please contact Vit DeBellis, Custom Solutions & Integrated Advertising Manager, at vdebellis@marvel.com. For Marvel subscription inquiries, please call 888-511-5480.

THE UNCANNY AVENGERS
STARS AND GARTERS

JIM ZUB
WRITER

SEAN IZAAKSE WITH
JUANAN RAMÍREZ (#29)
ARTISTS

TAMRA BONVILLAIN
COLOR ARTIST

VC's CLAYTON COWLES
LETTERER

R.B. SILVA (#26-29) WITH
JESUS ABURTOV (#26-27),
EDGAR DELGADO (#28),
JAVA TARTAGLIA (#29)
AND **TERRY DODSON** &
RACHEL DODSON (#30)
COVER ART

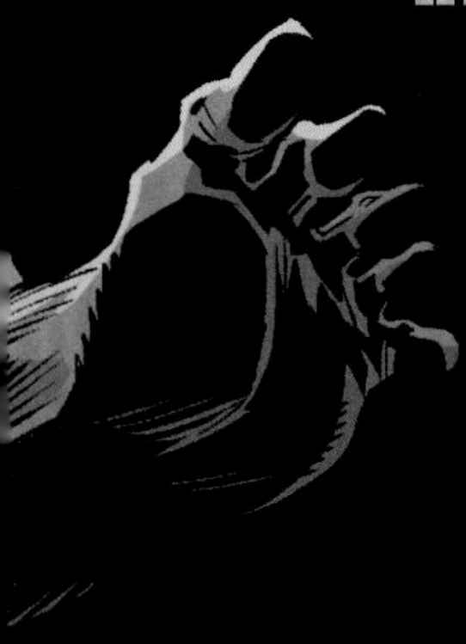

ALANNA SMITH
ASSISTANT EDITOR

TOM BREVOORT WITH
DANIEL KETCHUM
EDITORS

AVENGERS CREATED BY **STAN LEE** & **JACK KIRBY**

COLLECTION EDITOR: **JENNIFER GRÜNWALD**
ASSISTANT EDITOR: **CAITLIN O'CONNELL**
ASSOCIATE MANAGING EDITOR: **KATERI WOODY**
EDITOR, SPECIAL PROJECTS: **MARK D. BEAZLEY**
VP PRODUCTION & SPECIAL PROJECTS: **JEFF YOUNGQUIST**
SVP PRINT, SALES & MARKETING: **DAVID GABRIEL**
BOOK DESIGNER: **JAY BOWEN**

EDITOR IN CHIEF: **C.B. CEBULSKI**
CHIEF CREATIVE OFFICER: **JOE QUESADA**
PRESIDENT: **DAN BUCKLEY**
EXECUTIVE PRODUCER: **ALAN FINE**

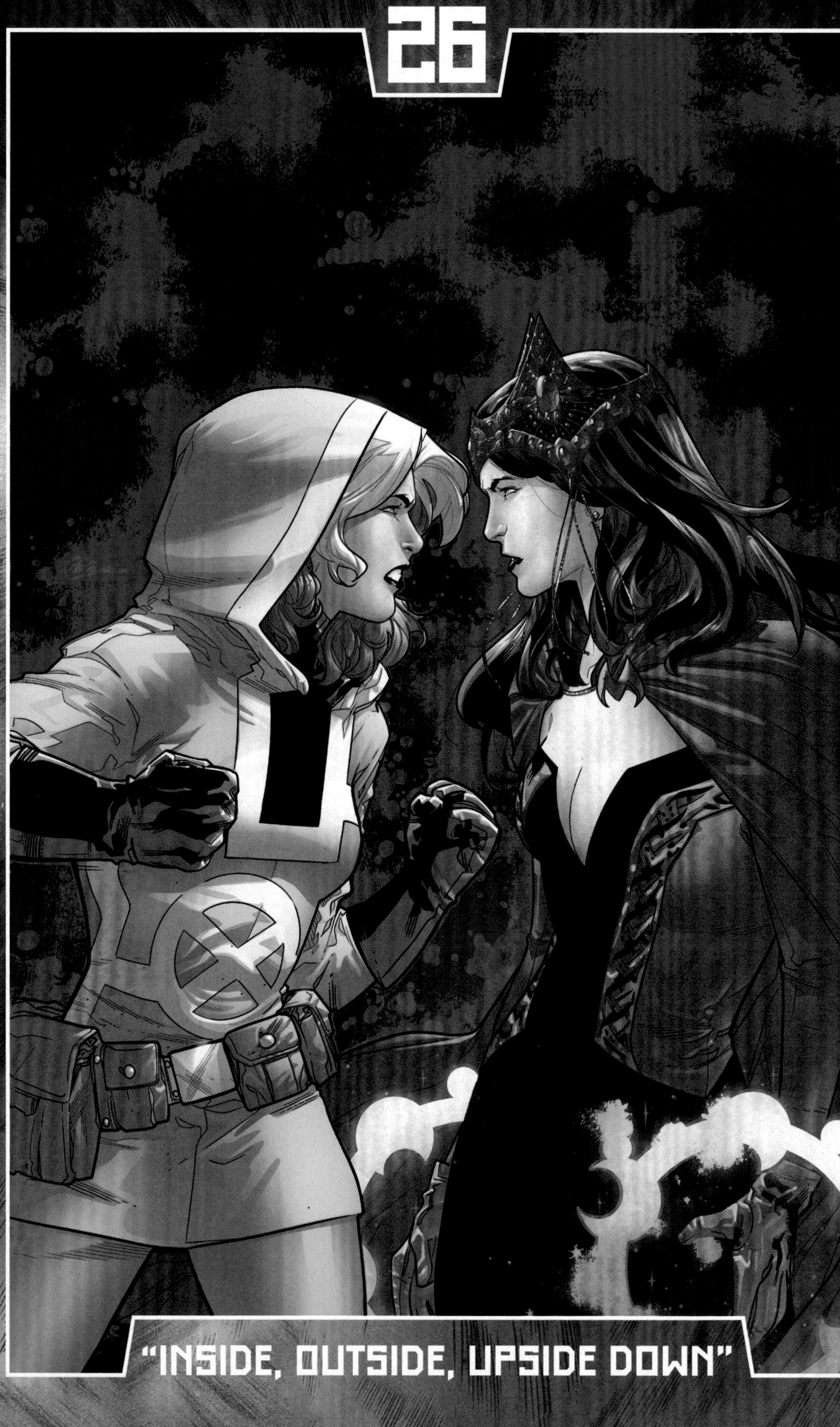
26
"INSIDE, OUTSIDE, UPSIDE DOWN"

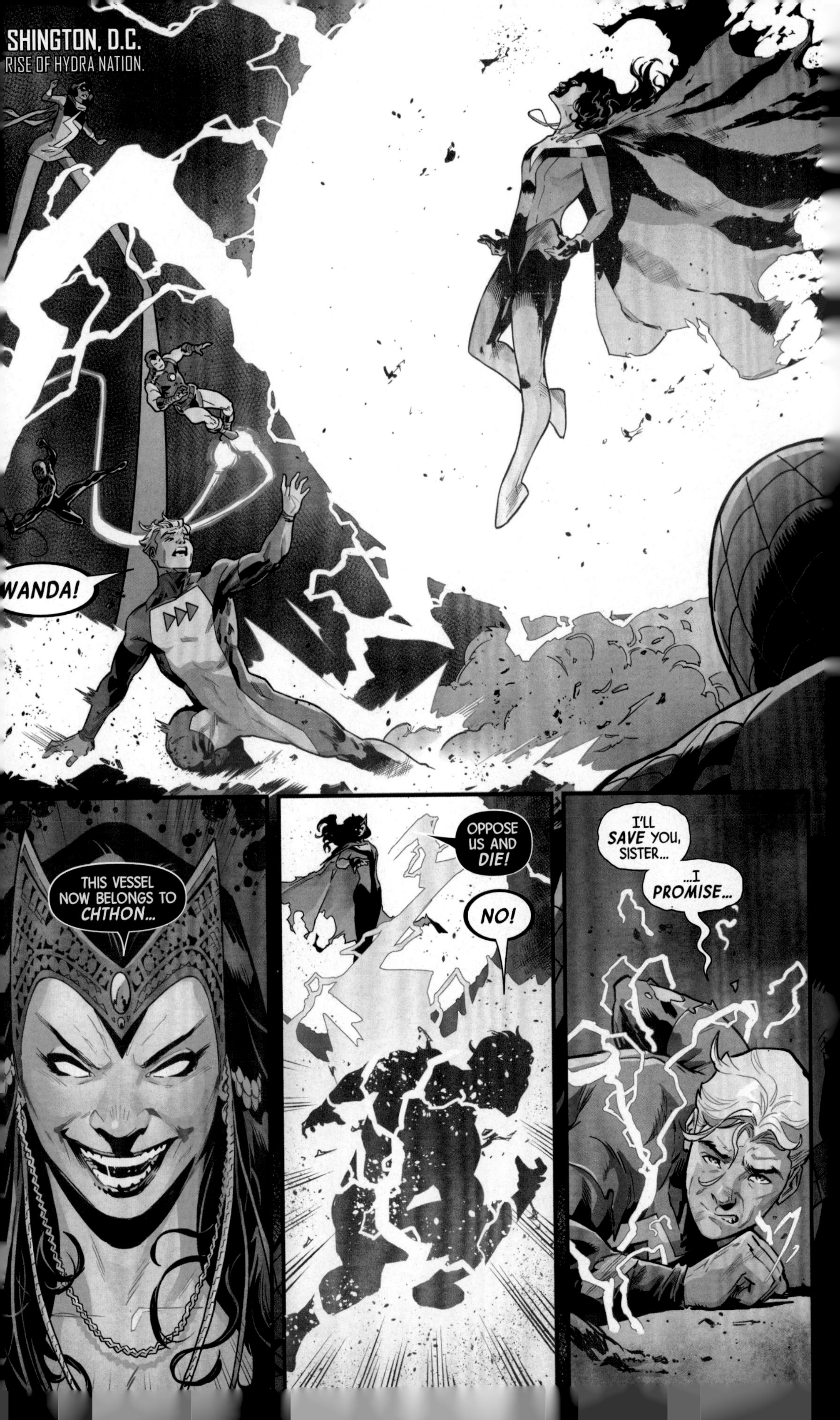
SHINGTON, D.C.
RISE OF HYDRA NATION.
WANDA!
THIS VESSEL NOW BELONGS TO CHTHON...
OPPOSE US AND DIE!
NO!
I'LL SAVE YOU, SISTER...
...I PROMISE...

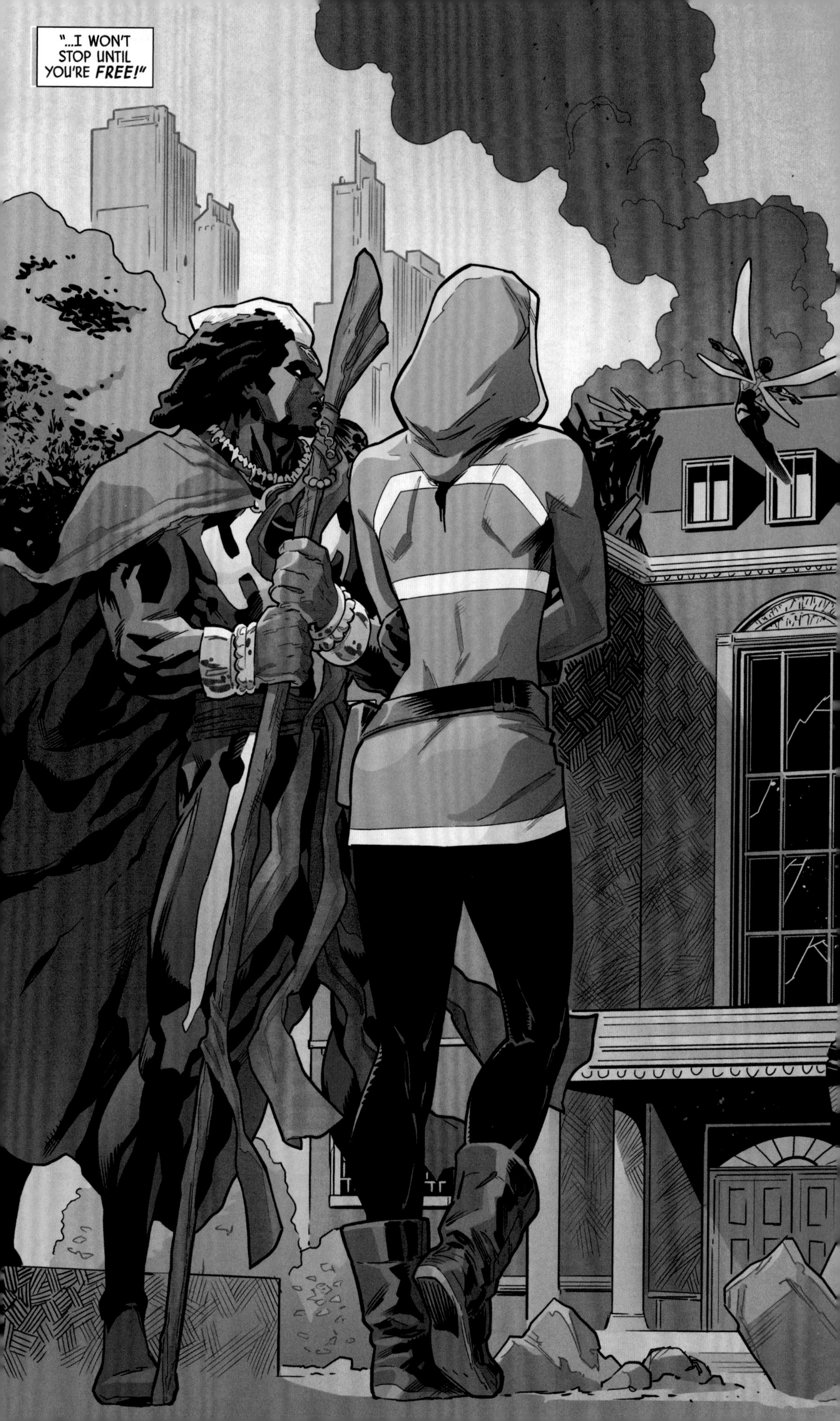
"...I WON'T STOP UNTIL YOU'RE FREE!"

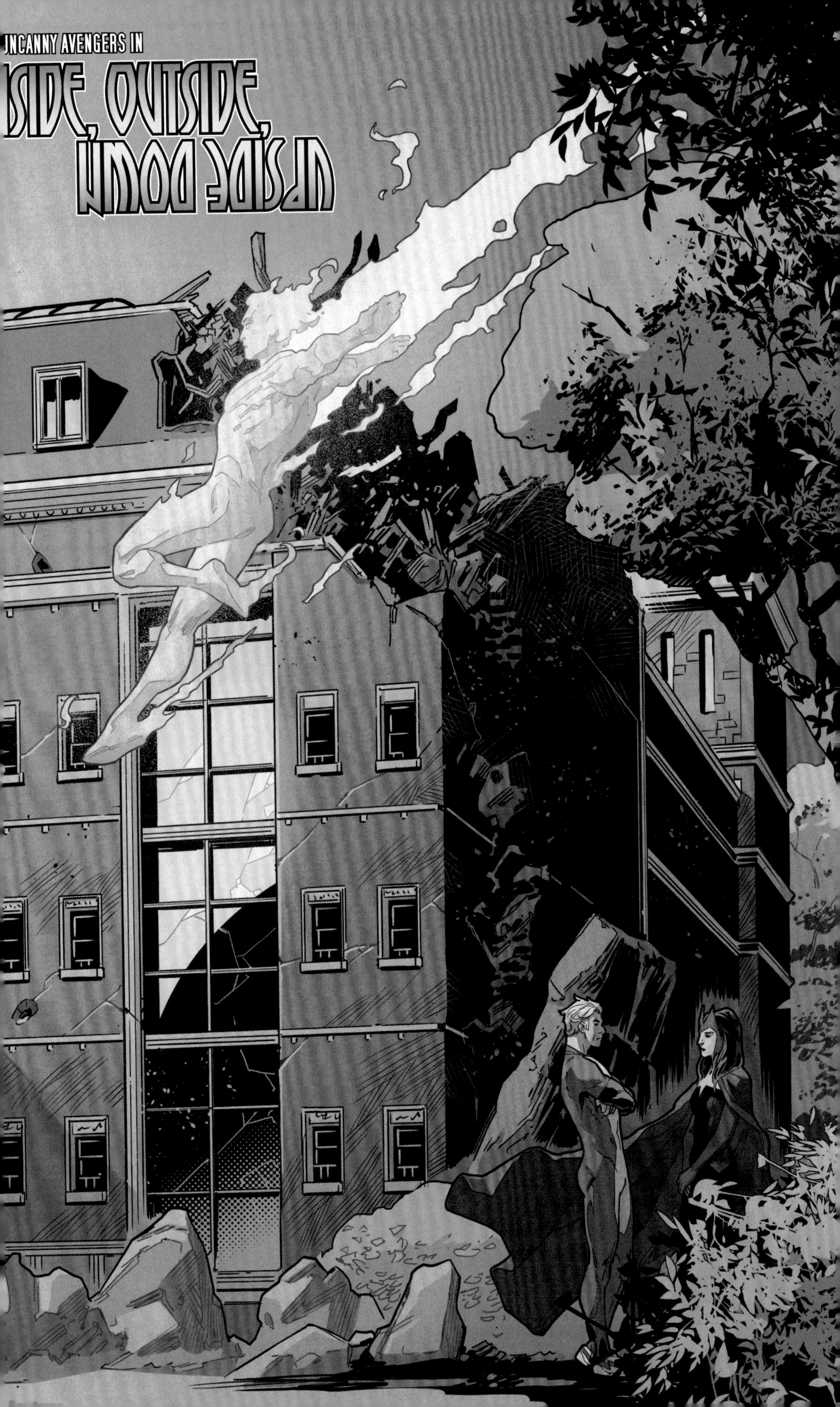
UNCANNY AVENGERS IN
SIDE, OUTSIDE,
UPSIDE DOWN

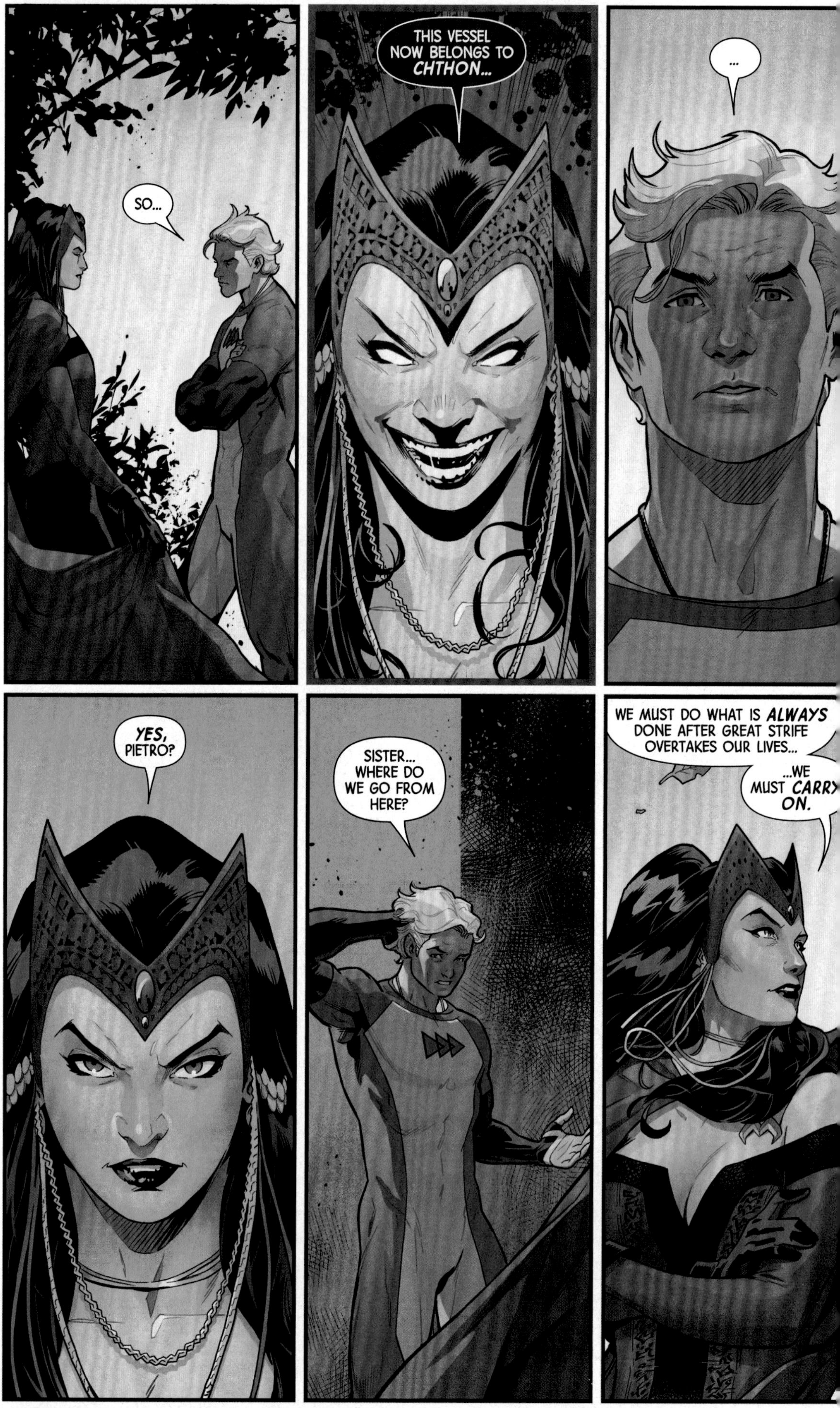
SO...
THIS VESSEL NOW BELONGS TO CHTHON...
...
YES, PIETRO?
SISTER... WHERE DO WE GO FROM HERE?
WE MUST DO WHAT IS ALWAYS DONE AFTER GREAT STRIFE OVERTAKES OUR LIVES...
...WE MUST CARRY ON.

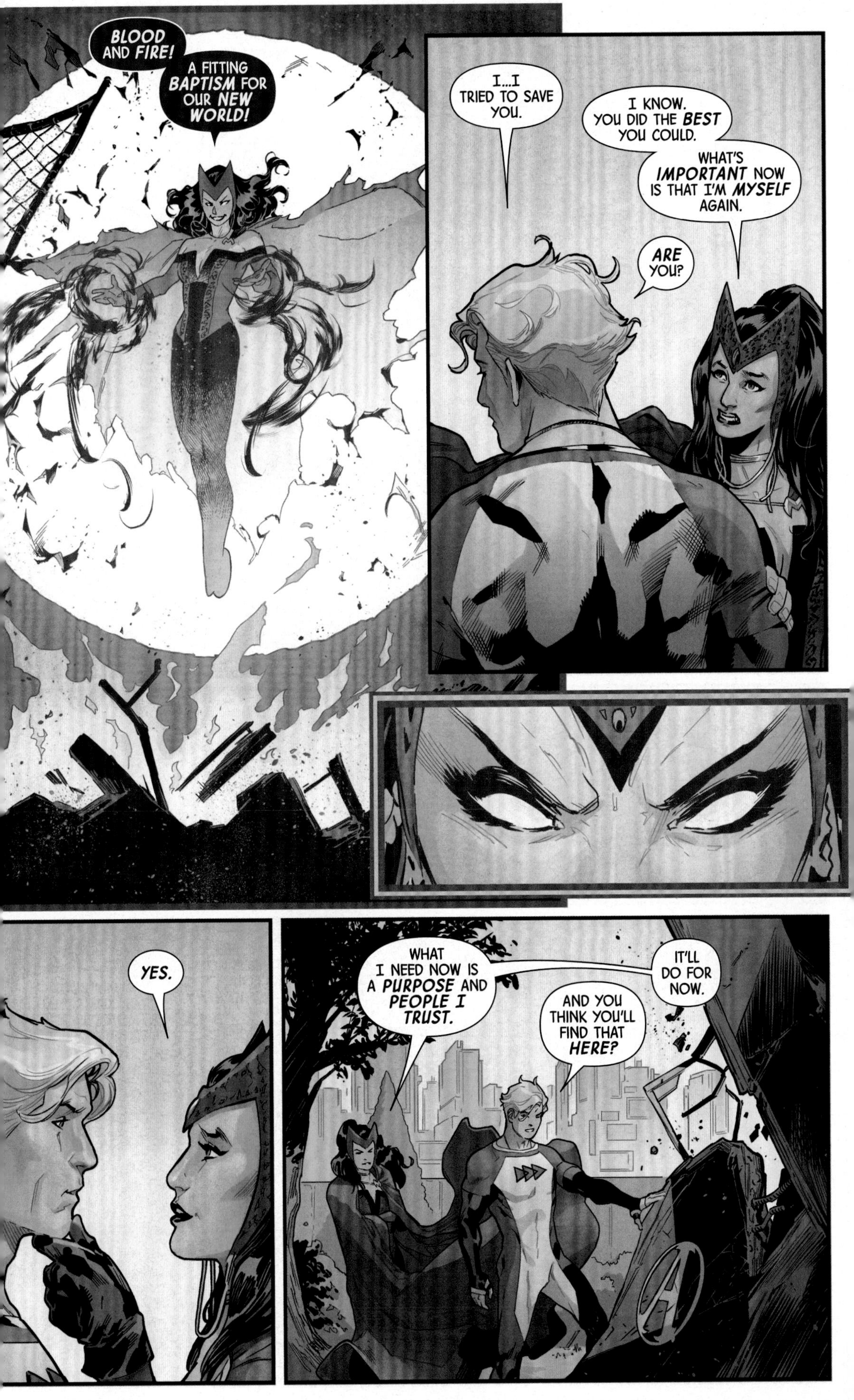
BLOOD AND FIRE!
A FITTING BAPTISM FOR OUR NEW WORLD!
I...I TRIED TO SAVE YOU.
I KNOW. YOU DID THE BEST YOU COULD.
WHAT'S IMPORTANT NOW IS THAT I'M MYSELF AGAIN.
ARE YOU?
YES.
WHAT I NEED NOW IS A PURPOSE AND PEOPLE I TRUST.
AND YOU THINK YOU'LL FIND THAT HERE?
IT'LL DO FOR NOW.

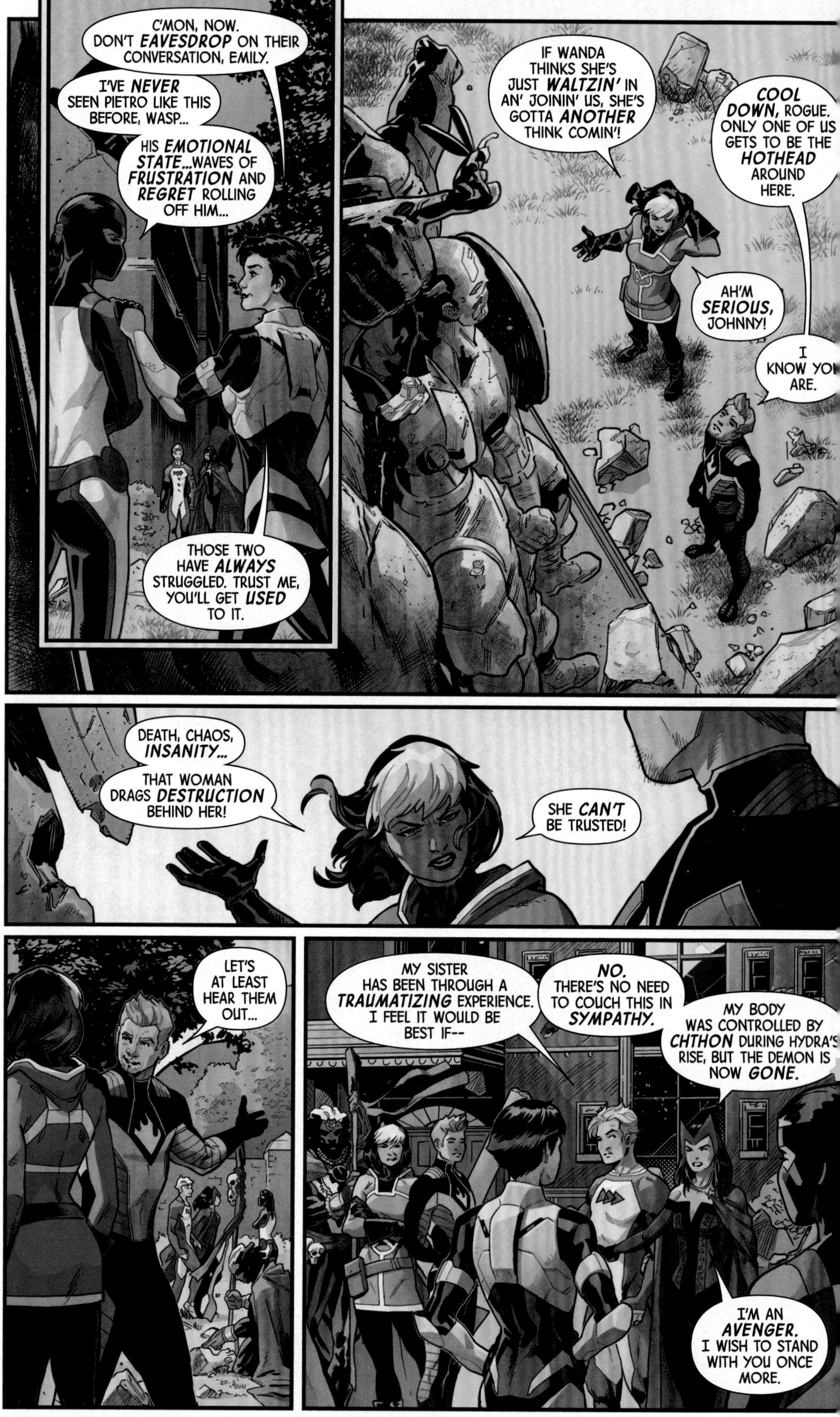
C'MON, NOW. DON'T EAVESDROP ON THEIR CONVERSATION, EMILY.
I'VE NEVER SEEN PIETRO LIKE THIS BEFORE, WASP...
HIS EMOTIONAL STATE...WAVES OF FRUSTRATION AND REGRET ROLLING OFF HIM...
THOSE TWO HAVE ALWAYS STRUGGLED. TRUST ME, YOU'LL GET USED TO IT.
IF WANDA THINKS SHE'S JUST WALTZIN' IN AN' JOININ' US, SHE'S GOTTA ANOTHER THINK COMIN'!
COOL DOWN, ROGUE. ONLY ONE OF US GETS TO BE THE HOTHEAD AROUND HERE.
AH'M SERIOUS, JOHNNY!
I KNOW YO ARE.
DEATH, CHAOS, INSANITY...
THAT WOMAN DRAGS DESTRUCTION BEHIND HER!
SHE CAN'T BE TRUSTED!
LET'S AT LEAST HEAR THEM OUT...
MY SISTER HAS BEEN THROUGH A TRAUMATIZING EXPERIENCE. I FEEL IT WOULD BE BEST IF--
NO. THERE'S NO NEED TO COUCH THIS IN SYMPATHY.
MY BODY WAS CONTROLLED BY CHTHON DURING HYDRA'S RISE, BUT THE DEMON IS NOW GONE.
I'M AN AVENGER. I WISH TO STAND WITH YOU ONCE MORE.

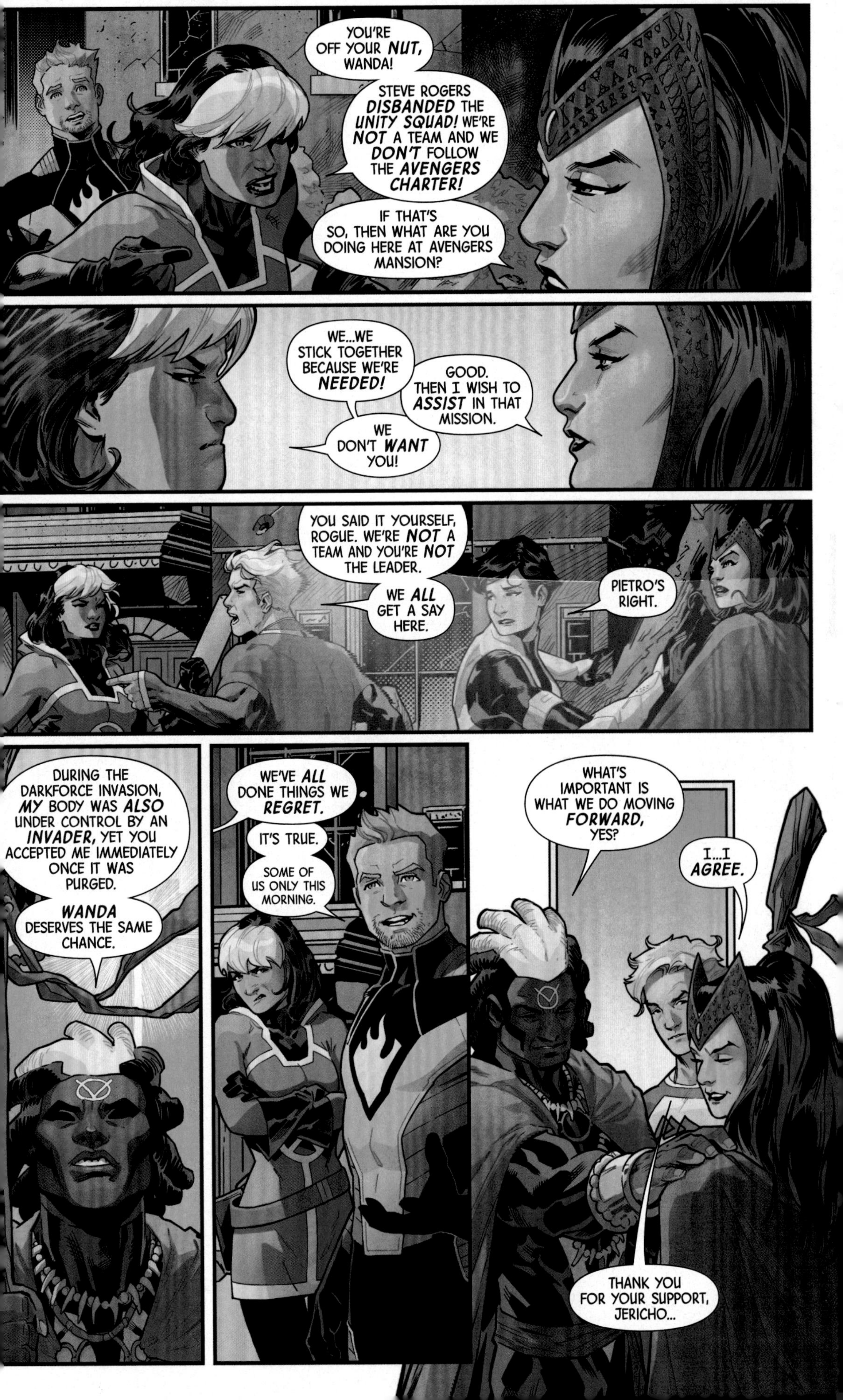

YOU'RE OFF YOUR NUT, WANDA!
STEVE ROGERS DISBANDED THE UNITY SQUAD! WE'RE NOT A TEAM AND WE DON'T FOLLOW THE AVENGERS CHARTER!
IF THAT'S SO, THEN WHAT ARE YOU DOING HERE AT AVENGERS MANSION?
WE...WE STICK TOGETHER BECAUSE WE'RE NEEDED!
GOOD. THEN I WISH TO ASSIST IN THAT MISSION.
WE DON'T WANT YOU!
YOU SAID IT YOURSELF, ROGUE. WE'RE NOT A TEAM AND YOU'RE NOT THE LEADER.
WE ALL GET A SAY HERE.
PIETRO'S RIGHT.
DURING THE DARKFORCE INVASION, MY BODY WAS ALSO UNDER CONTROL BY AN INVADER, YET YOU ACCEPTED ME IMMEDIATELY ONCE IT WAS PURGED.
WANDA DESERVES THE SAME CHANCE.
WE'VE ALL DONE THINGS WE REGRET.
IT'S TRUE.
SOME OF US ONLY THIS MORNING.
WHAT'S IMPORTANT IS WHAT WE DO MOVING FORWARD, YES?
I...I AGREE.
THANK YOU FOR YOUR SUPPORT, JERICHO...

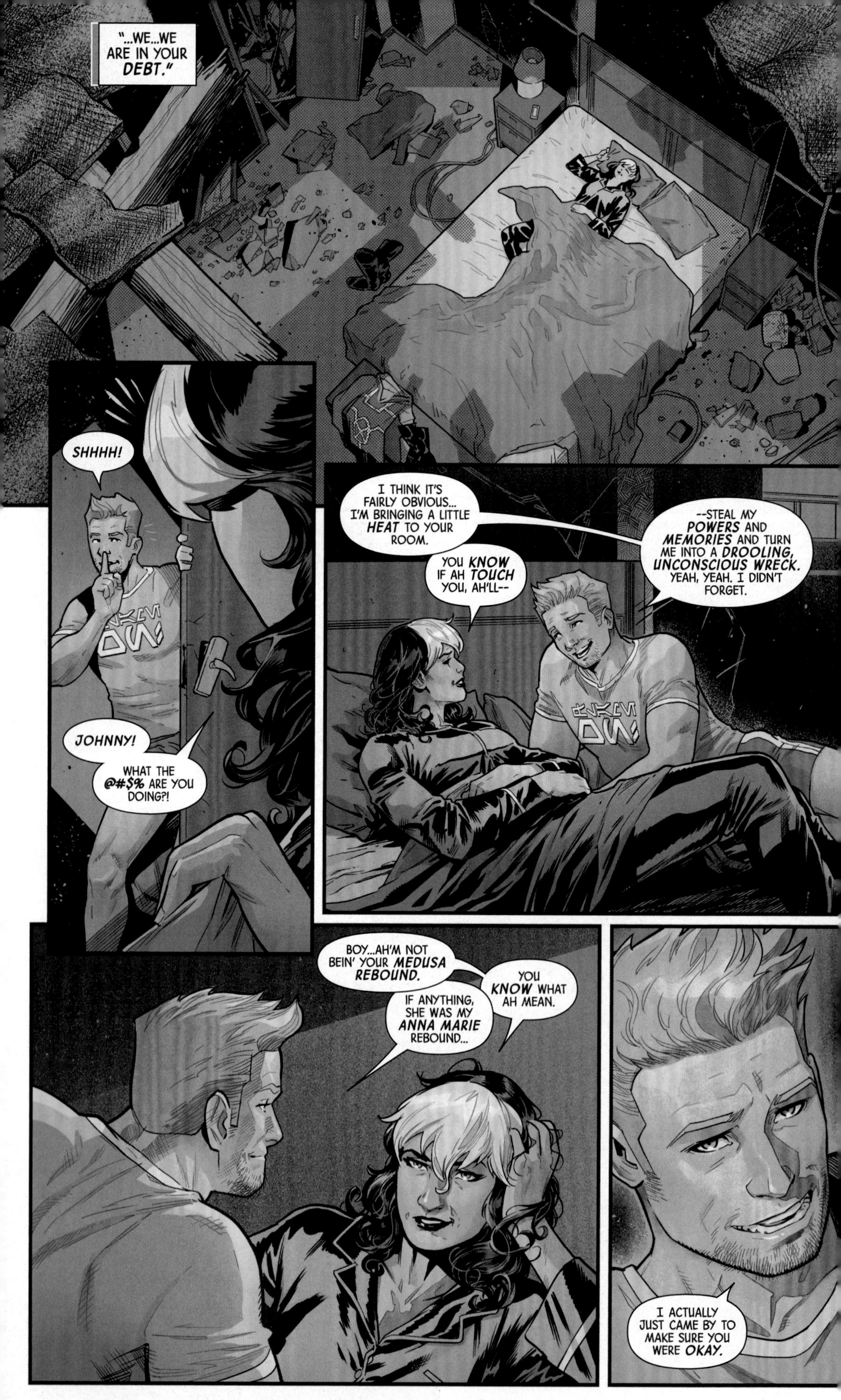
"...WE...WE ARE IN YOUR DEBT."
SHHHH!
JOHNNY!
WHAT THE @#$% ARE YOU DOING?!
I THINK IT'S FAIRLY OBVIOUS... I'M BRINGING A LITTLE HEAT TO YOUR ROOM.
YOU KNOW IF AH TOUCH YOU, AH'LL--
--STEAL MY POWERS AND MEMORIES AND TURN ME INTO A DROOLING, UNCONSCIOUS WRECK. YEAH, YEAH. I DIDN'T FORGET.
BOY...AH'M NOT BEIN' YOUR MEDUSA REBOUND.
IF ANYTHING, SHE WAS MY ANNA MARIE REBOUND...
YOU KNOW WHAT AH MEAN.
I ACTUALLY JUST CAME BY TO MAKE SURE YOU WERE OKAY.

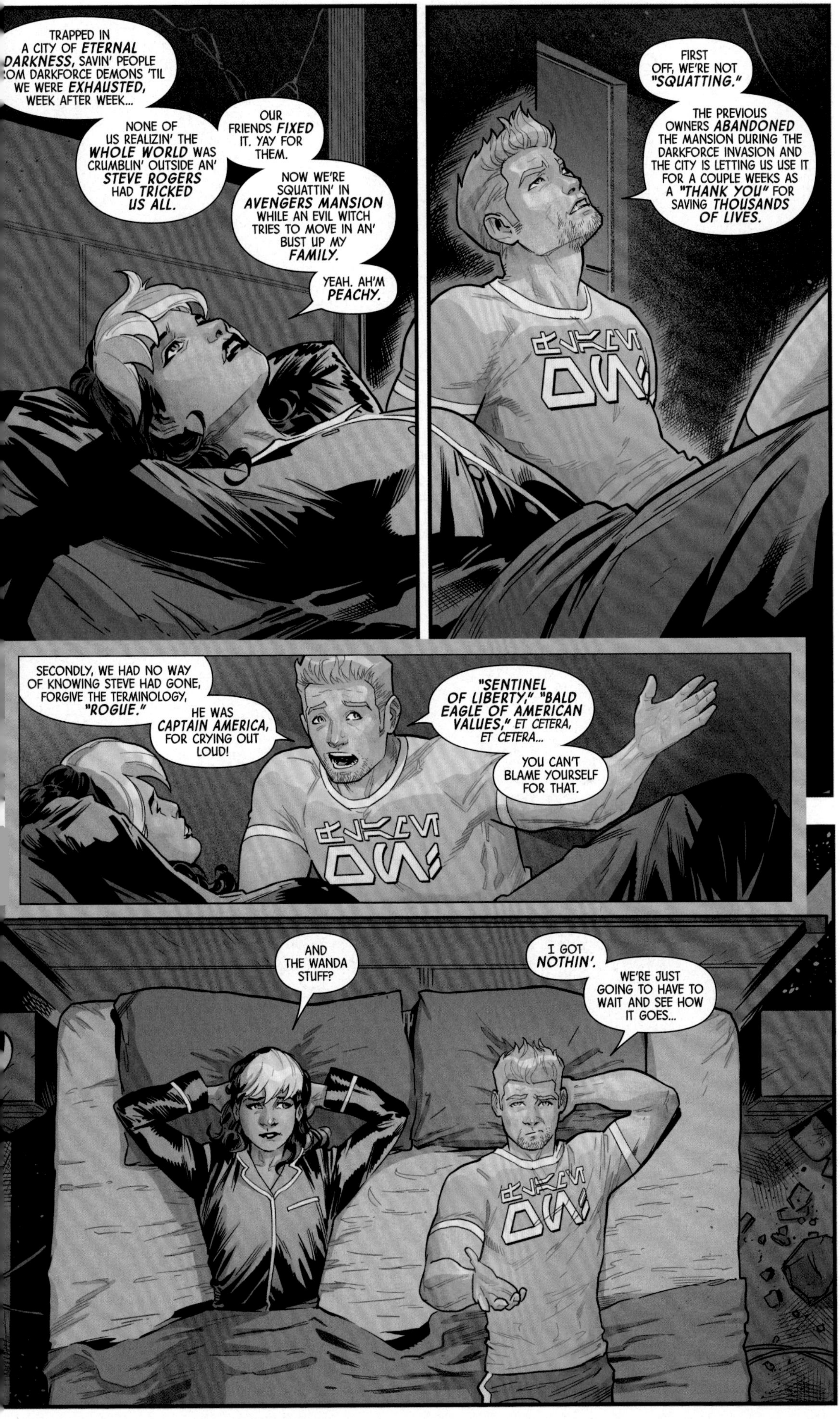
TRAPPED IN A CITY OF ETERNAL DARKNESS, SAVIN' PEOPLE ROM DARKFORCE DEMONS 'TIL WE WERE EXHAUSTED, WEEK AFTER WEEK...
NONE OF US REALIZIN' THE WHOLE WORLD WAS CRUMBLIN' OUTSIDE AN' STEVE ROGERS HAD TRICKED US ALL.
OUR FRIENDS FIXED IT. YAY FOR THEM.
NOW WE'RE SQUATTIN' IN AVENGERS MANSION WHILE AN EVIL WITCH TRIES TO MOVE IN AN' BUST UP MY FAMILY.
YEAH. AH'M PEACHY.
FIRST OFF, WE'RE NOT "SQUATTING."
THE PREVIOUS OWNERS ABANDONED THE MANSION DURING THE DARKFORCE INVASION AND THE CITY IS LETTING US USE IT FOR A COUPLE WEEKS AS A "THANK YOU" FOR SAVING THOUSANDS OF LIVES.
SECONDLY, WE HAD NO WAY OF KNOWING STEVE HAD GONE, FORGIVE THE TERMINOLOGY, "ROGUE."
HE WAS CAPTAIN AMERICA, FOR CRYING OUT LOUD!
"SENTINEL OF LIBERTY," "BALD EAGLE OF AMERICAN VALUES," ET CETERA, ET CETERA...
YOU CAN'T BLAME YOURSELF FOR THAT.
AND THE WANDA STUFF?
I GOT NOTHIN'.
WE'RE JUST GOING TO HAVE TO WAIT AND SEE HOW IT GOES...

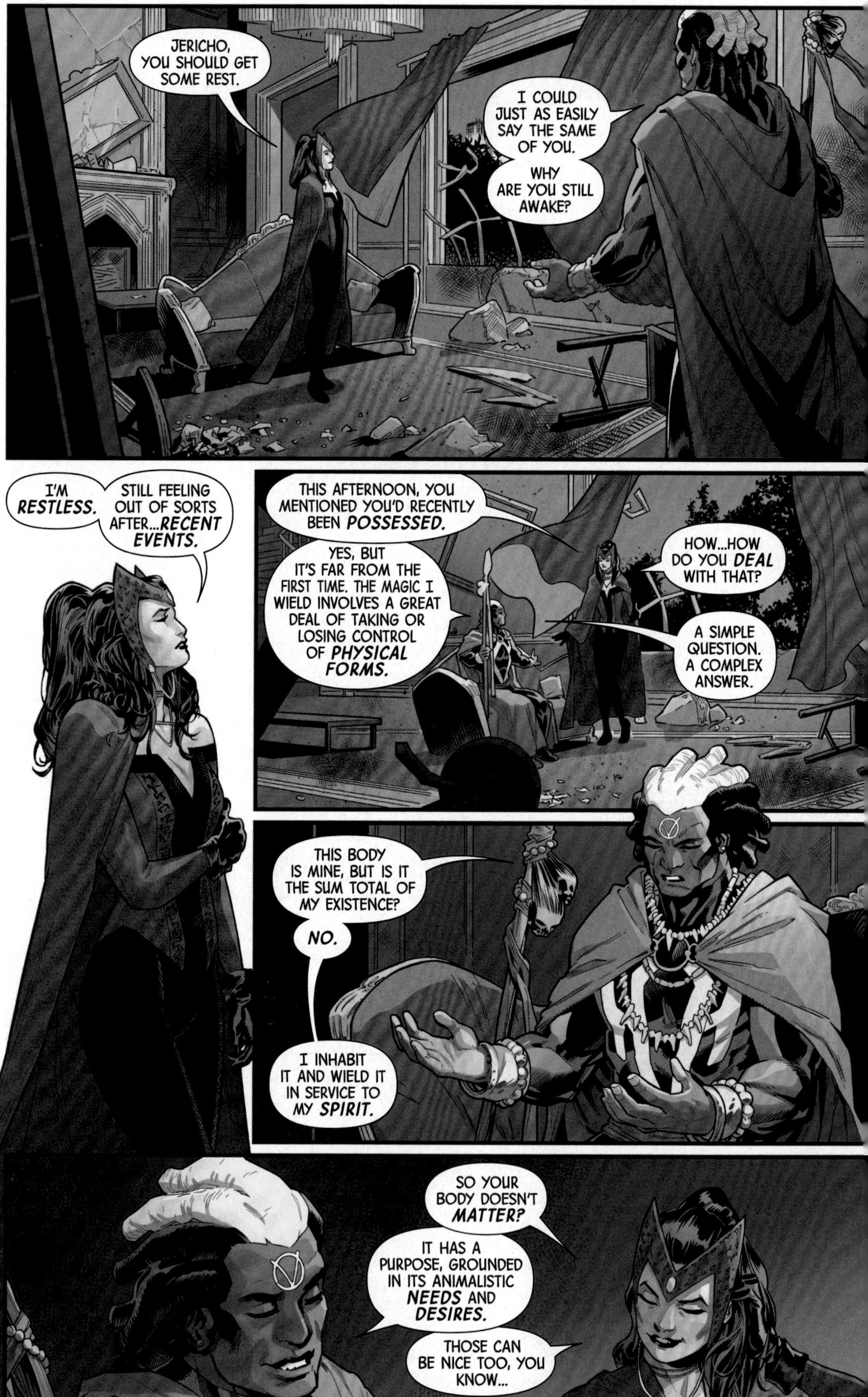

JERICHO, YOU SHOULD GET SOME REST.
I COULD JUST AS EASILY SAY THE SAME OF YOU.
WHY ARE YOU STILL AWAKE?
I'M *RESTLESS.*
STILL FEELING OUT OF SORTS AFTER...*RECENT EVENTS.*
THIS AFTERNOON, YOU MENTIONED YOU'D RECENTLY BEEN *POSSESSED.*
YES, BUT IT'S FAR FROM THE FIRST TIME. THE MAGIC I WIELD INVOLVES A GREAT DEAL OF TAKING OR LOSING CONTROL OF *PHYSICAL FORMS.*
HOW...HOW DO YOU *DEAL* WITH THAT?
A SIMPLE QUESTION. A COMPLEX ANSWER.
THIS BODY IS MINE, BUT IS IT THE SUM TOTAL OF MY EXISTENCE?
NO.
I INHABIT IT AND WIELD IT IN SERVICE TO MY *SPIRIT.*
SO YOUR BODY DOESN'T *MATTER?*
IT HAS A PURPOSE, GROUNDED IN ITS ANIMALISTIC *NEEDS* AND *DESIRES.*
THOSE CAN BE NICE TOO, YOU KNOW...
HEH.

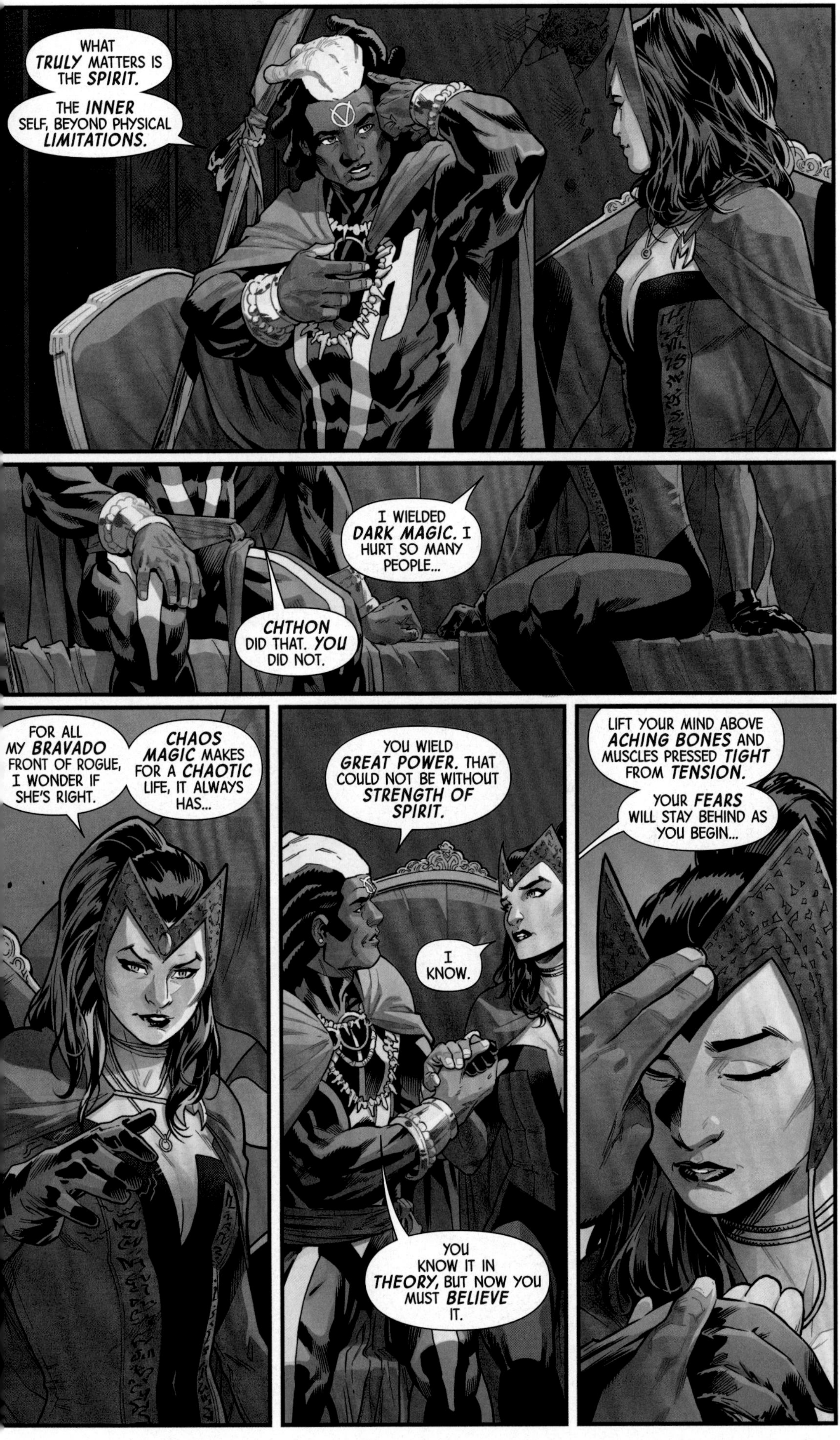
WHAT TRULY MATTERS IS THE SPIRIT.
THE INNER SELF, BEYOND PHYSICAL LIMITATIONS.
I WIELDED DARK MAGIC. I HURT SO MANY PEOPLE...
CHTHON DID THAT. YOU DID NOT.
FOR ALL MY BRAVADO FRONT OF ROGUE, I WONDER IF SHE'S RIGHT.
CHAOS MAGIC MAKES FOR A CHAOTIC LIFE, IT ALWAYS HAS...
YOU WIELD GREAT POWER. THAT COULD NOT BE WITHOUT STRENGTH OF SPIRIT.
I KNOW.
YOU KNOW IT IN THEORY, BUT NOW YOU MUST BELIEVE IT.
LIFT YOUR MIND ABOVE ACHING BONES AND MUSCLES PRESSED TIGHT FROM TENSION.
YOUR FEARS WILL STAY BEHIND AS YOU BEGIN...

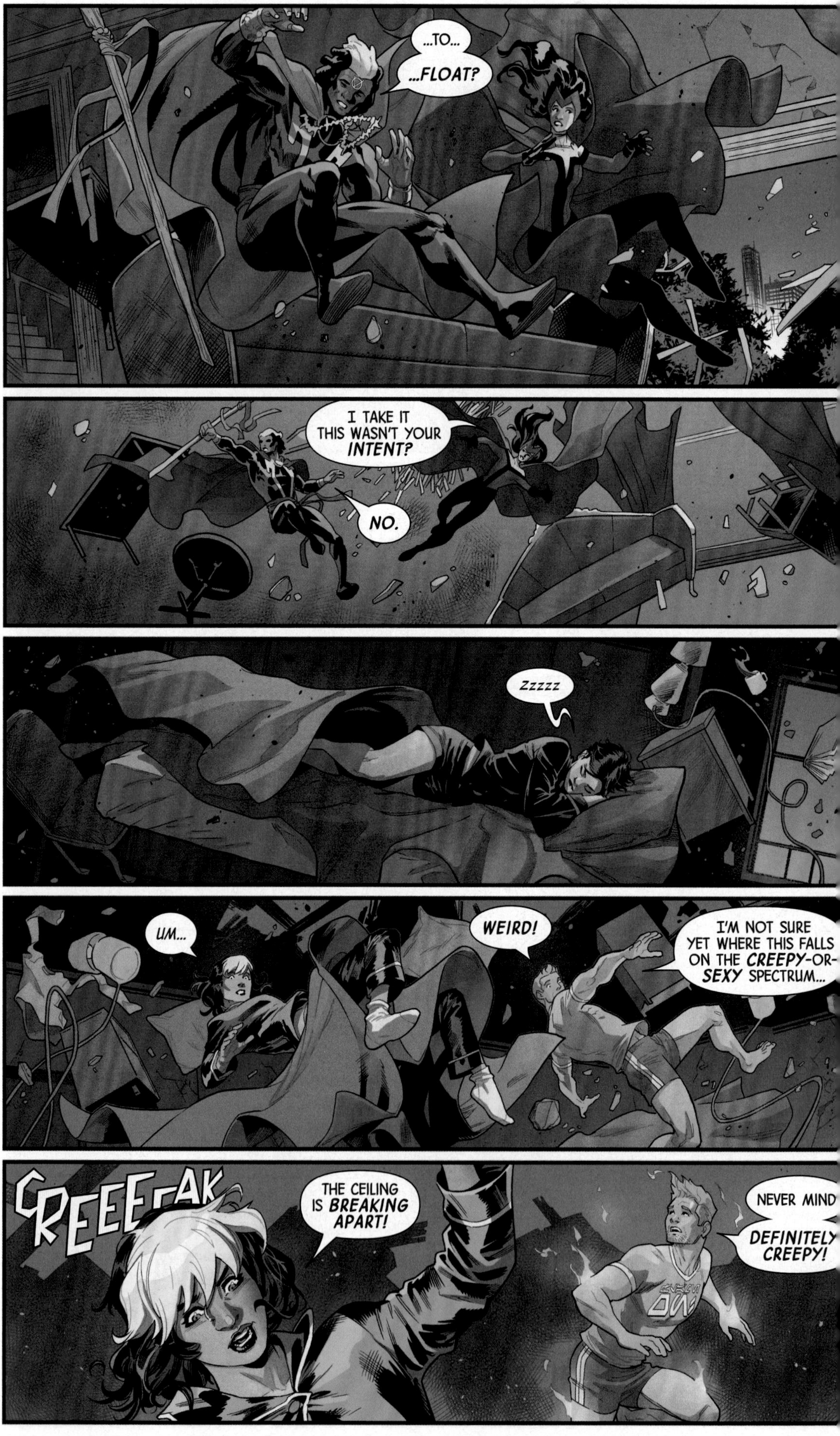
...TO...
...FLOAT?
I TAKE IT THIS WASN'T YOUR INTENT?
NO.
Zzzzz
UM...
WEIRD!
I'M NOT SURE YET WHERE THIS FALLS ON THE CREEPY-OR-SEXY SPECTRUM...
CREEEEAK
THE CEILING IS BREAKING APART!
NEVER MIND
DEFINITELY CREEPY!

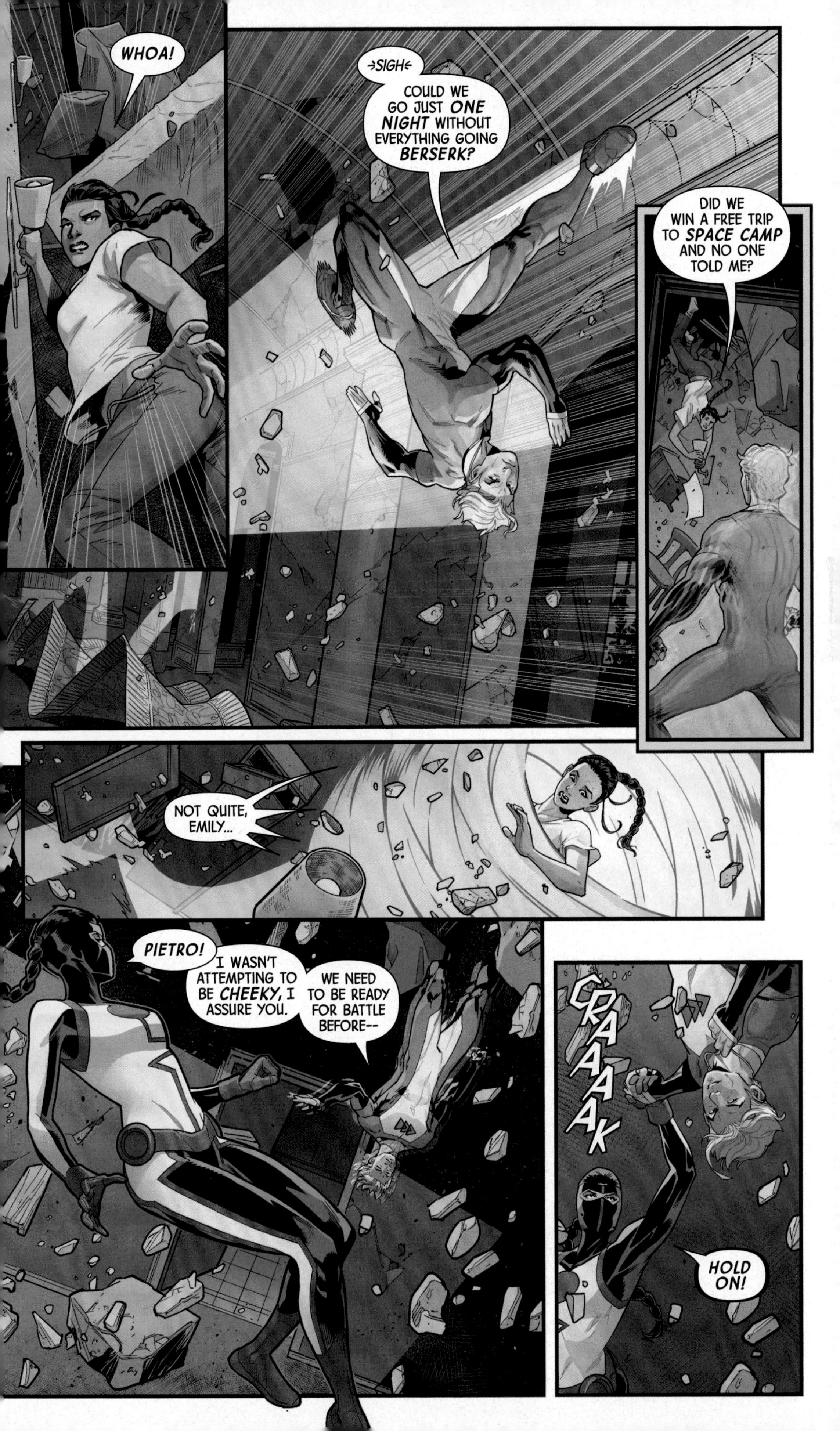
WHOA!
→SIGH←
COULD WE GO JUST ONE NIGHT WITHOUT EVERYTHING GOING BERSERK?
DID WE WIN A FREE TRIP TO SPACE CAMP AND NO ONE TOLD ME?
NOT QUITE, EMILY...
PIETRO!
I WASN'T ATTEMPTING TO BE CHEEKY, I ASSURE YOU.
WE NEED TO BE READY FOR BATTLE BEFORE--
CRAAAAK
HOLD ON!

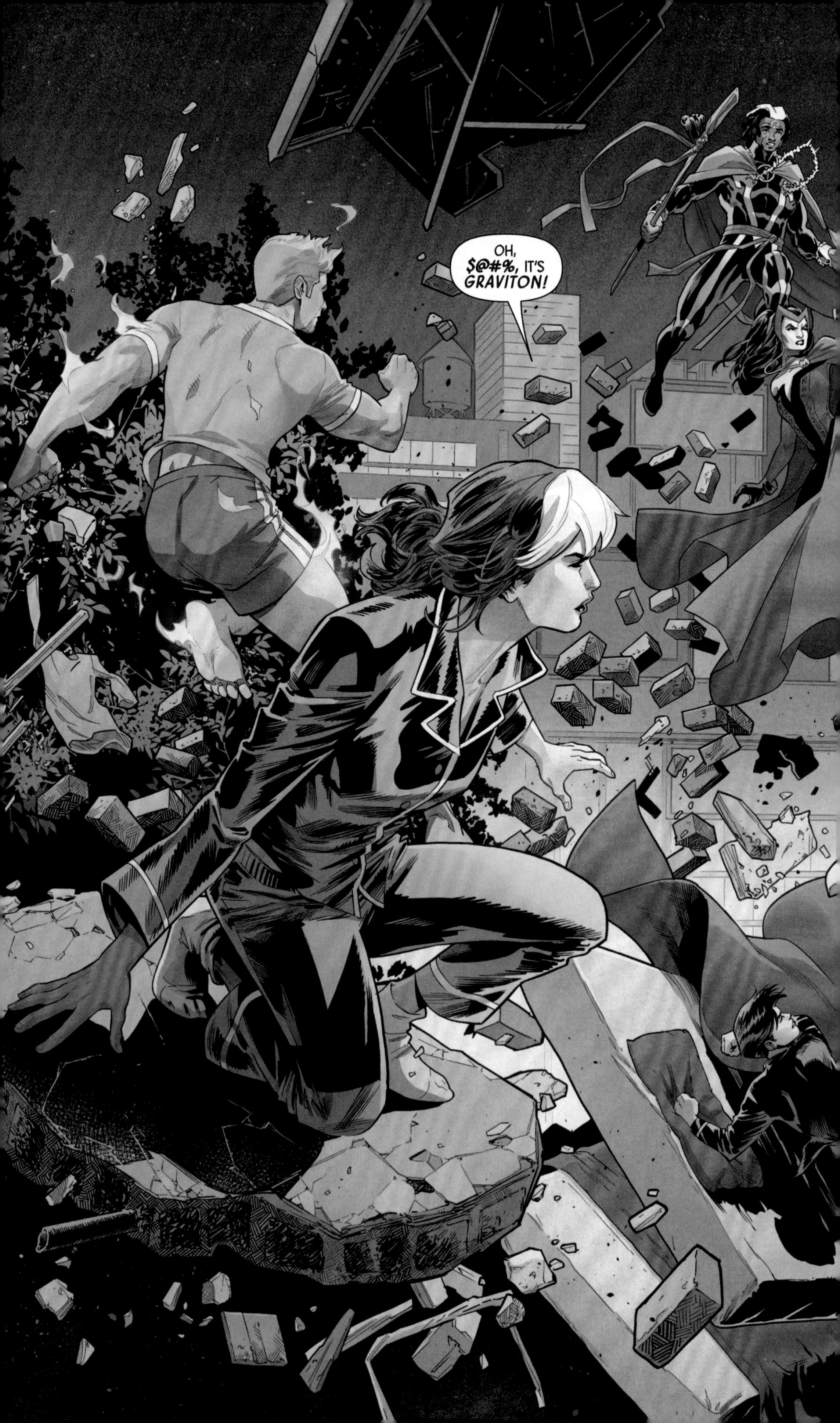
OH, $@#%, IT'S GRAVITON!

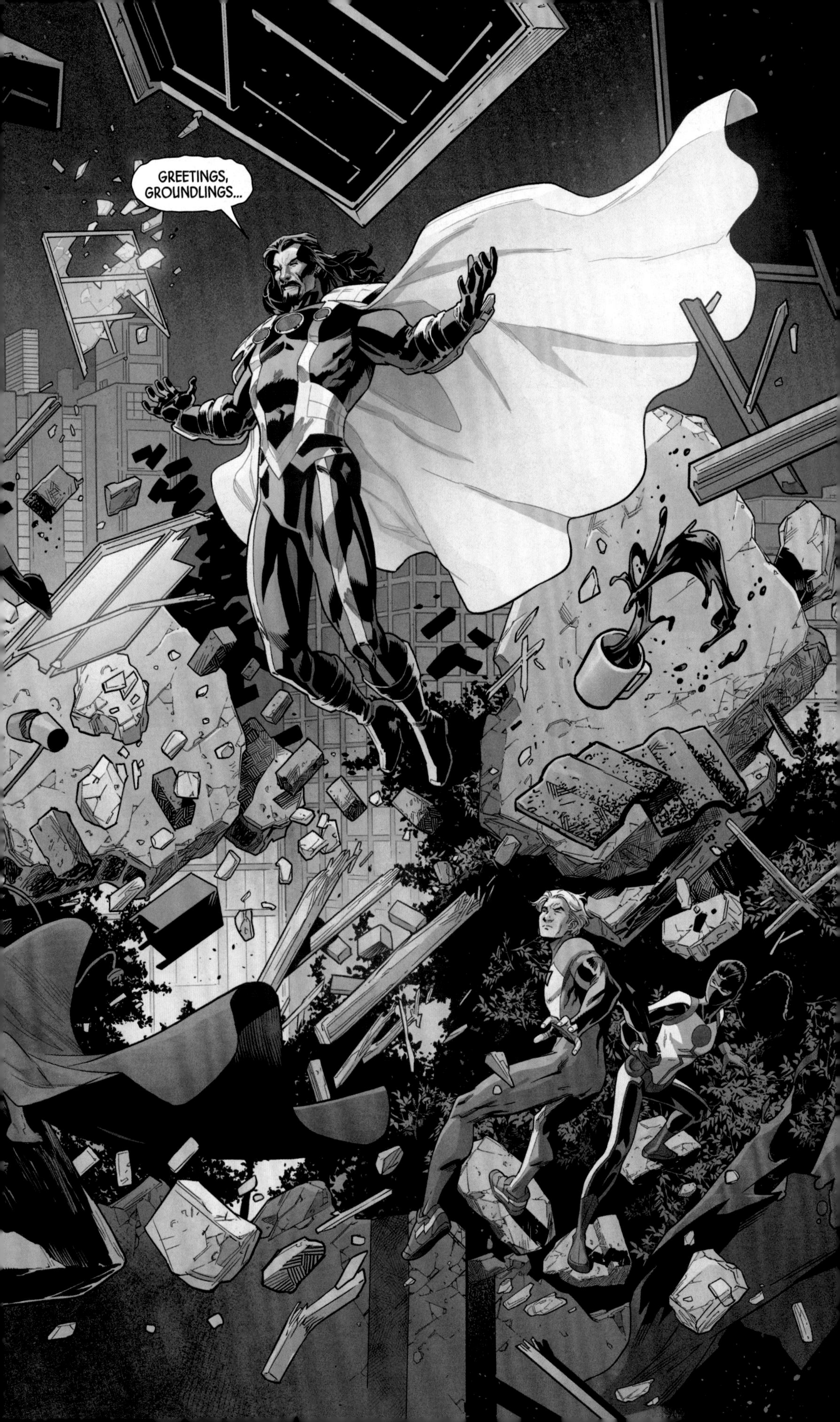
GREETINGS, GROUNDLINGS...

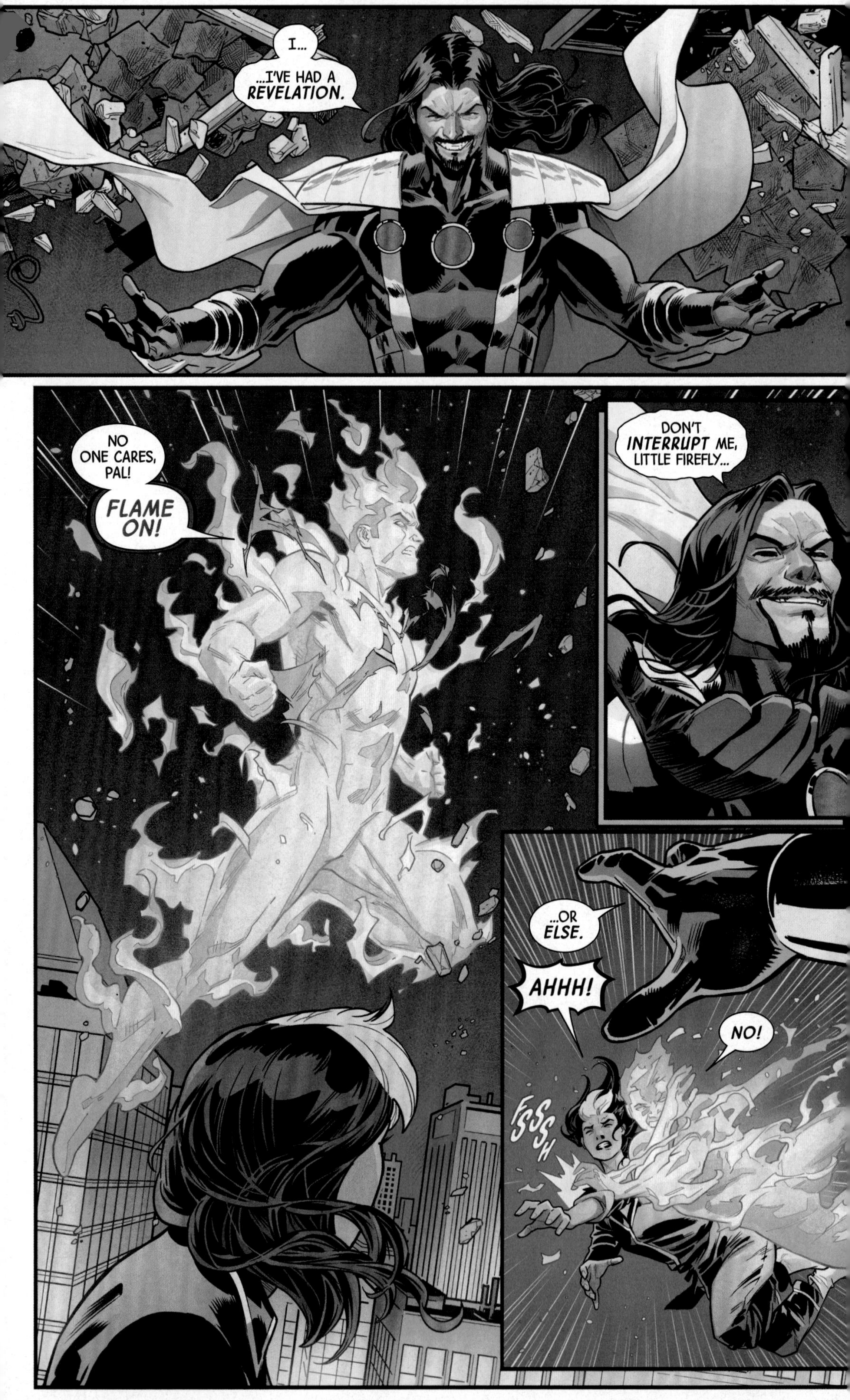
I...
...I'VE HAD A REVELATION.
NO ONE CARES, PAL!
FLAME ON!
DON'T INTERRUPT ME, LITTLE FIREFLY...
...OR ELSE.
AHHH!
NO!
FSSSH

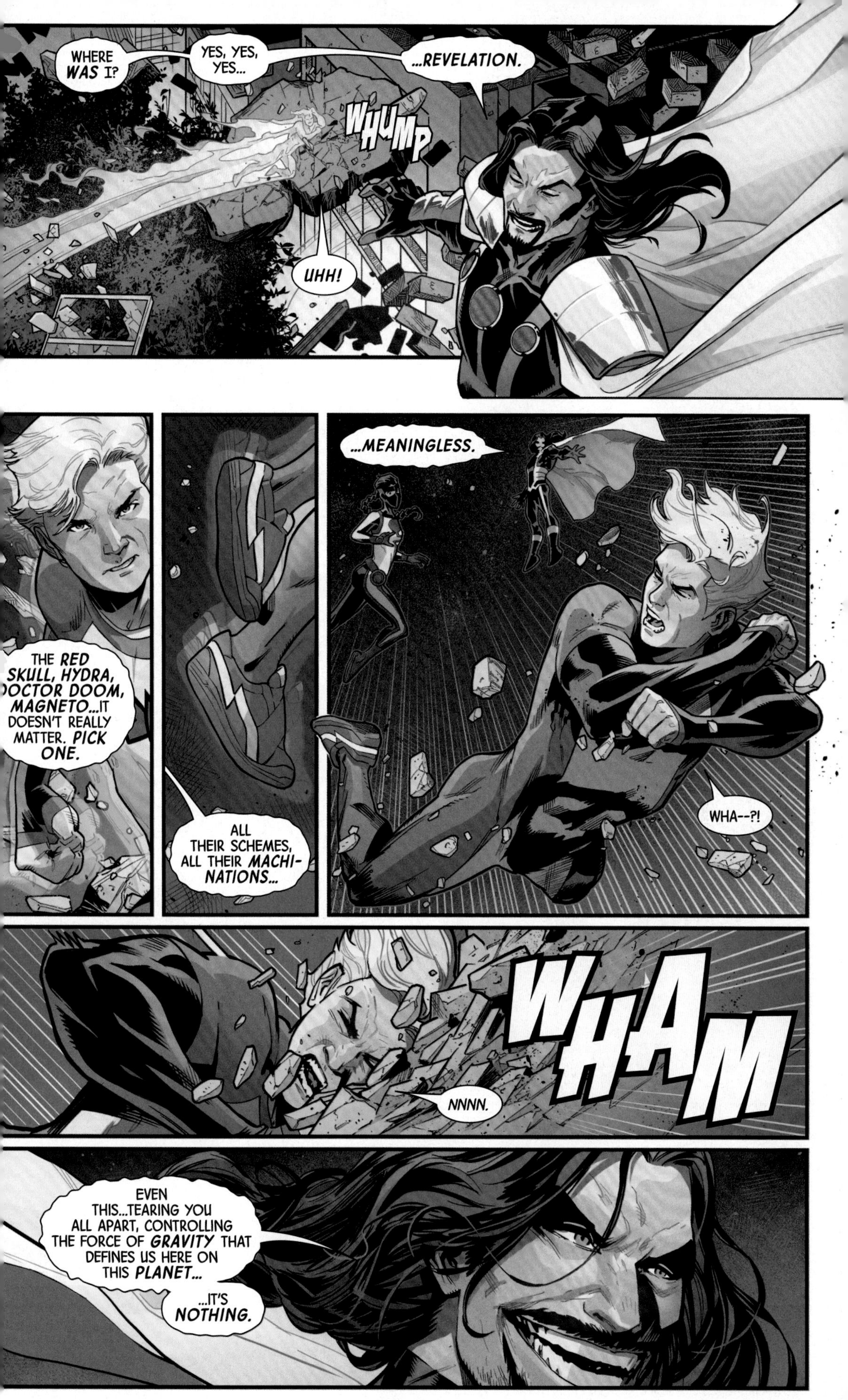
WHERE WAS I?
YES, YES, YES...
...REVELATION.
WHUMP
UHH!
THE RED SKULL, HYDRA, DOCTOR DOOM, MAGNETO...IT DOESN'T REALLY MATTER. PICK ONE.
ALL THEIR SCHEMES, ALL THEIR MACHI-NATIONS...
...MEANINGLESS.
WHA--?!
WHAM
NNNN.
EVEN THIS...TEARING YOU ALL APART, CONTROLLING THE FORCE OF GRAVITY THAT DEFINES US HERE ON THIS PLANET...
...IT'S NOTHING.

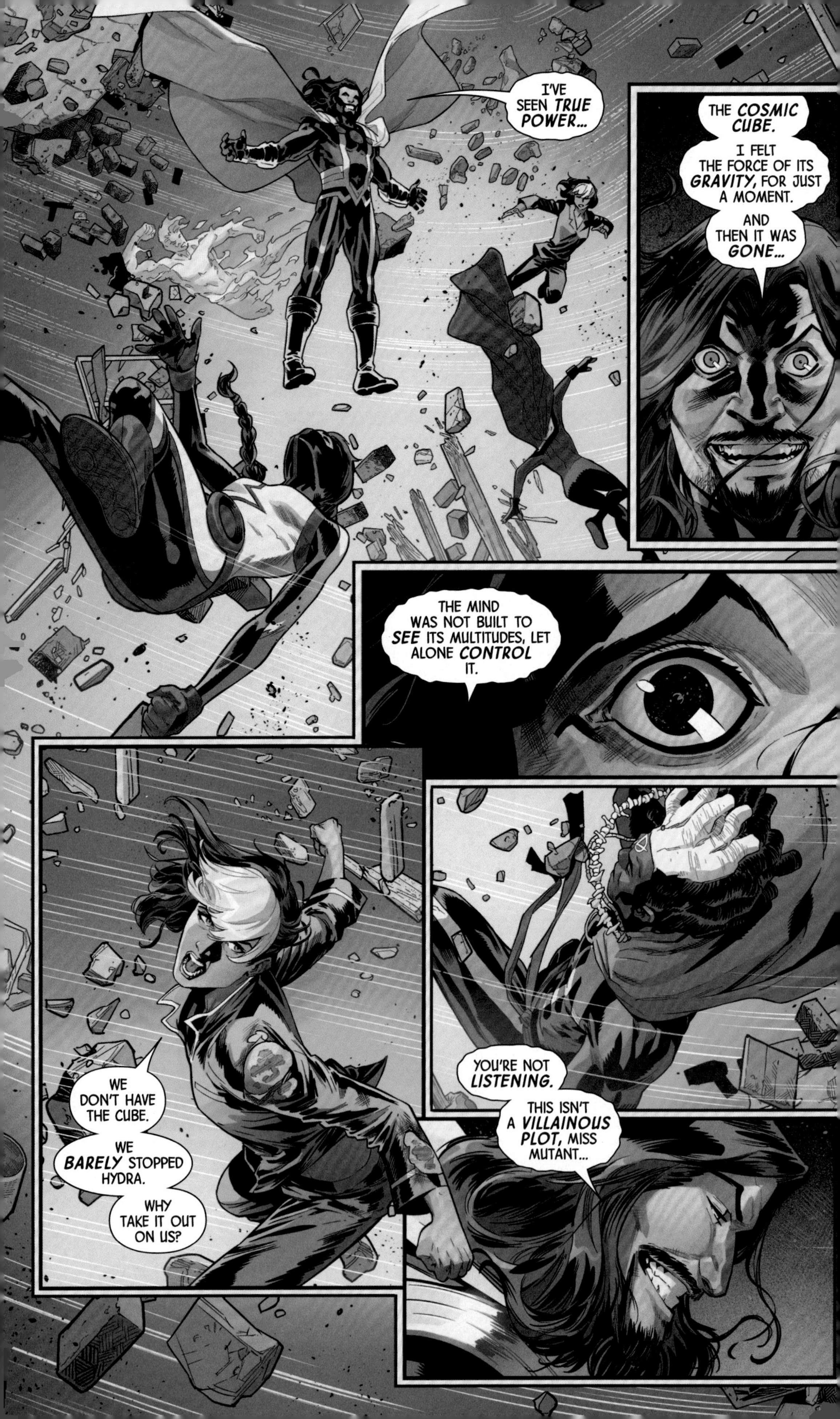
I'VE SEEN *TRUE POWER*...
THE *COSMIC CUBE.*
I FELT THE FORCE OF ITS *GRAVITY*, FOR JUST A MOMENT.
AND THEN IT WAS *GONE*...
THE MIND WAS NOT BUILT TO *SEE* ITS MULTITUDES, LET ALONE *CONTROL* IT.
WE DON'T HAVE THE CUBE.
WE *BARELY* STOPPED HYDRA.
WHY TAKE IT OUT ON US?
YOU'RE NOT *LISTENING.*
THIS ISN'T A *VILLAINOUS PLOT*, MISS MUTANT...

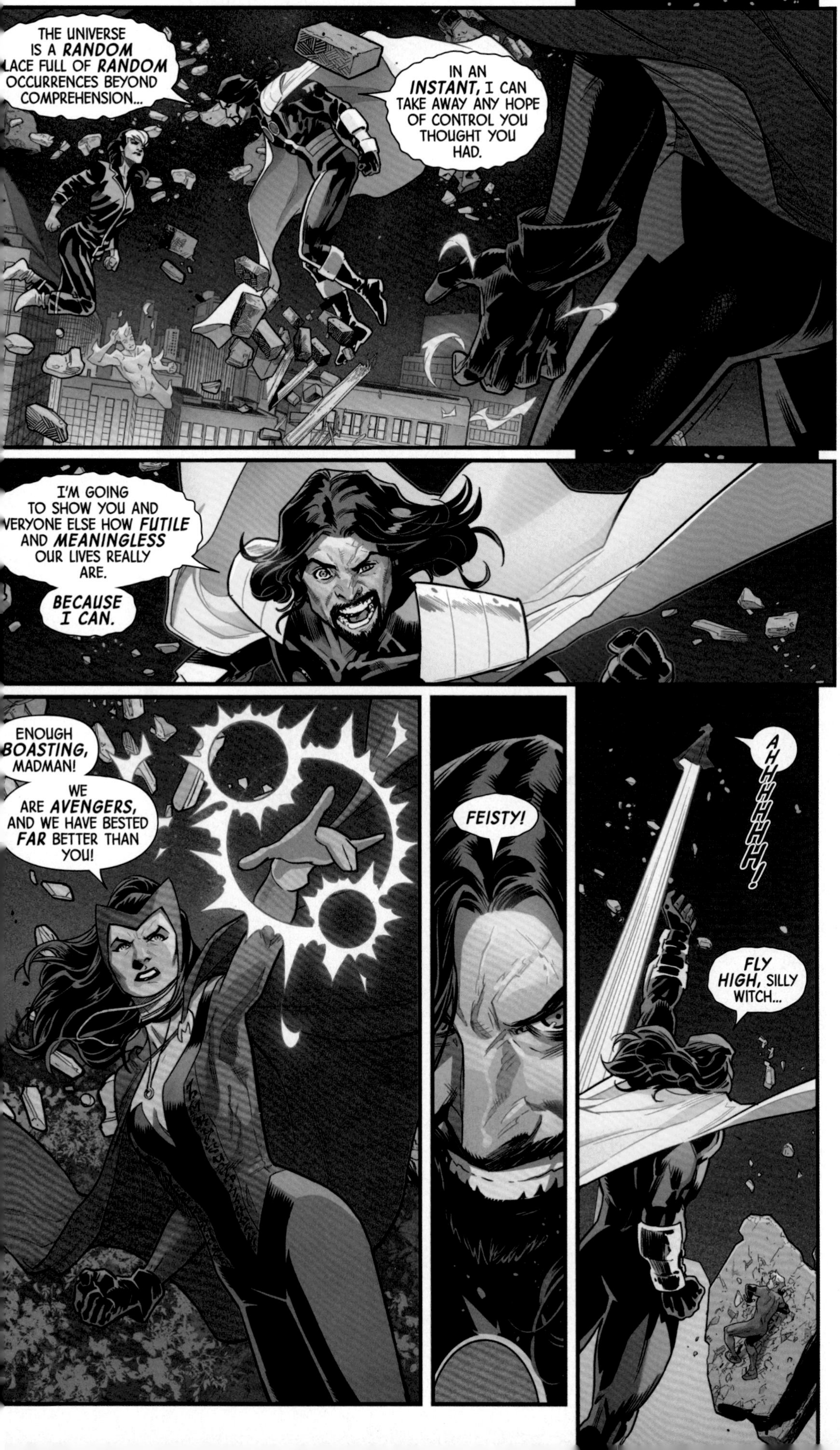
THE UNIVERSE IS A RANDOM LACE FULL OF RANDOM OCCURRENCES BEYOND COMPREHENSION...
IN AN INSTANT, I CAN TAKE AWAY ANY HOPE OF CONTROL YOU THOUGHT YOU HAD.
I'M GOING TO SHOW YOU AND VERYONE ELSE HOW FUTILE AND MEANINGLESS OUR LIVES REALLY ARE.
BECAUSE I CAN.
ENOUGH BOASTING, MADMAN!
WE ARE AVENGERS, AND WE HAVE BESTED FAR BETTER THAN YOU!
FEISTY!
AHHHHHHH!
FLY HIGH, SILLY WITCH...

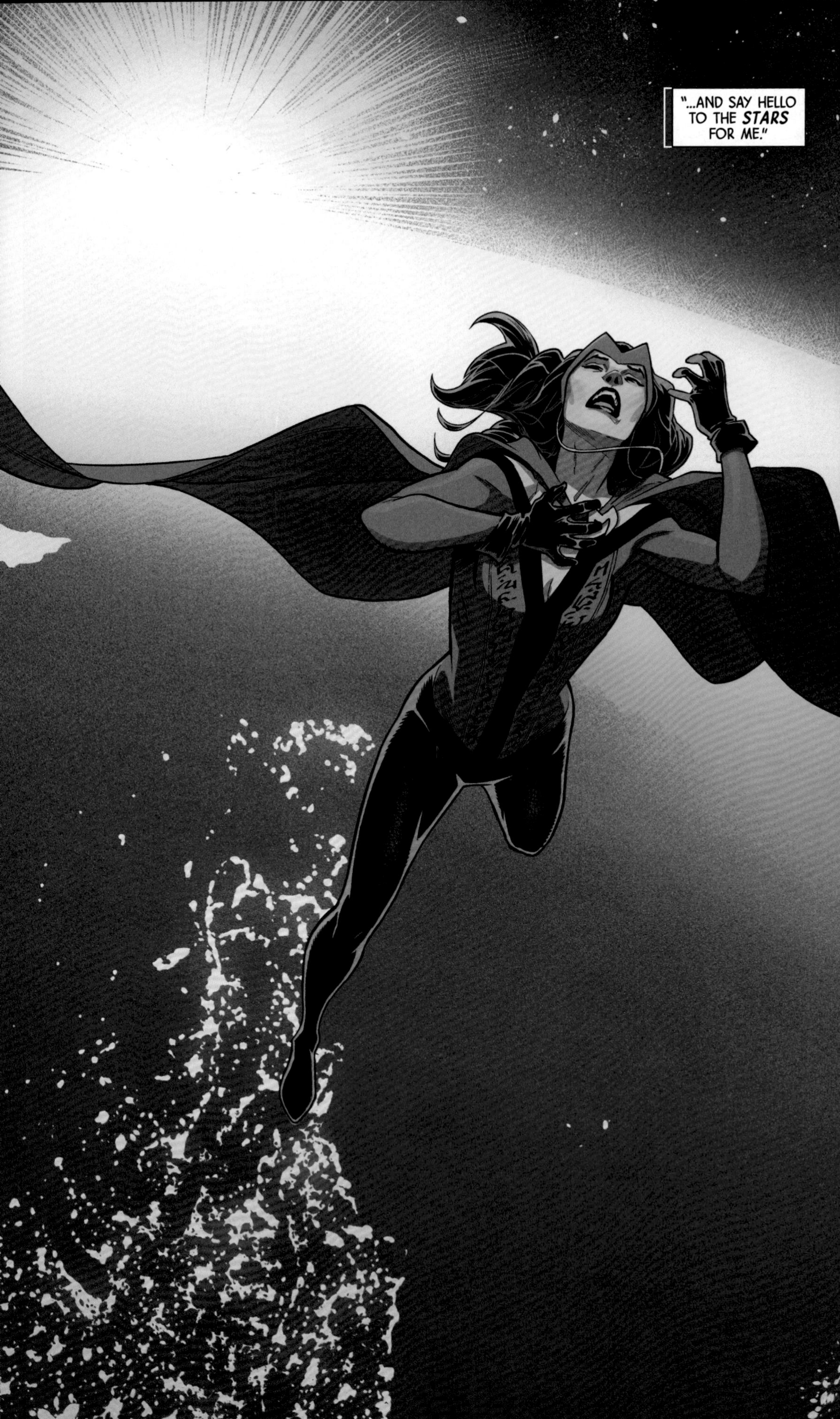
"...AND SAY HELLO TO THE STARS FOR ME."

#27 VENOMIZED VILLAINS VARIANT
BY MIKE HAWTHORNE

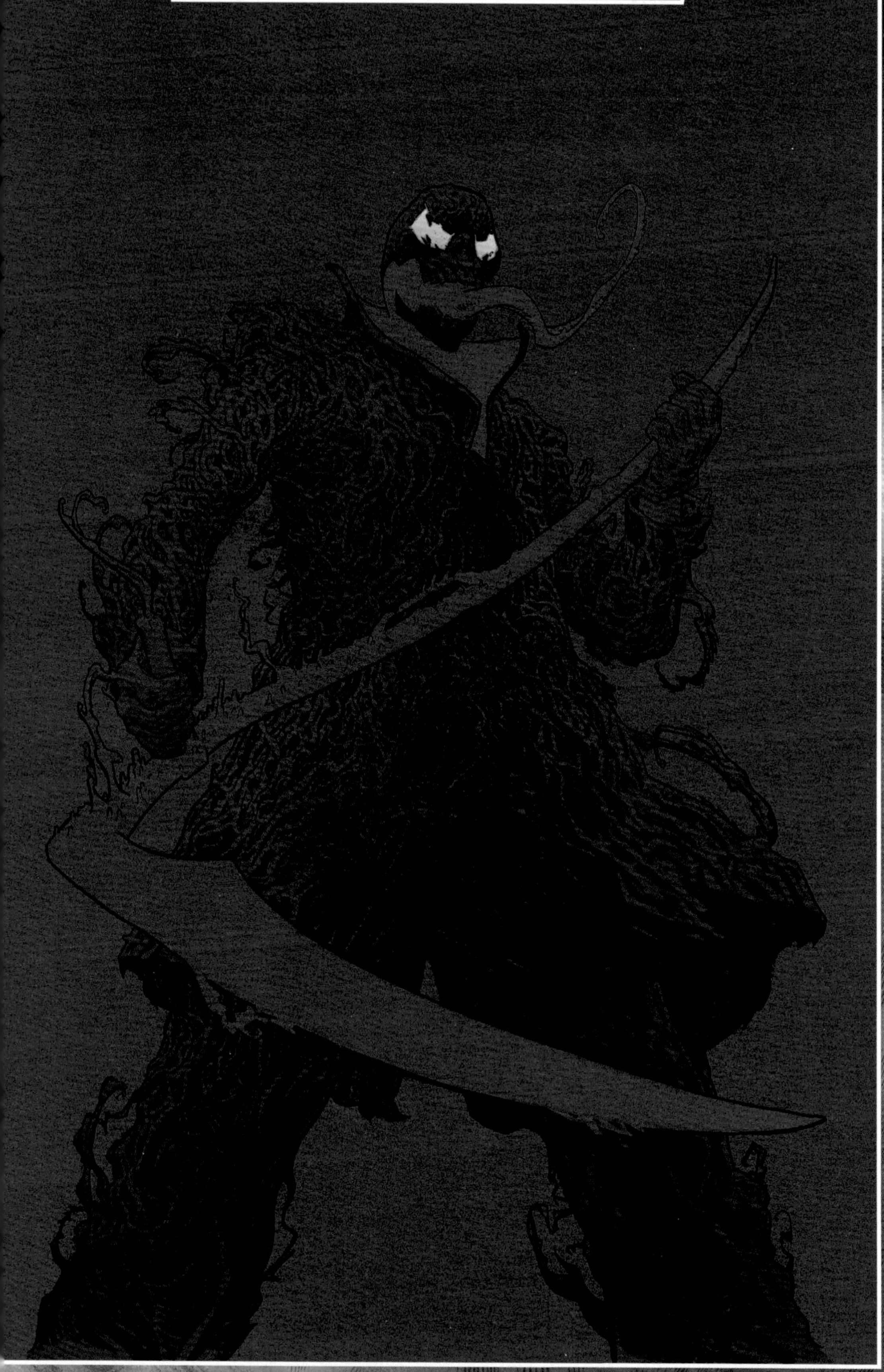

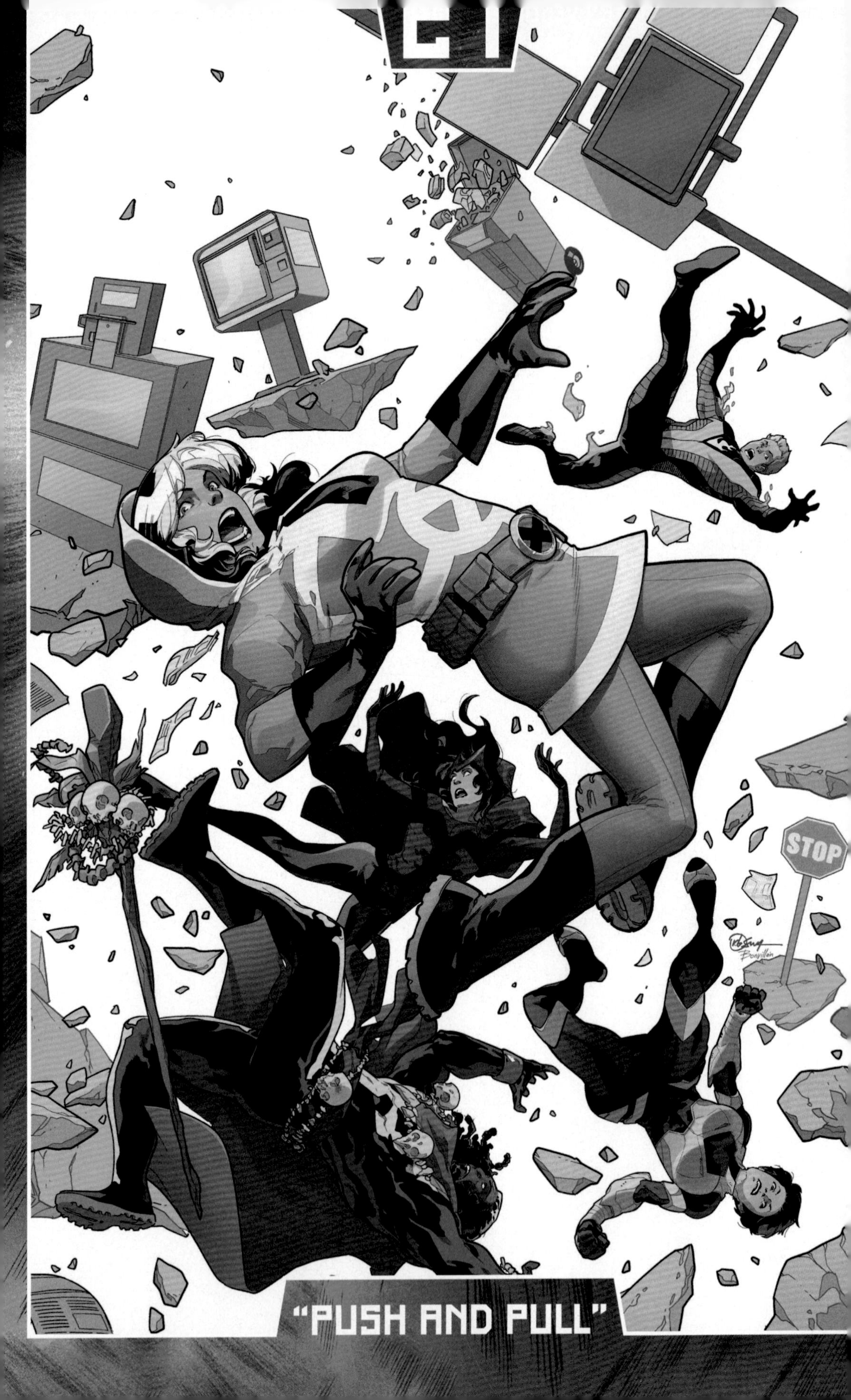
STOP

“PUSH AND PULL”

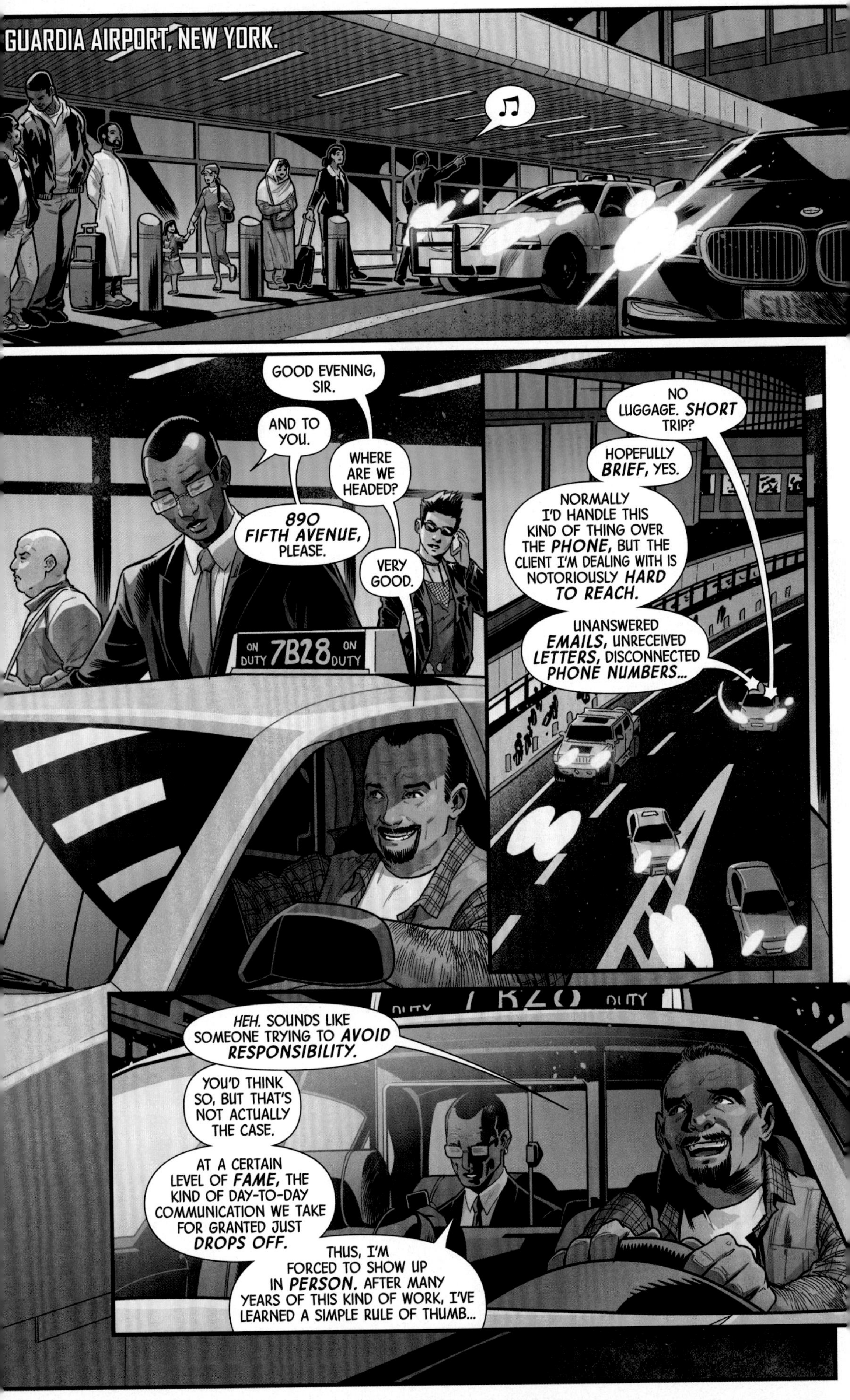

GUARDIA AIRPORT, NEW YORK.
♫
GOOD EVENING, SIR.
AND TO YOU.
WHERE ARE WE HEADED?
890 FIFTH AVENUE, PLEASE.
VERY GOOD.
ON DUTY 7B28 ON DUTY
NO LUGGAGE. SHORT TRIP?
HOPEFULLY BRIEF, YES.
NORMALLY I'D HANDLE THIS KIND OF THING OVER THE PHONE, BUT THE CLIENT I'M DEALING WITH IS NOTORIOUSLY HARD TO REACH.
UNANSWERED EMAILS, UNRECEIVED LETTERS, DISCONNECTED PHONE NUMBERS...
HEH. SOUNDS LIKE SOMEONE TRYING TO AVOID RESPONSIBILITY.
YOU'D THINK SO, BUT THAT'S NOT ACTUALLY THE CASE.
AT A CERTAIN LEVEL OF FAME, THE KIND OF DAY-TO-DAY COMMUNICATION WE TAKE FOR GRANTED JUST DROPS OFF.
THUS, I'M FORCED TO SHOW UP IN PERSON. AFTER MANY YEARS OF THIS KIND OF WORK, I'VE LEARNED A SIMPLE RULE OF THUMB...

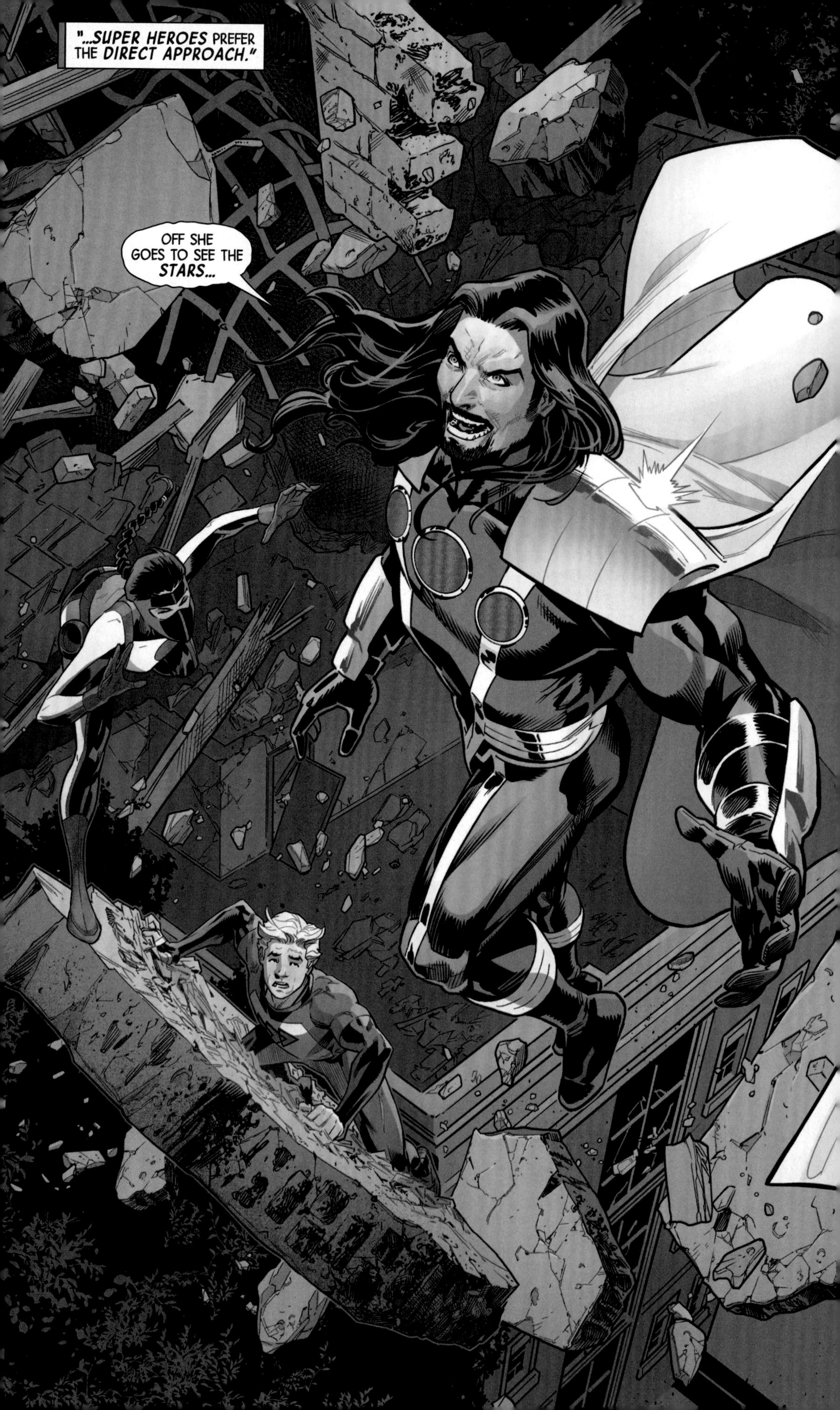
"...SUPER HEROES PREFER THE DIRECT APPROACH."
OFF SHE GOES TO SEE THE STARS...

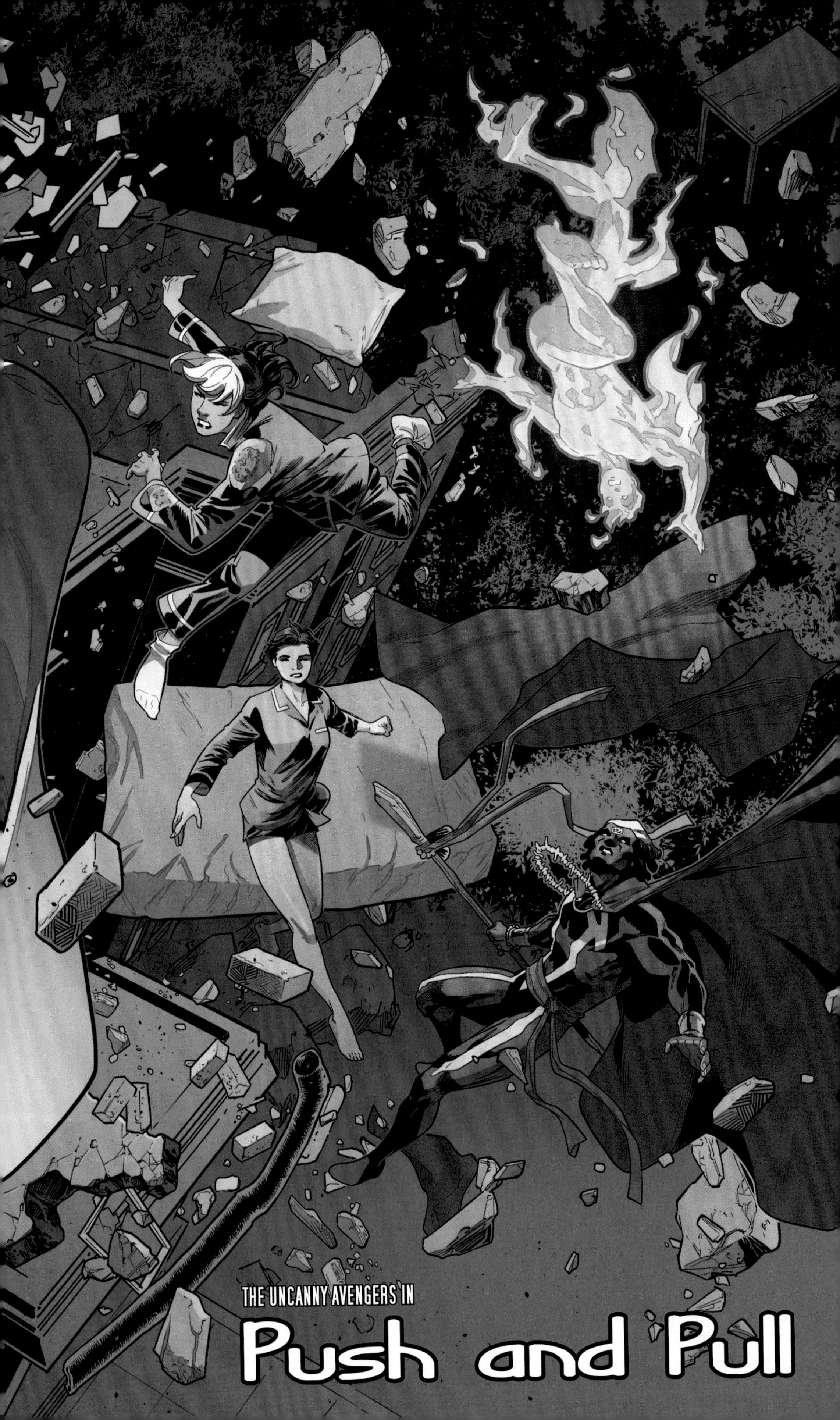
THE UNCANNY AVENGERS IN
Push and Pull

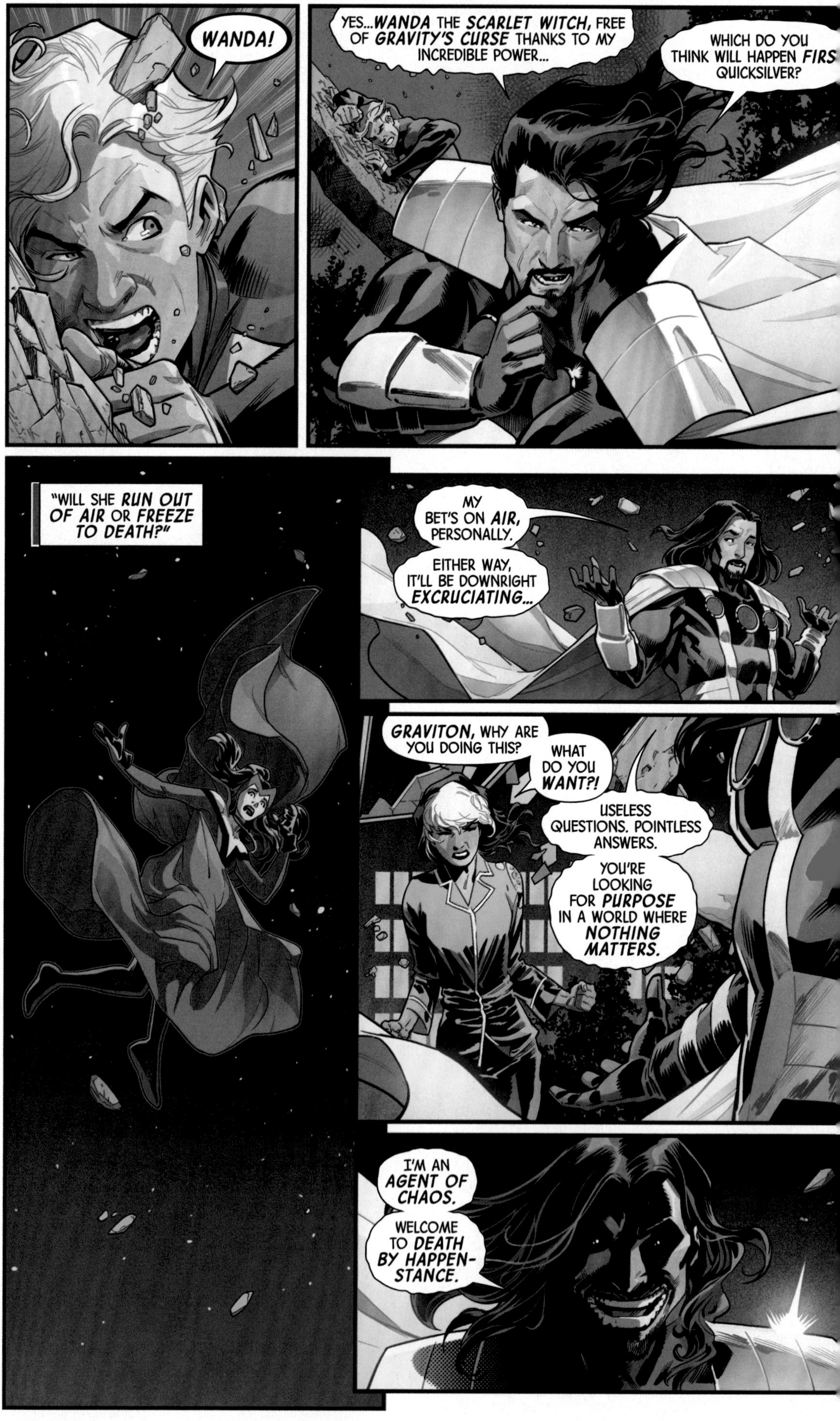
WANDA!
YES...WANDA THE SCARLET WITCH, FREE OF GRAVITY'S CURSE THANKS TO MY INCREDIBLE POWER...
WHICH DO YOU THINK WILL HAPPEN FIRS
QUICKSILVER?
"WILL SHE RUN OUT OF AIR OR FREEZE TO DEATH?"
MY BET'S ON AIR, PERSONALLY.
EITHER WAY, IT'LL BE DOWNRIGHT EXCRUCIATING...
GRAVITON, WHY ARE YOU DOING THIS?
WHAT DO YOU WANT?!
USELESS QUESTIONS. POINTLESS ANSWERS.
YOU'RE LOOKING FOR PURPOSE IN A WORLD WHERE NOTHING MATTERS.
I'M AN AGENT OF CHAOS.
WELCOME TO DEATH BY HAPPEN-STANCE.

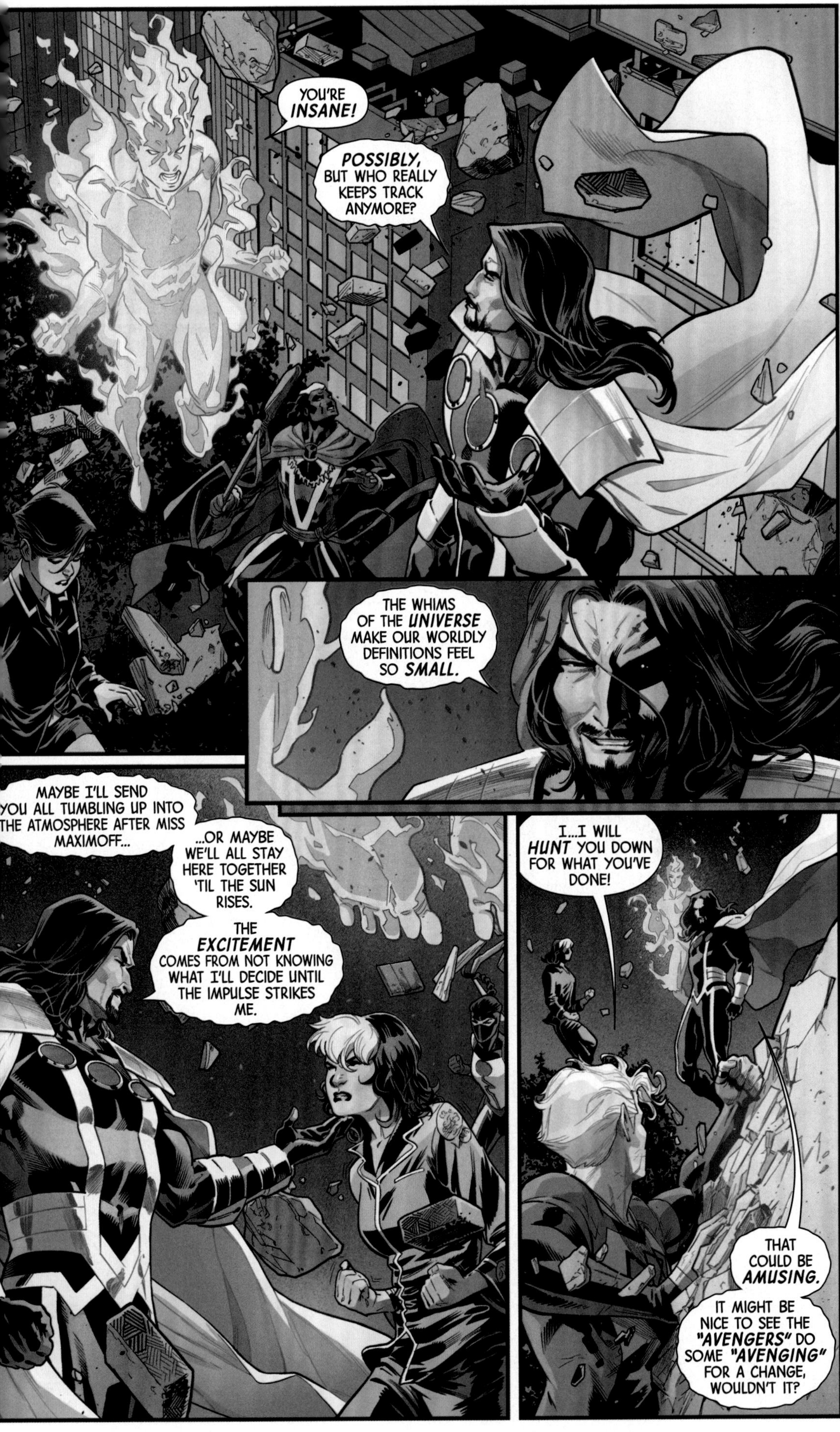
YOU'RE INSANE!
POSSIBLY, BUT WHO REALLY KEEPS TRACK ANYMORE?
THE WHIMS OF THE UNIVERSE MAKE OUR WORLDLY DEFINITIONS FEEL SO SMALL.
MAYBE I'LL SEND YOU ALL TUMBLING UP INTO THE ATMOSPHERE AFTER MISS MAXIMOFF...
...OR MAYBE WE'LL ALL STAY HERE TOGETHER 'TIL THE SUN RISES.
THE EXCITEMENT COMES FROM NOT KNOWING WHAT I'LL DECIDE UNTIL THE IMPULSE STRIKES ME.
I...I WILL HUNT YOU DOWN FOR WHAT YOU'VE DONE!
THAT COULD BE AMUSING.
IT MIGHT BE NICE TO SEE THE "AVENGERS" DO SOME "AVENGING" FOR A CHANGE, WOULDN'T IT?

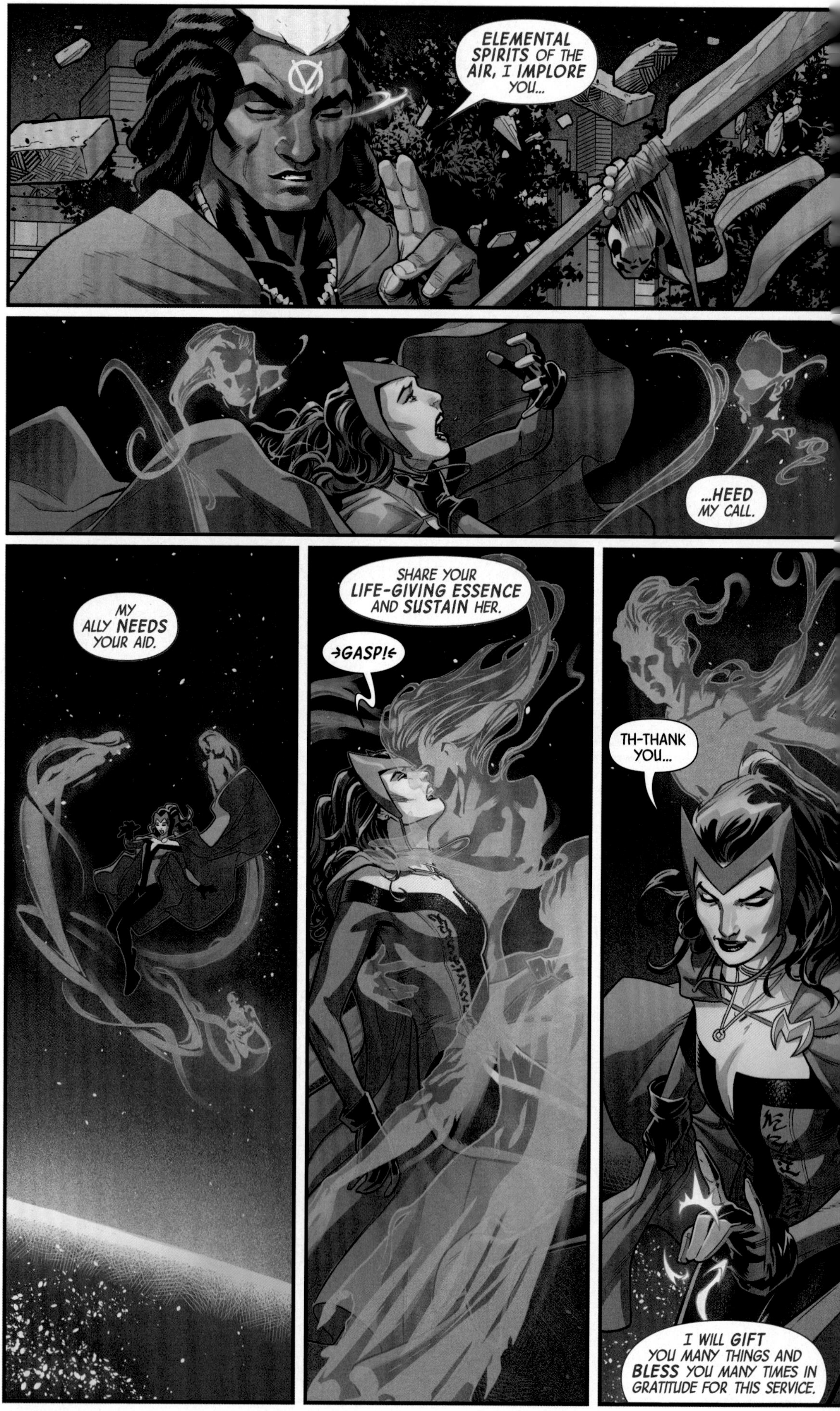
ELEMENTAL SPIRITS OF THE AIR, I IMPLORE YOU...
...HEED MY CALL.
MY ALLY NEEDS YOUR AID.
SHARE YOUR LIFE-GIVING ESSENCE AND SUSTAIN HER.
GASP!
TH-THANK YOU...
I WILL GIFT YOU MANY THINGS AND BLESS YOU MANY TIMES IN GRATITUDE FOR THIS SERVICE.

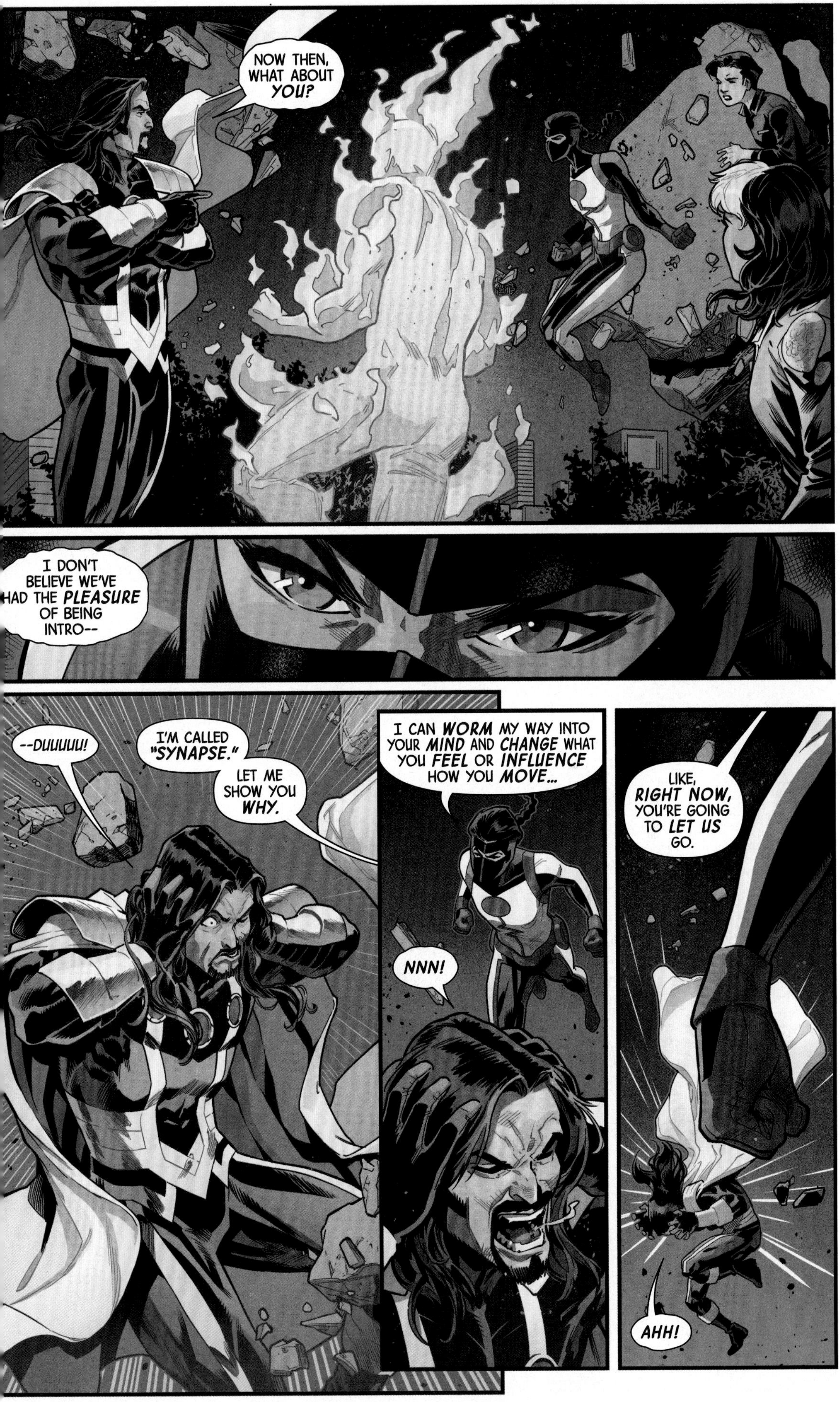

NOW THEN, WHAT ABOUT *YOU?*
I DON'T BELIEVE WE'VE HAD THE *PLEASURE* OF BEING INTRO--
--DUUUUU!
I'M CALLED *"SYNAPSE."*
LET ME SHOW YOU *WHY.*
I CAN *WORM* MY WAY INTO YOUR *MIND* AND *CHANGE* WHAT YOU *FEEL* OR *INFLUENCE* HOW YOU *MOVE*...
NNN!
LIKE, *RIGHT NOW,* YOU'RE GOING TO *LET US* GO.
AHH!

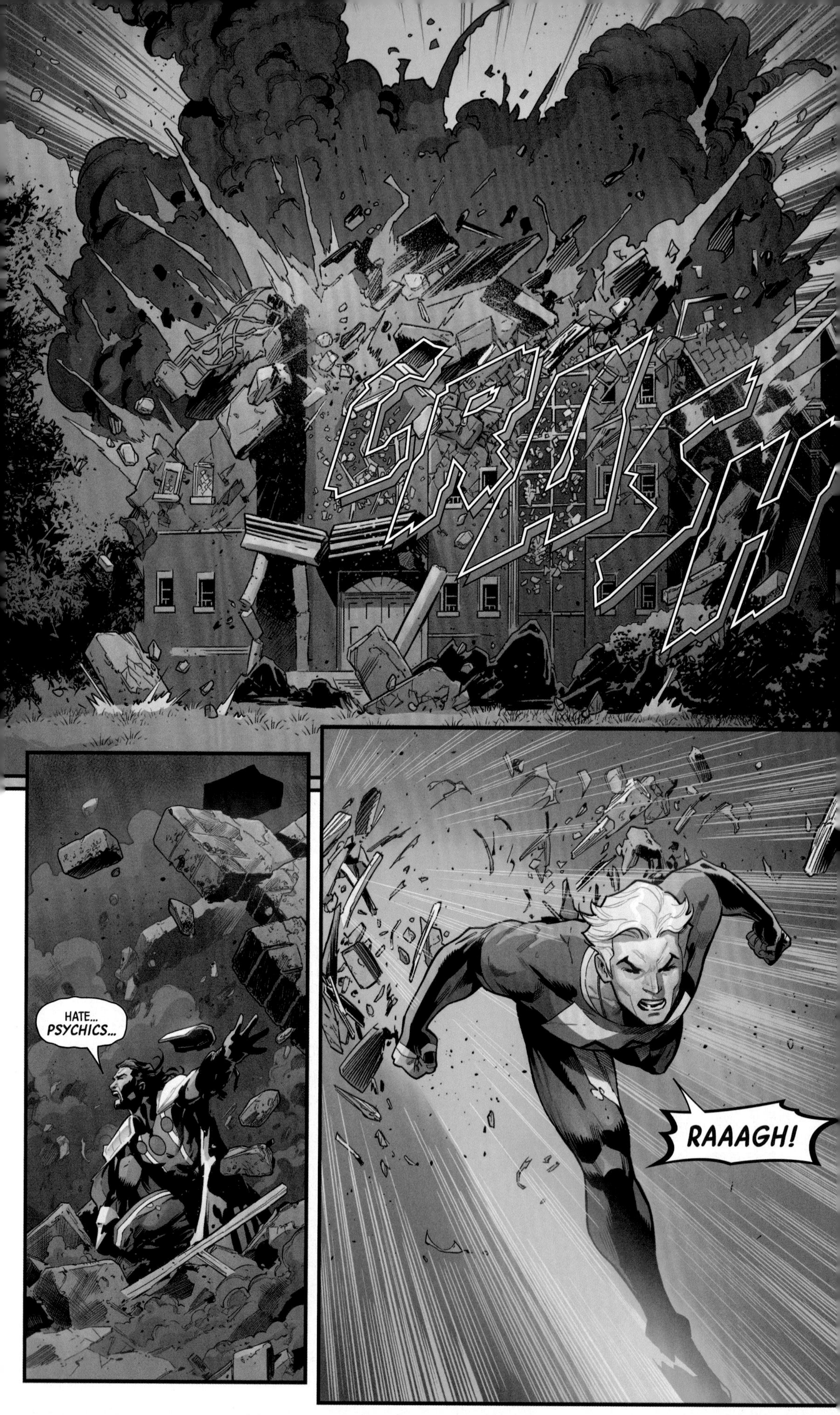
CRASH
HATE... PSYCHICS...
RAAAGH!

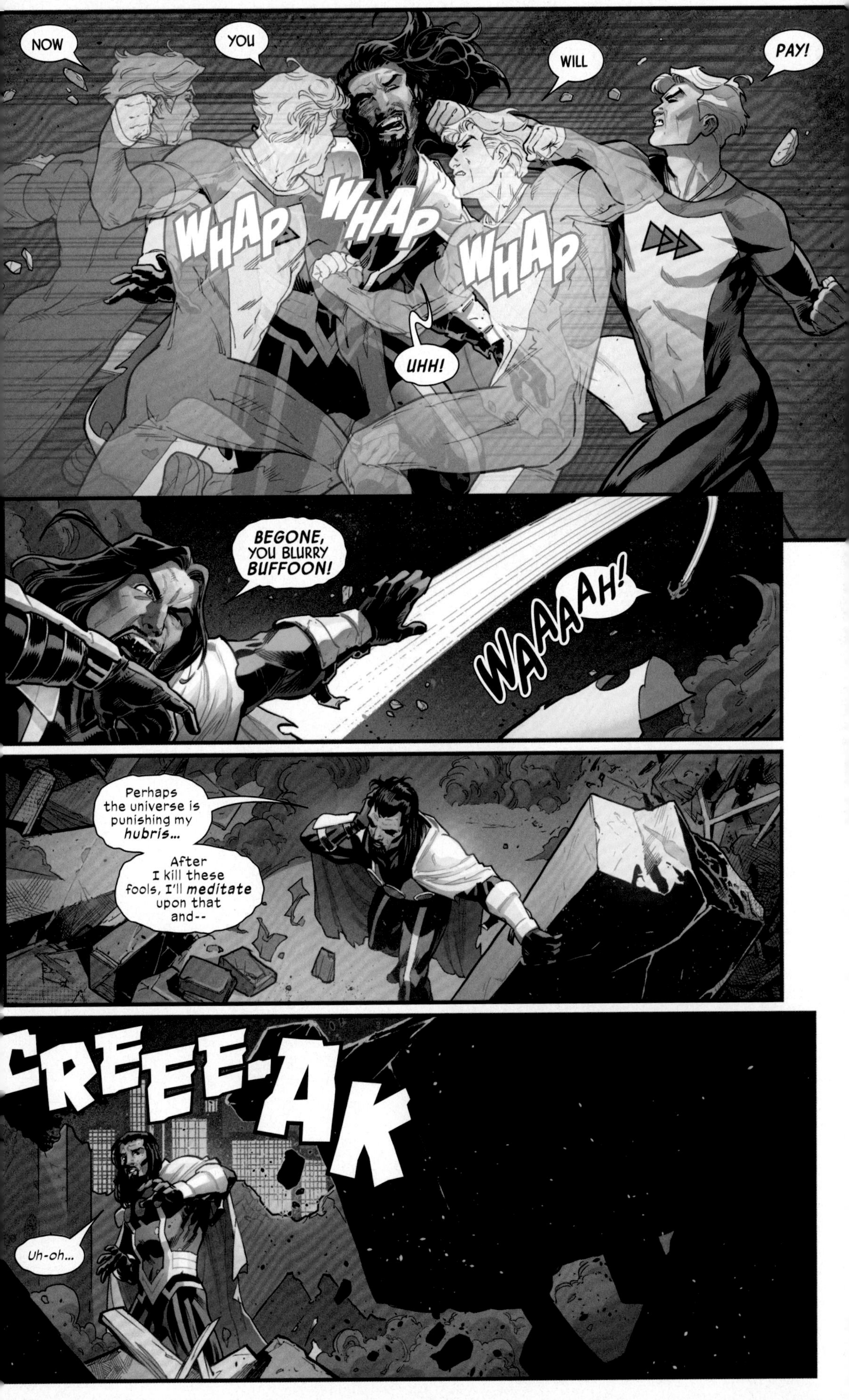
NOW
YOU
WILL
PAY!
WHAP
WHAP
WHAP
UHH!
BEGONE, YOU BLURRY BUFFOON!
WAAAAH!
Perhaps the universe is punishing my *hubris*...
After I kill these fools, I'll *meditate* upon that and--
CREEE-AK
Uh-oh...

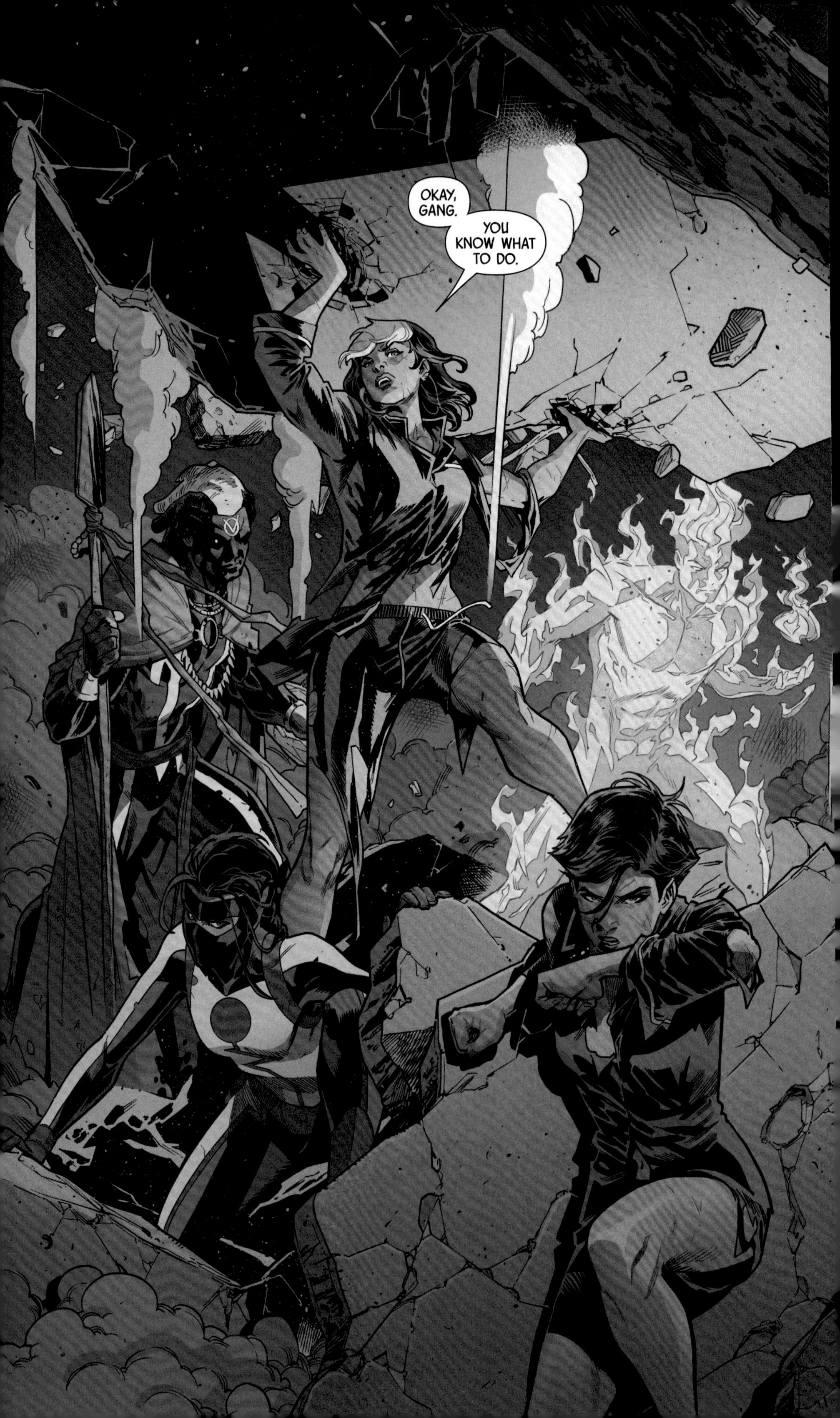

OKAY, GANG.
YOU KNOW WHAT TO DO.

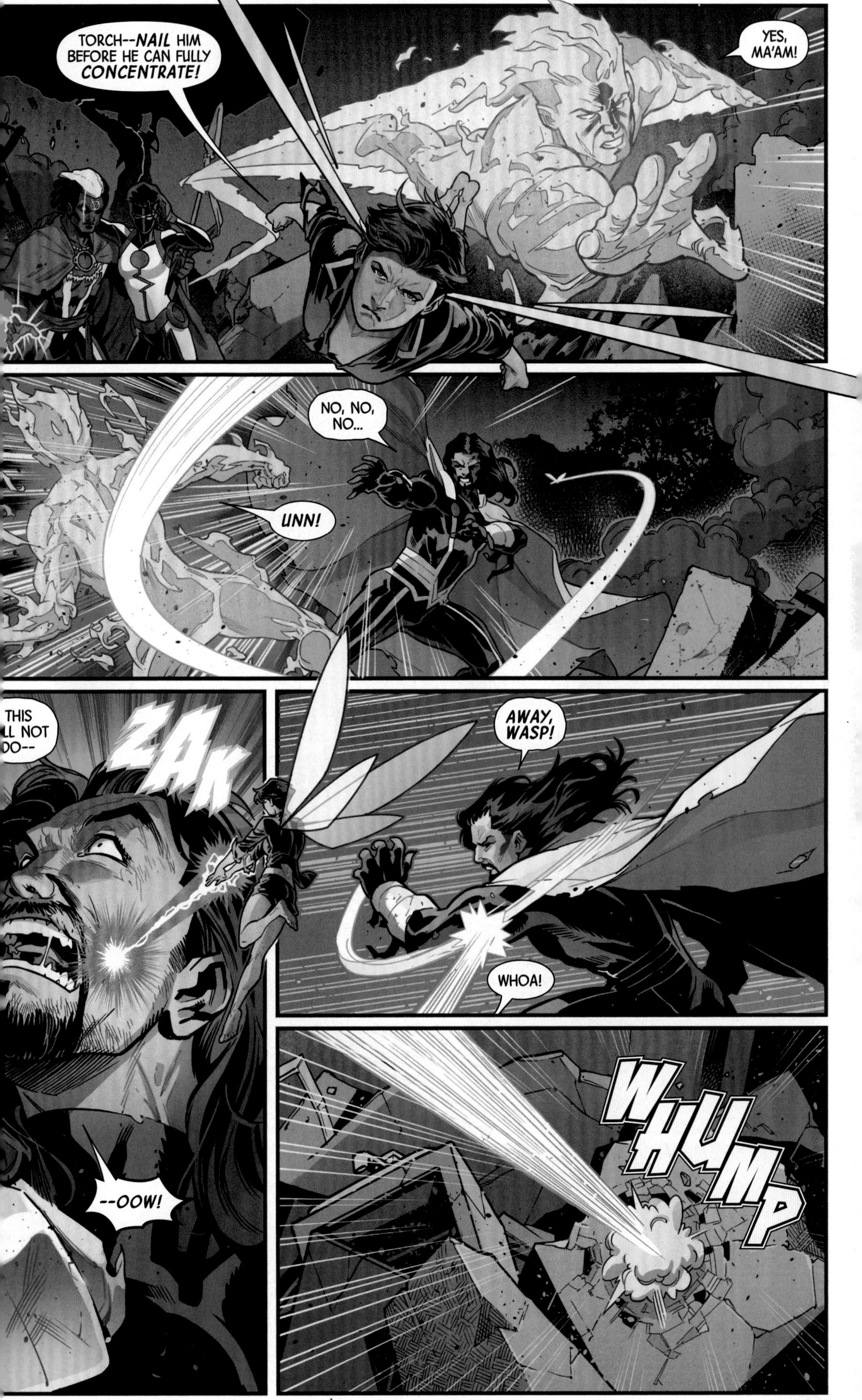
TORCH--NAIL HIM BEFORE HE CAN FULLY CONCENTRATE!
YES, MA'AM!
NO, NO, NO...
UNN!
THIS
LL NOT
DO--
ZAK
--OOW!
AWAY, WASP!
WHOA!
WHUMP

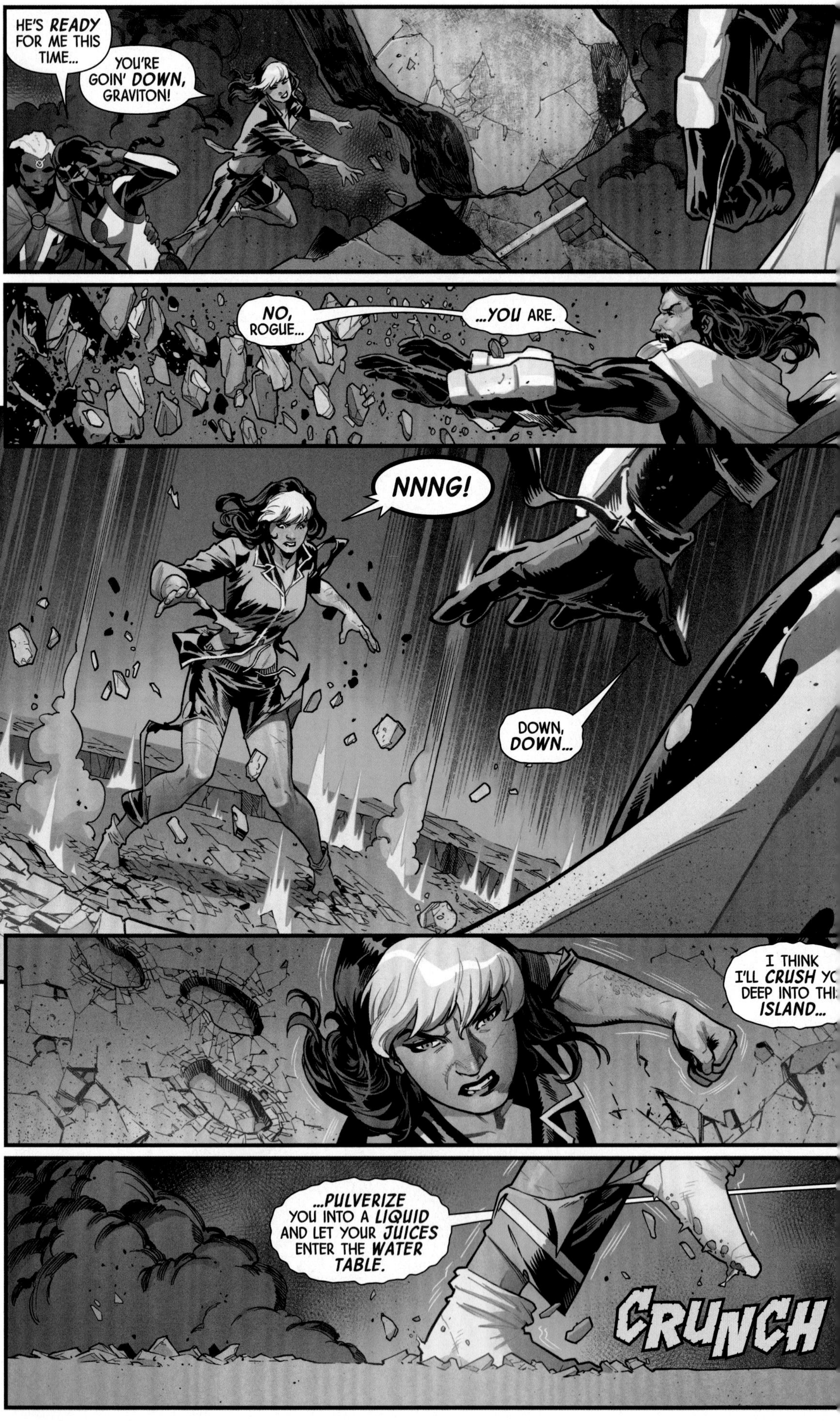
HE'S READY FOR ME THIS TIME...
YOU'RE GOIN' DOWN, GRAVITON!
NO, ROGUE...
...YOU ARE.
NNNG!
DOWN, DOWN...
I THINK I'LL CRUSH YO DEEP INTO THI ISLAND...
...PULVERIZE YOU INTO A LIQUID AND LET YOUR JUICES ENTER THE WATER TABLE.
CRUNCH

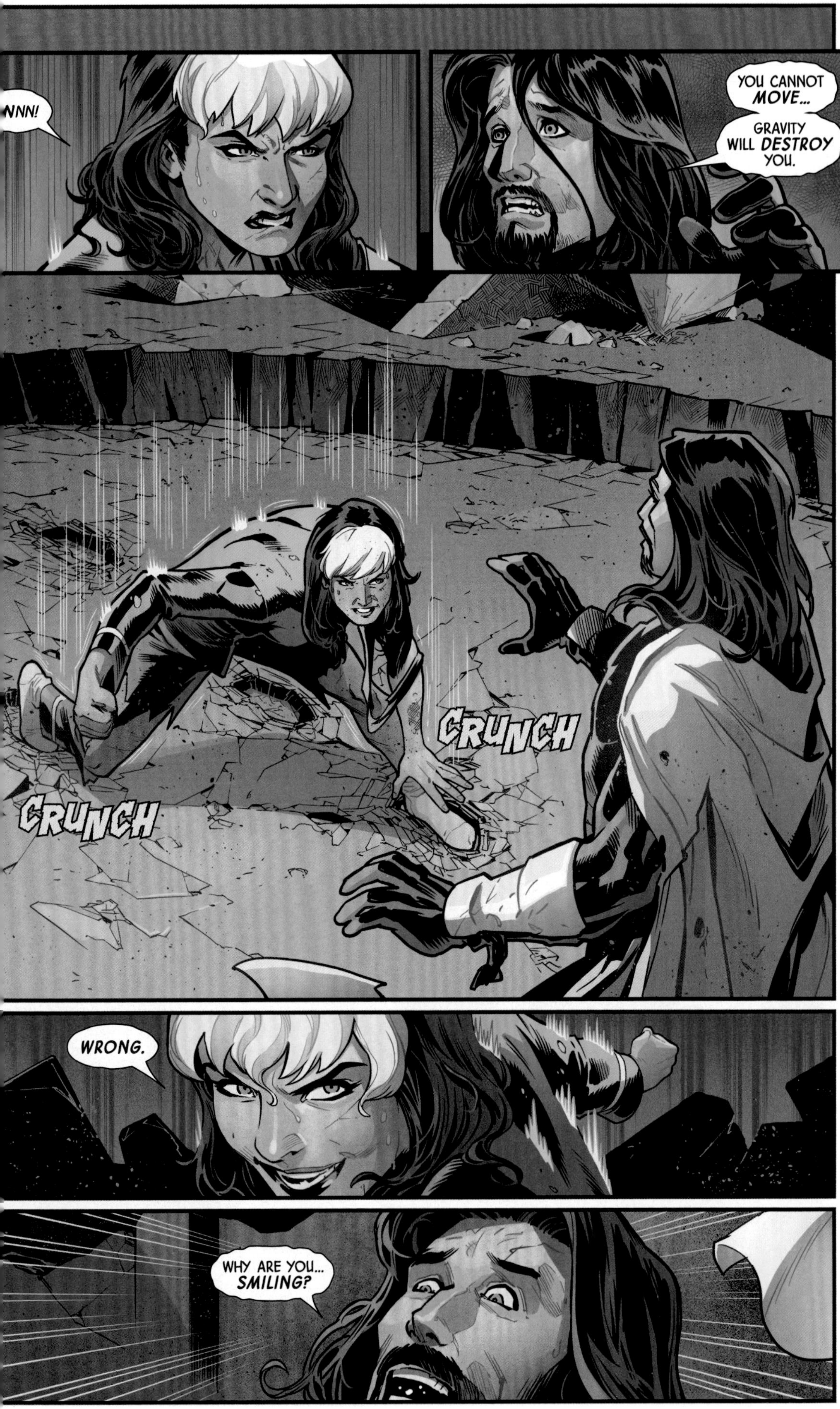
NNN!
YOU CANNOT MOVE...
GRAVITY WILL DESTROY YOU.
CRUNCH
CRUNCH
WRONG.
WHY ARE YOU... SMILING?

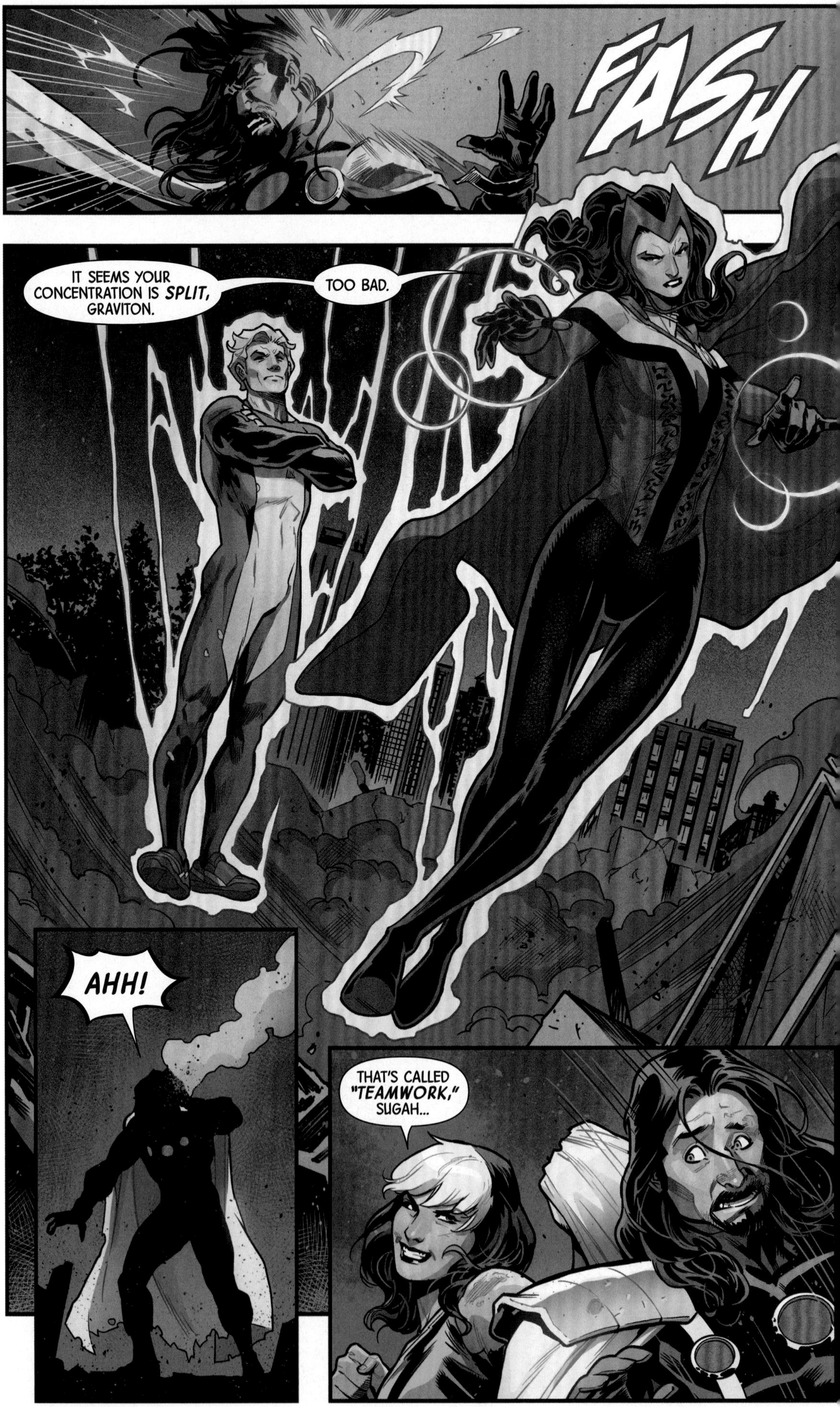
FASH
IT SEEMS YOUR CONCENTRATION IS SPLIT, GRAVITON.
TOO BAD.
AHH!
THAT'S CALLED "TEAMWORK," SUGAH...

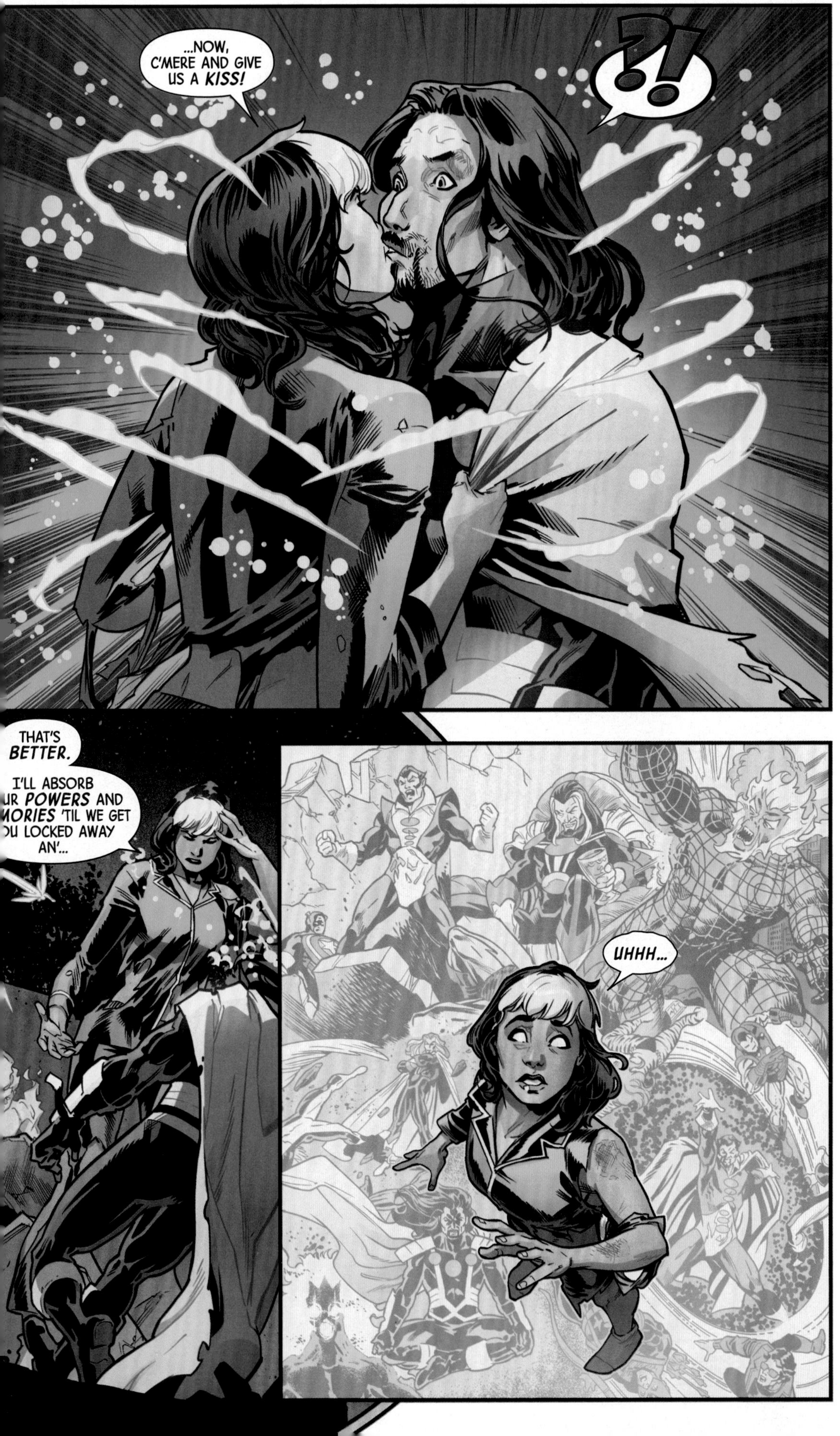

...NOW, C'MERE AND GIVE US A KISS!
?!
THAT'S BETTER.
I'LL ABSORB UR POWERS AND MORIES 'TIL WE GET U LOCKED AWAY AN'...
UHHH...

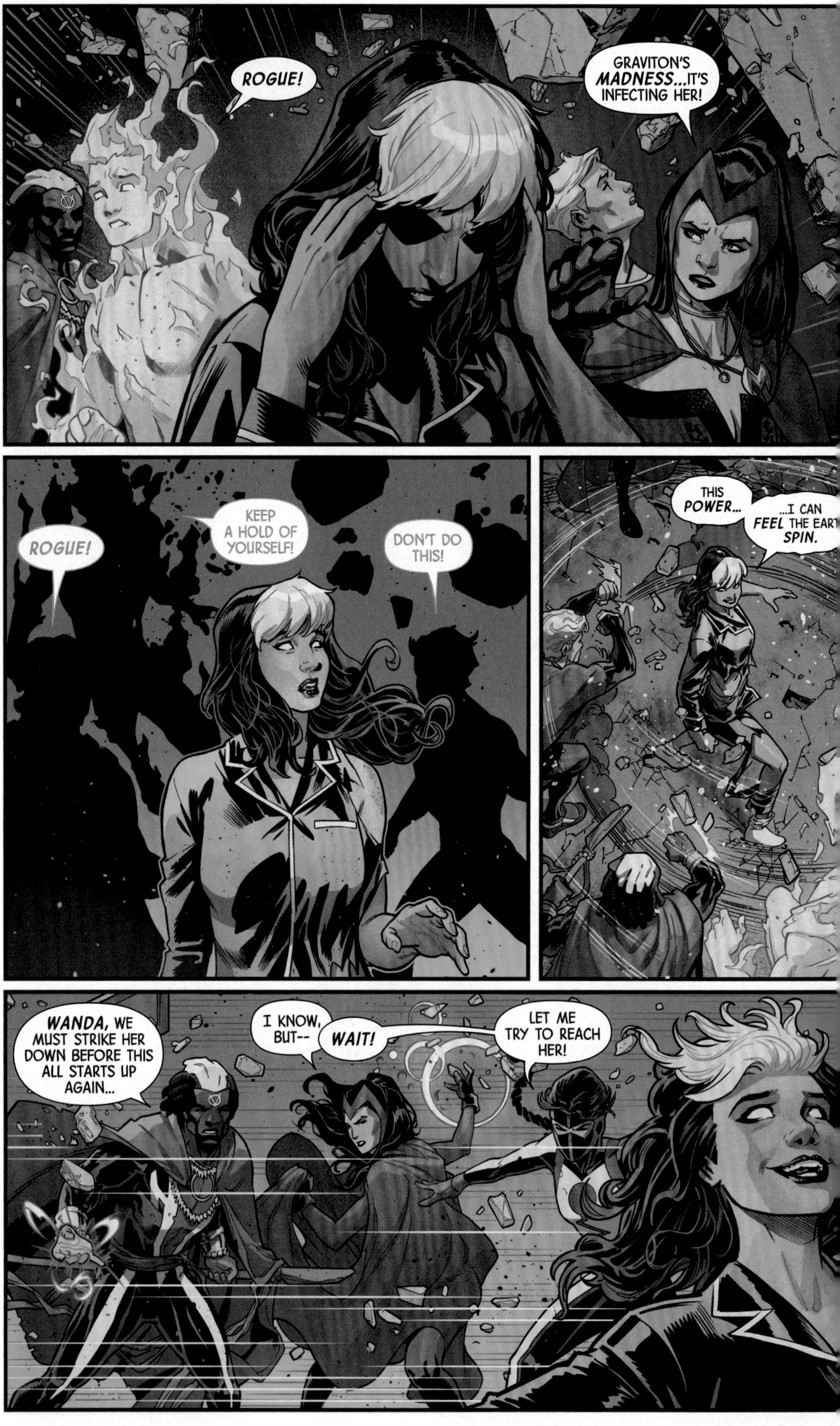
ROGUE!
GRAVITON'S MADNESS...IT'S INFECTING HER!
ROGUE!
KEEP A HOLD OF YOURSELF!
DON'T DO THIS!
THIS POWER...
...I CAN FEEL THE EART SPIN.
WANDA, WE MUST STRIKE HER DOWN BEFORE THIS ALL STARTS UP AGAIN...
I KNOW, BUT--
WAIT!
LET ME TRY TO REACH HER!

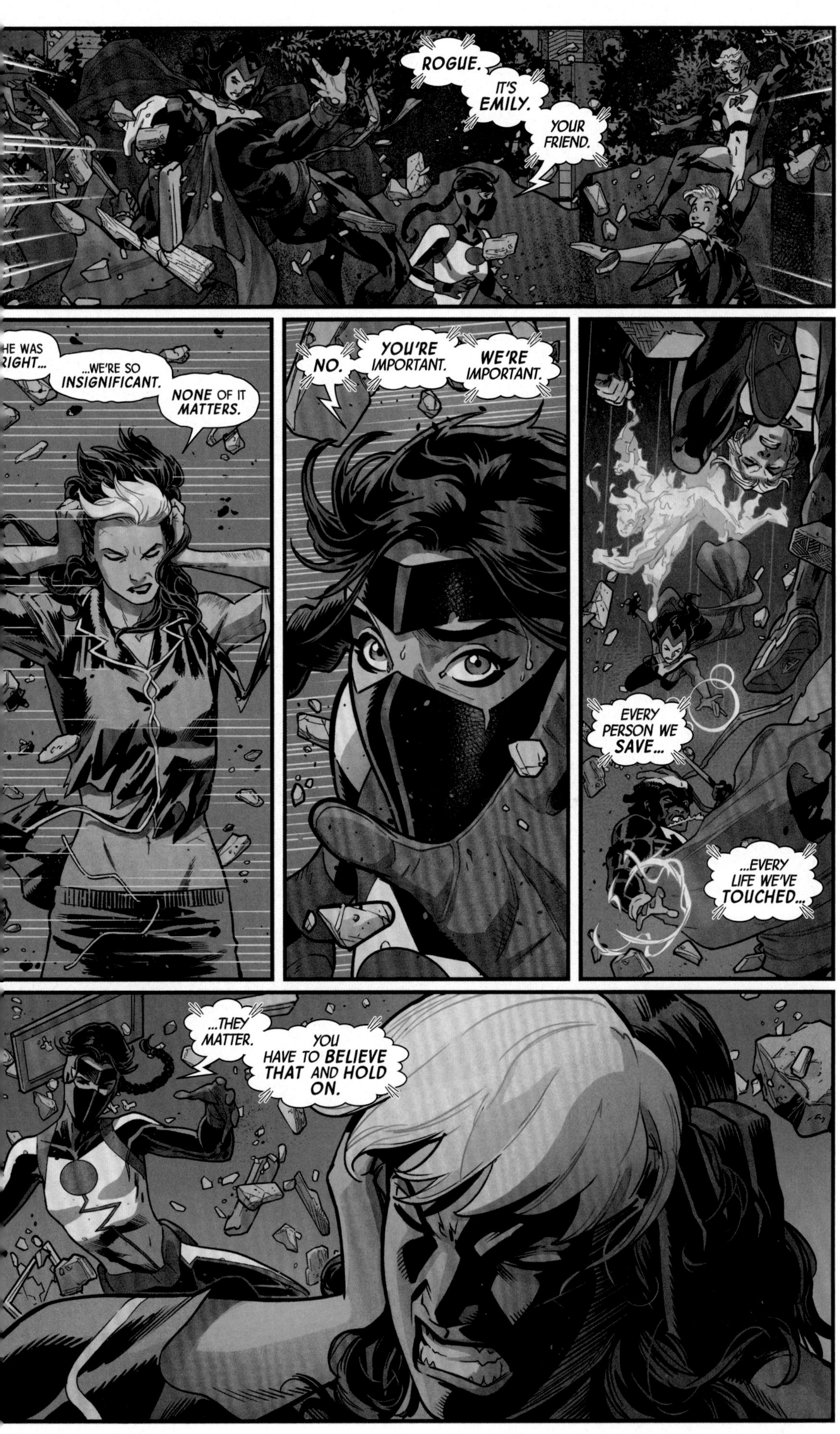
ROGUE.
IT'S EMILY.
YOUR FRIEND.
HE WAS RIGHT...
...WE'RE SO INSIGNIFICANT.
NONE OF IT MATTERS.
NO.
YOU'RE IMPORTANT.
WE'RE IMPORTANT.
EVERY PERSON WE SAVE...
...EVERY LIFE WE'VE TOUCHED...
...THEY MATTER.
YOU HAVE TO BELIEVE THAT AND HOLD ON.

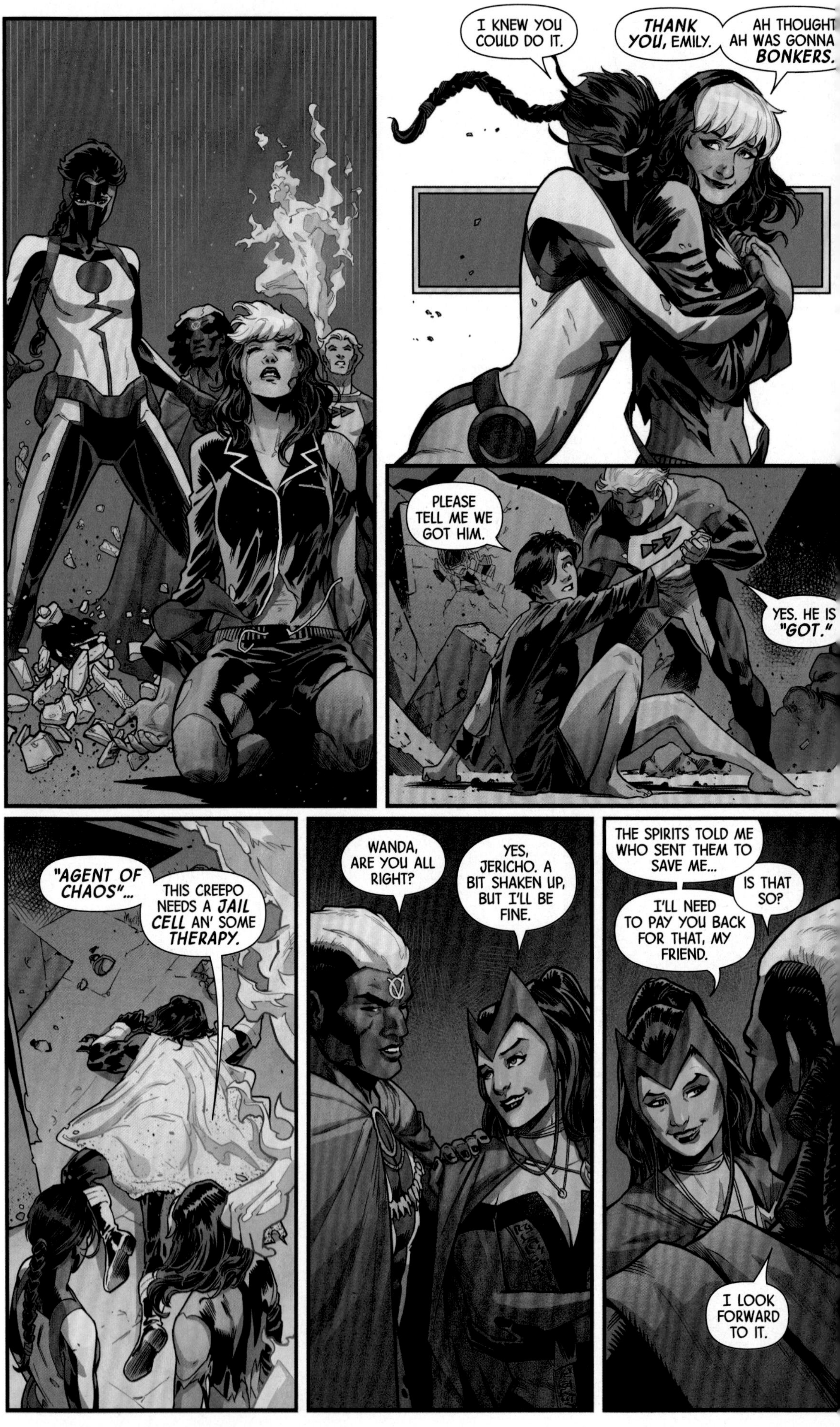
I KNEW YOU COULD DO IT.
THANK YOU, EMILY.
AH THOUGHT AH WAS GONNA BONKERS.
PLEASE TELL ME WE GOT HIM.
YES. HE IS "GOT."
"AGENT OF CHAOS"...
THIS CREEPO NEEDS A JAIL CELL AN' SOME THERAPY.
WANDA, ARE YOU ALL RIGHT?
YES, JERICHO. A BIT SHAKEN UP, BUT I'LL BE FINE.
THE SPIRITS TOLD ME WHO SENT THEM TO SAVE ME...
I'LL NEED TO PAY YOU BACK FOR THAT, MY FRIEND.
IS THAT SO?
I LOOK FORWARD TO IT.

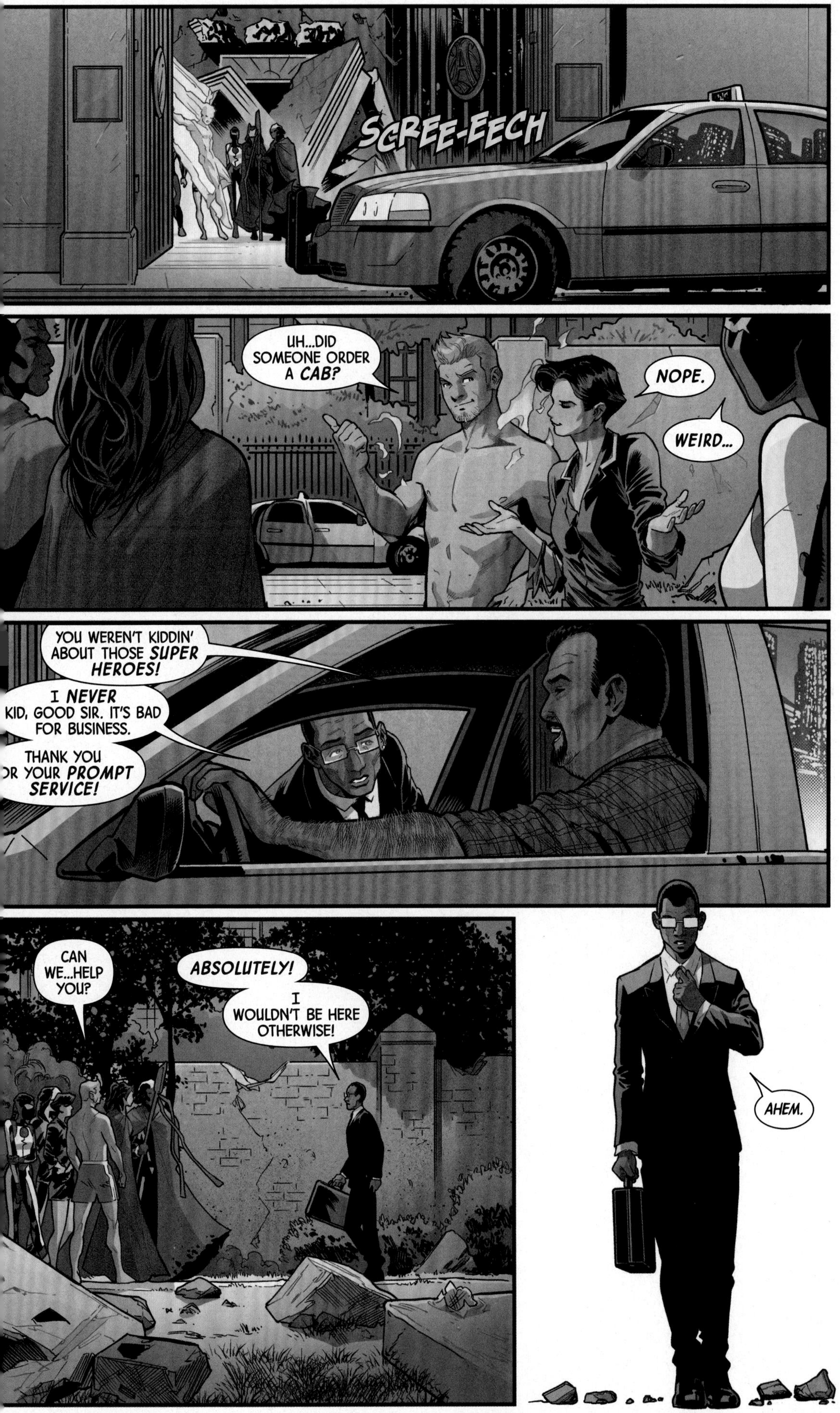
SCREE-EECH
UH...DID SOMEONE ORDER A CAB?
NOPE.
WEIRD...
YOU WEREN'T KIDDIN' ABOUT THOSE SUPER HEROES!
I NEVER KID, GOOD SIR. IT'S BAD FOR BUSINESS.
THANK YOU FOR YOUR PROMPT SERVICE!
CAN WE...HELP YOU?
ABSOLUTELY!
I WOULDN'T BE HERE OTHERWISE!
AHEM.

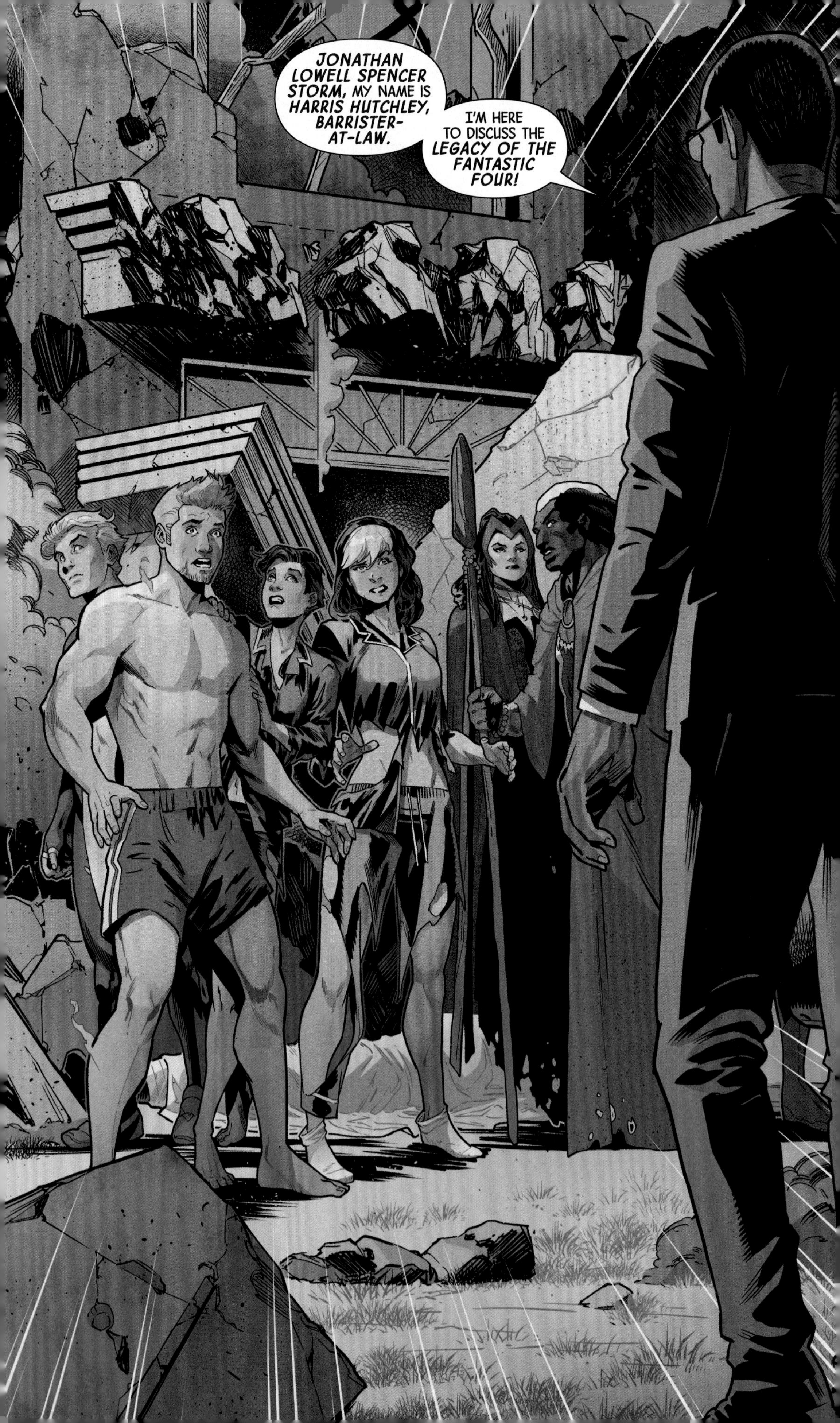
JONATHAN LOWELL SPENCER STORM, MY NAME IS HARRIS HUTCHLEY, BARRISTER-AT-LAW.
I'M HERE TO DISCUSS THE LEGACY OF THE FANTASTIC FOUR!

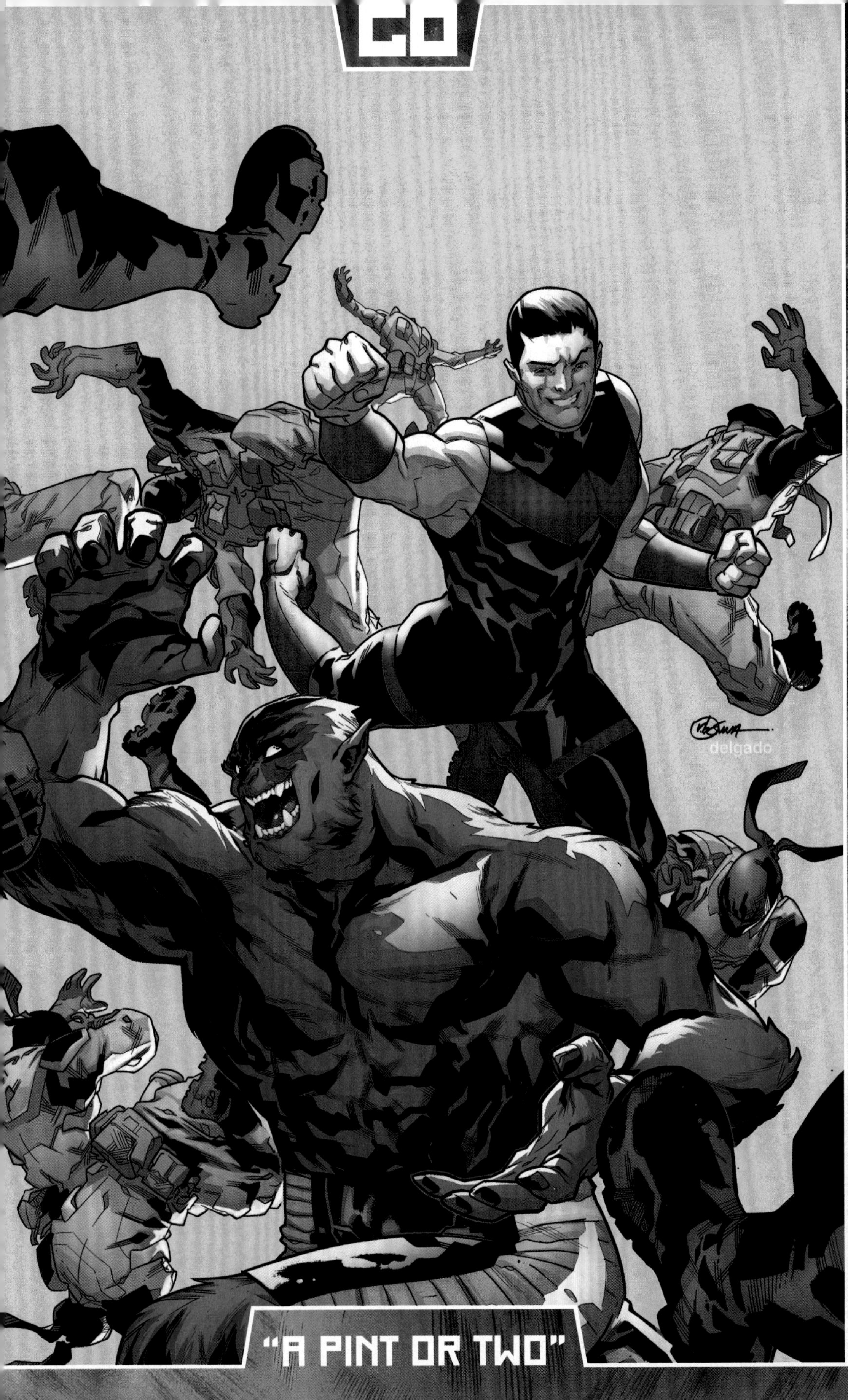
60
delgado
"A PINT OR TWO"

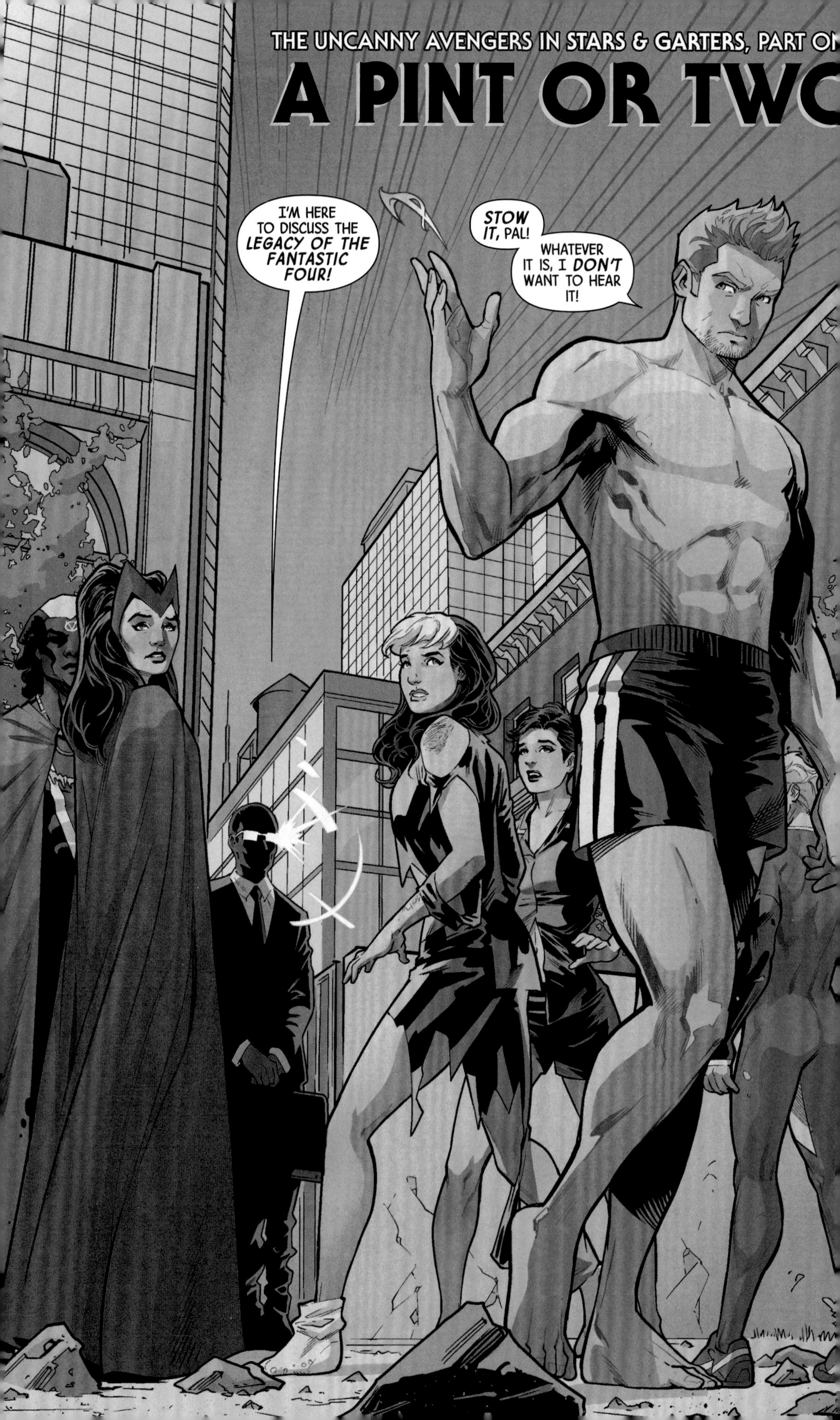
THE UNCANNY AVENGERS IN STARS & GARTERS, PART ON
A PINT OR TWO
I'M HERE TO DISCUSS THE LEGACY OF THE FANTASTIC FOUR!
STOW IT, PAL!
WHATEVER IT IS, I DON'T WANT TO HEAR IT!

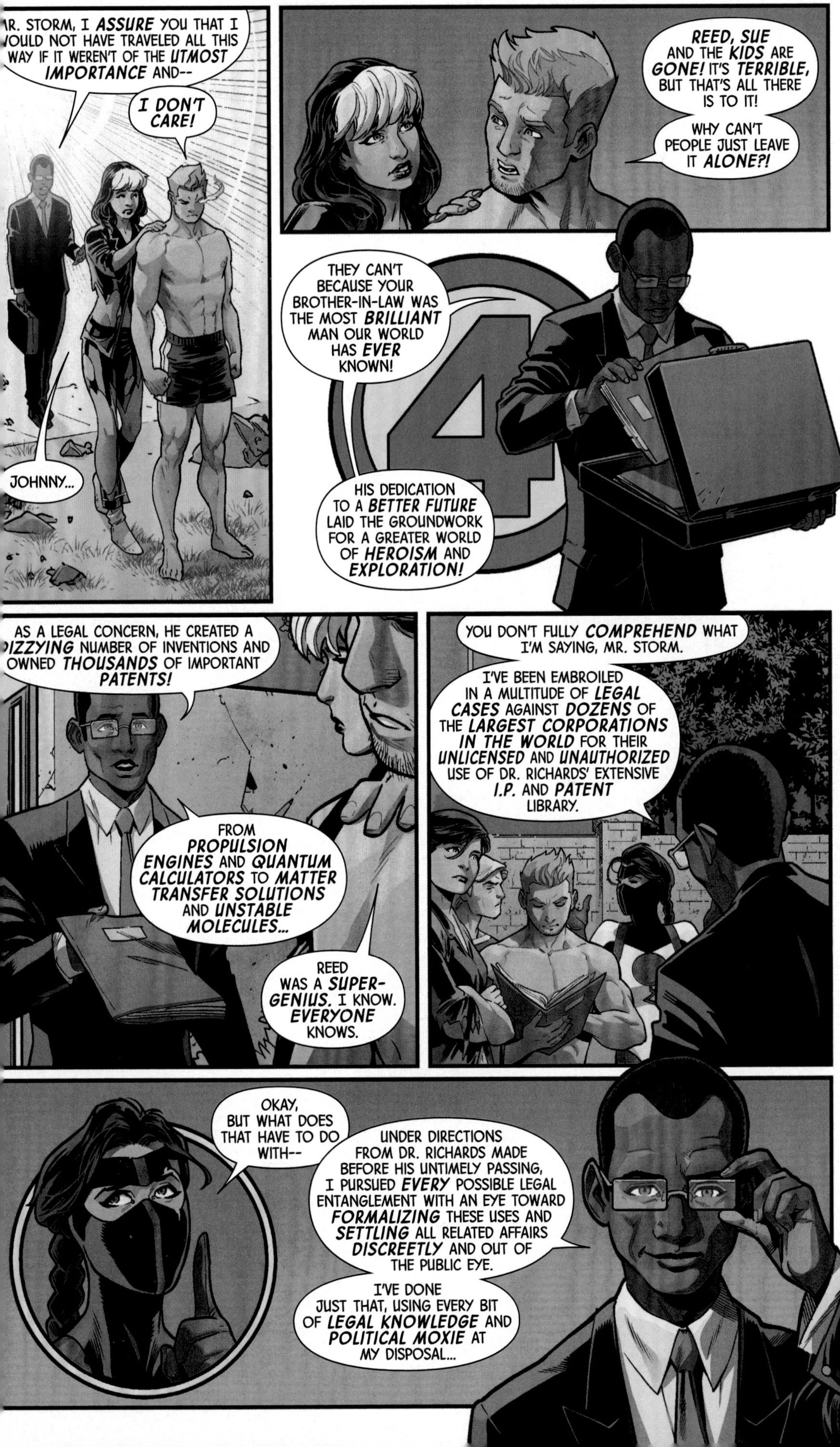

R. STORM, I ASSURE YOU THAT I OULD NOT HAVE TRAVELED ALL THIS WAY IF IT WEREN'T OF THE UTMOST IMPORTANCE AND--
I DON'T CARE!
JOHNNY...
REED, SUE AND THE KIDS ARE GONE! IT'S TERRIBLE, BUT THAT'S ALL THERE IS TO IT!
WHY CAN'T PEOPLE JUST LEAVE IT ALONE?!
THEY CAN'T BECAUSE YOUR BROTHER-IN-LAW WAS THE MOST BRILLIANT MAN OUR WORLD HAS EVER KNOWN!
HIS DEDICATION TO A BETTER FUTURE LAID THE GROUNDWORK FOR A GREATER WORLD OF HEROISM AND EXPLORATION!
AS A LEGAL CONCERN, HE CREATED A IZZYING NUMBER OF INVENTIONS AND OWNED THOUSANDS OF IMPORTANT PATENTS!
FROM PROPULSION ENGINES AND QUANTUM CALCULATORS TO MATTER TRANSFER SOLUTIONS AND UNSTABLE MOLECULES...
REED WAS A SUPER-GENIUS. I KNOW. EVERYONE KNOWS.
YOU DON'T FULLY COMPREHEND WHAT I'M SAYING, MR. STORM.
I'VE BEEN EMBROILED IN A MULTITUDE OF LEGAL CASES AGAINST DOZENS OF THE LARGEST CORPORATIONS IN THE WORLD FOR THEIR UNLICENSED AND UNAUTHORIZED USE OF DR. RICHARDS' EXTENSIVE I.P. AND PATENT LIBRARY.
OKAY, BUT WHAT DOES THAT HAVE TO DO WITH--
UNDER DIRECTIONS FROM DR. RICHARDS MADE BEFORE HIS UNTIMELY PASSING, I PURSUED EVERY POSSIBLE LEGAL ENTANGLEMENT WITH AN EYE TOWARD FORMALIZING THESE USES AND SETTLING ALL RELATED AFFAIRS DISCREETLY AND OUT OF THE PUBLIC EYE.
I'VE DONE JUST THAT, USING EVERY BIT OF LEGAL KNOWLEDGE AND POLITICAL MOXIE AT MY DISPOSAL...

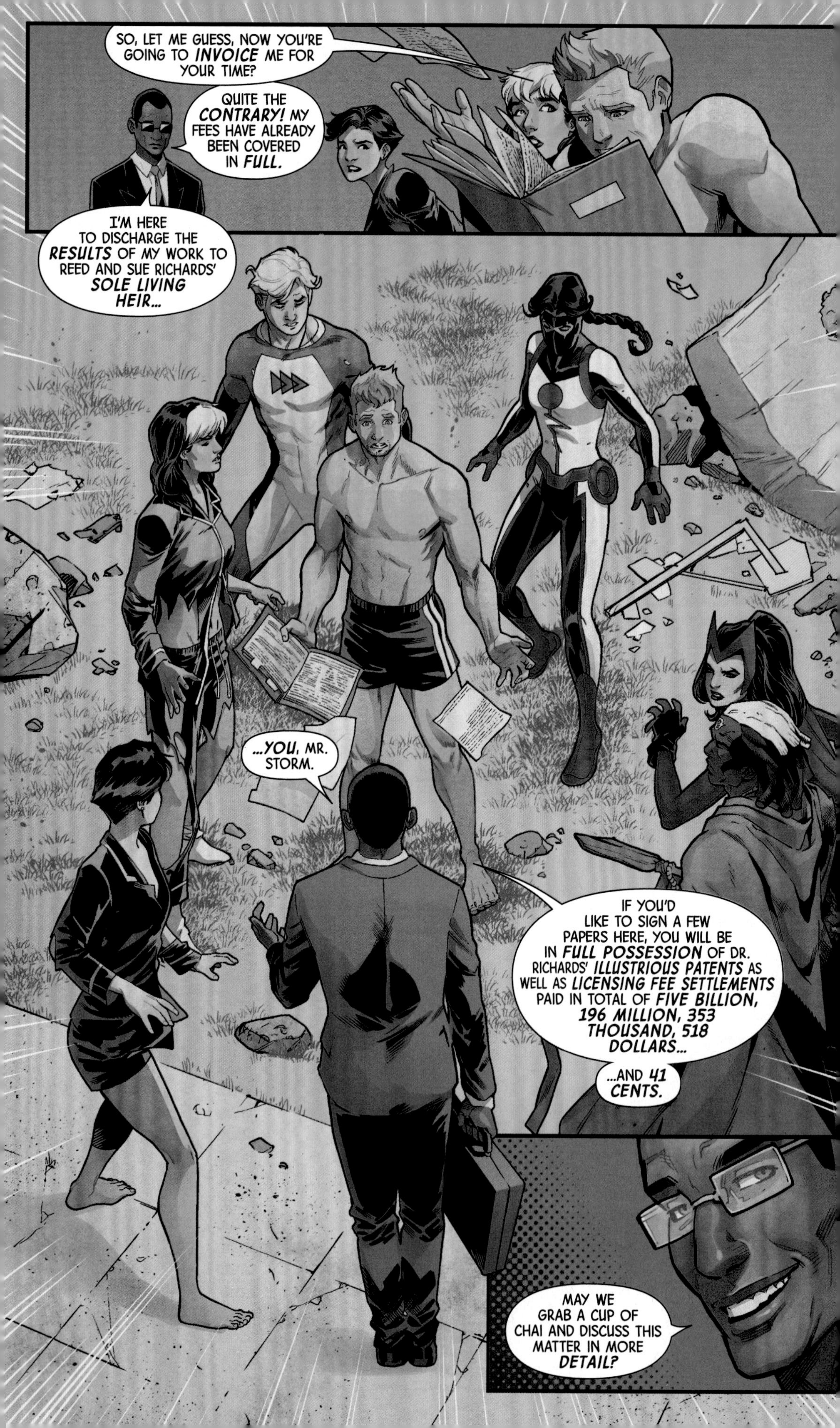
SO, LET ME GUESS, NOW YOU'RE GOING TO INVOICE ME FOR YOUR TIME?
QUITE THE CONTRARY! MY FEES HAVE ALREADY BEEN COVERED IN FULL.
I'M HERE TO DISCHARGE THE RESULTS OF MY WORK TO REED AND SUE RICHARDS' SOLE LIVING HEIR...
...YOU, MR. STORM.
IF YOU'D LIKE TO SIGN A FEW PAPERS HERE, YOU WILL BE IN FULL POSSESSION OF DR. RICHARDS' ILLUSTRIOUS PATENTS AS WELL AS LICENSING FEE SETTLEMENTS PAID IN TOTAL OF FIVE BILLION, 196 MILLION, 353 THOUSAND, 518 DOLLARS...
...AND 41 CENTS.
MAY WE GRAB A CUP OF CHAI AND DISCUSS THIS MATTER IN MORE DETAIL?

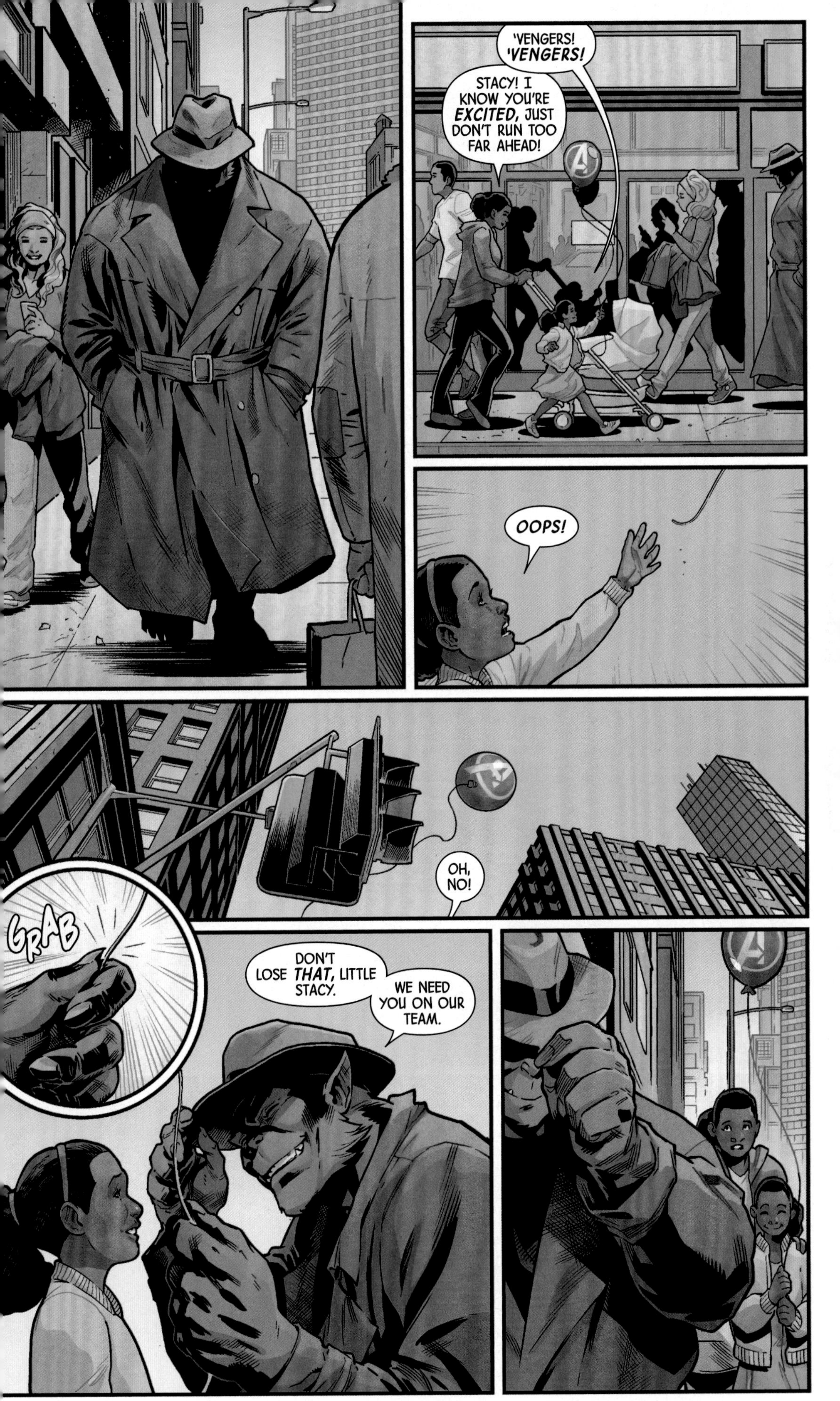
'VENGERS! 'VENGERS!
STACY! I KNOW YOU'RE EXCITED, JUST DON'T RUN TOO FAR AHEAD!
OOPS!
OH, NO!
GRAB
DON'T LOSE THAT, LITTLE STACY.
WE NEED YOU ON OUR TEAM.

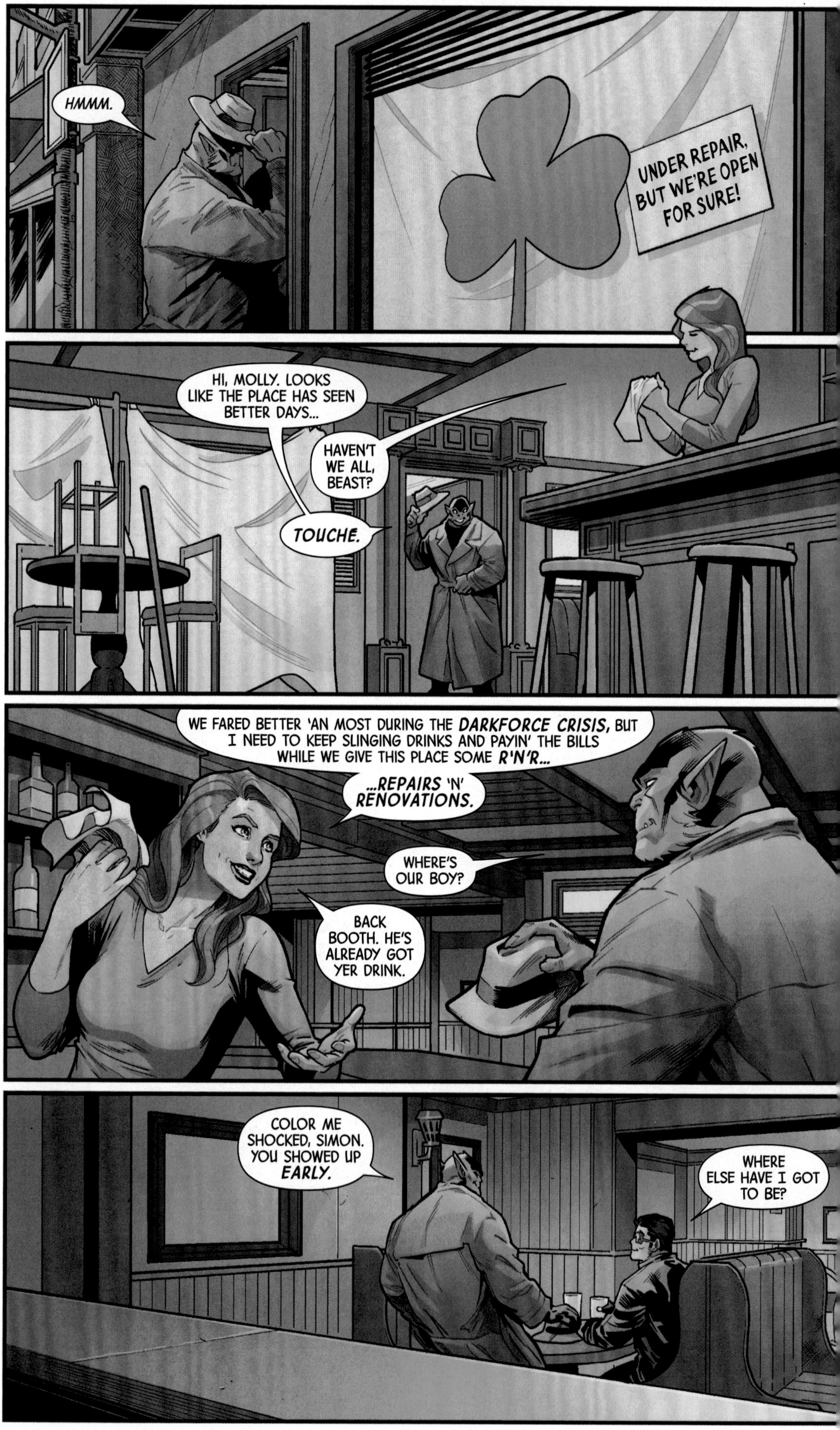
HMMM.
UNDER REPAIR, BUT WE'RE OPEN FOR SURE!
HI, MOLLY. LOOKS LIKE THE PLACE HAS SEEN BETTER DAYS...
HAVEN'T WE ALL, BEAST?
TOUCHÉ.
WE FARED BETTER 'AN MOST DURING THE DARKFORCE CRISIS, BUT I NEED TO KEEP SLINGING DRINKS AND PAYIN' THE BILLS WHILE WE GIVE THIS PLACE SOME R'N'R...
...REPAIRS 'N' RENOVATIONS.
WHERE'S OUR BOY?
BACK BOOTH. HE'S ALREADY GOT YER DRINK.
COLOR ME SHOCKED, SIMON. YOU SHOWED UP EARLY.
WHERE ELSE HAVE I GOT TO BE?

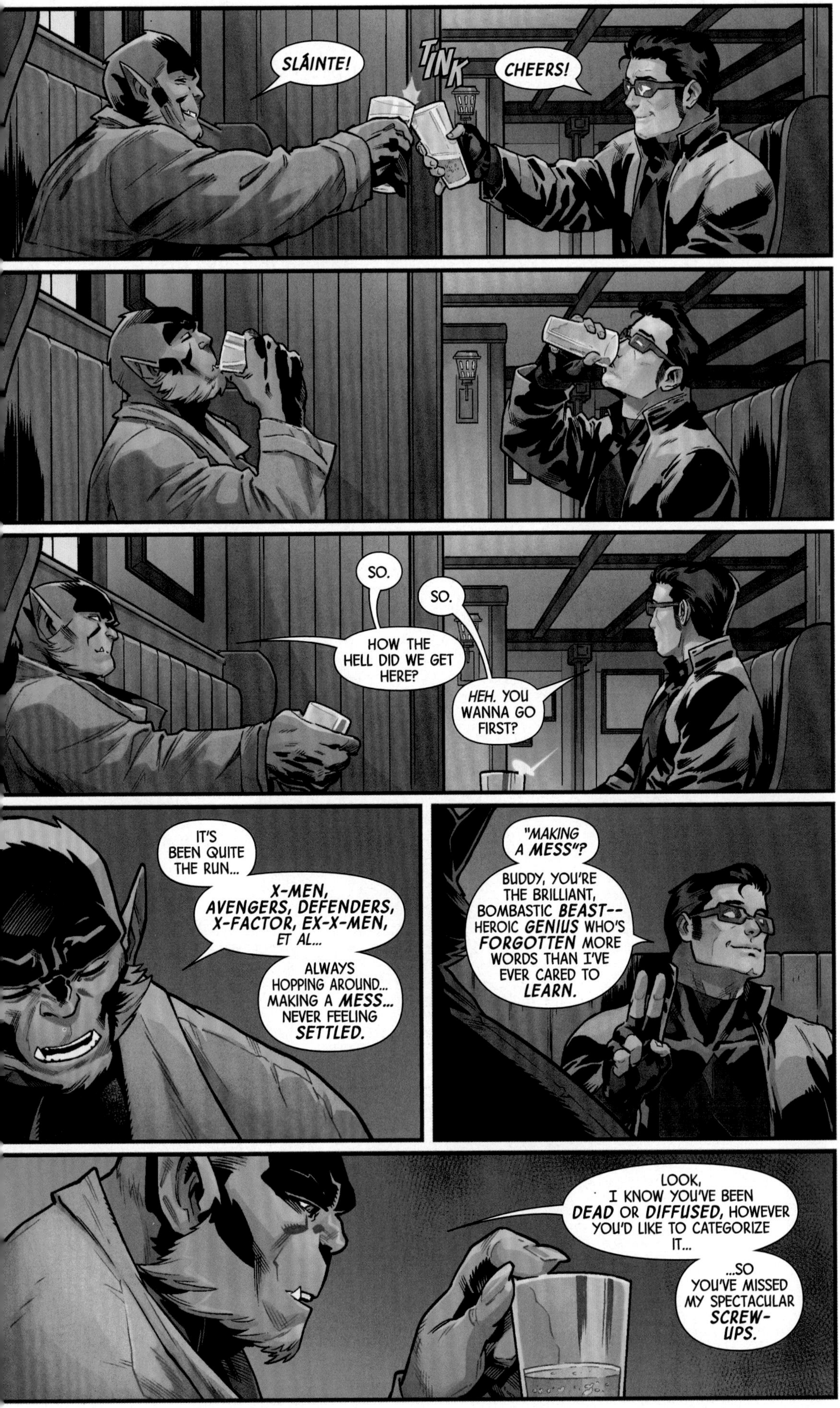
SLÁINTE!
TINK
CHEERS!
SO.
SO.
HOW THE HELL DID WE GET HERE?
HEH. YOU WANNA GO FIRST?
IT'S BEEN QUITE THE RUN...
X-MEN, AVENGERS, DEFENDERS, X-FACTOR, EX-X-MEN, ET AL...
ALWAYS HOPPING AROUND... MAKING A MESS... NEVER FEELING SETTLED.
"MAKING A MESS"?
BUDDY, YOU'RE THE BRILLIANT, BOMBASTIC BEAST--HEROIC GENIUS WHO'S FORGOTTEN MORE WORDS THAN I'VE EVER CARED TO LEARN.
LOOK, I KNOW YOU'VE BEEN DEAD OR DIFFUSED, HOWEVER YOU'D LIKE TO CATEGORIZE IT...
...SO YOU'VE MISSED MY SPECTACULAR SCREW-UPS.

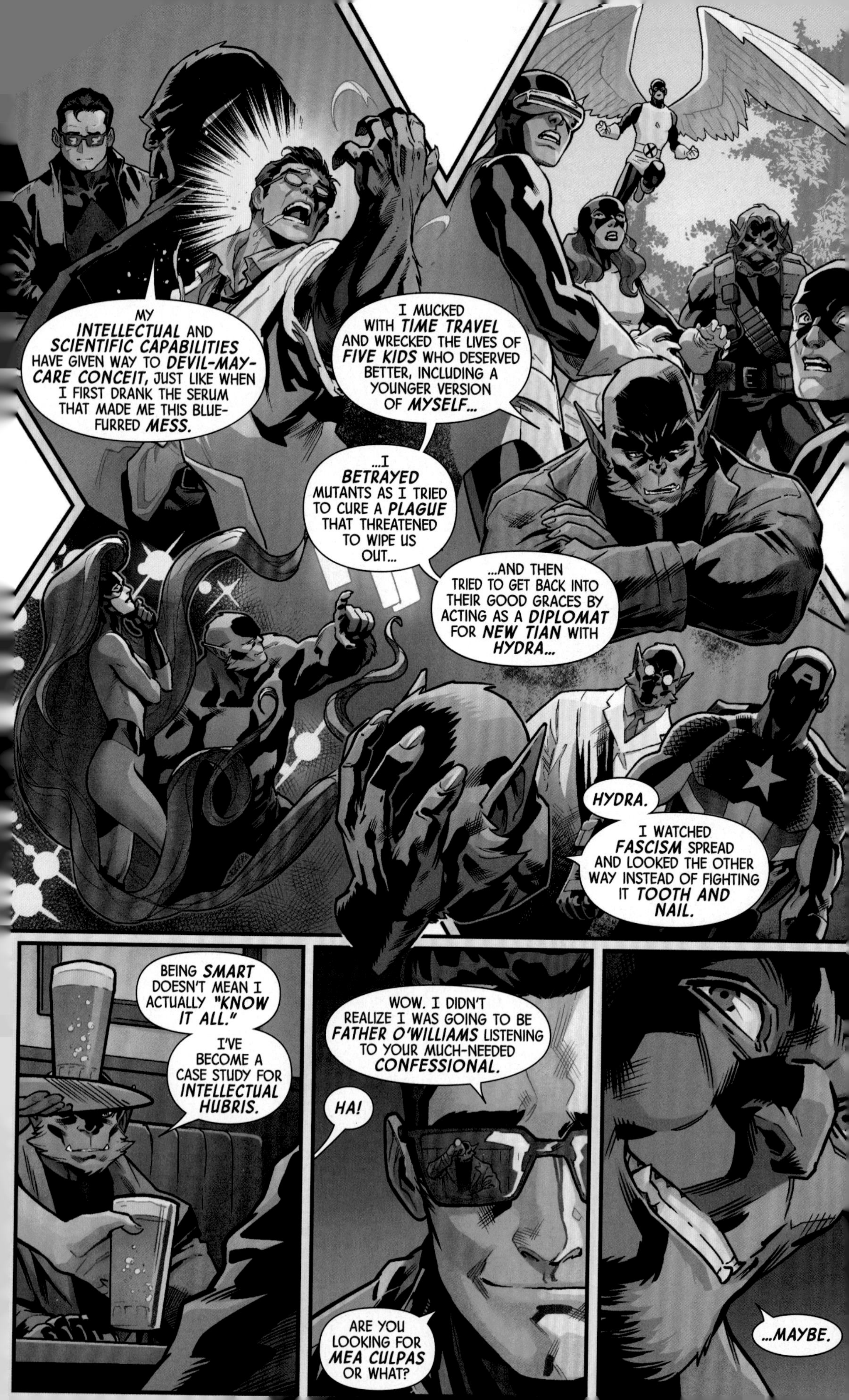
MY INTELLECTUAL AND SCIENTIFIC CAPABILITIES HAVE GIVEN WAY TO DEVIL-MAY-CARE CONCEIT, JUST LIKE WHEN I FIRST DRANK THE SERUM THAT MADE ME THIS BLUE-FURRED MESS.
I MUCKED WITH TIME TRAVEL AND WRECKED THE LIVES OF FIVE KIDS WHO DESERVED BETTER, INCLUDING A YOUNGER VERSION OF MYSELF...
...I BETRAYED MUTANTS AS I TRIED TO CURE A PLAGUE THAT THREATENED TO WIPE US OUT...
...AND THEN TRIED TO GET BACK INTO THEIR GOOD GRACES BY ACTING AS A DIPLOMAT FOR NEW TIAN WITH HYDRA...
HYDRA.
I WATCHED FASCISM SPREAD AND LOOKED THE OTHER WAY INSTEAD OF FIGHTING IT TOOTH AND NAIL.
BEING SMART DOESN'T MEAN I ACTUALLY "KNOW IT ALL."
I'VE BECOME A CASE STUDY FOR INTELLECTUAL HUBRIS.
WOW. I DIDN'T REALIZE I WAS GOING TO BE FATHER O'WILLIAMS LISTENING TO YOUR MUCH-NEEDED CONFESSIONAL.
HA!
ARE YOU LOOKING FOR MEA CULPAS OR WHAT?
...MAYBE.

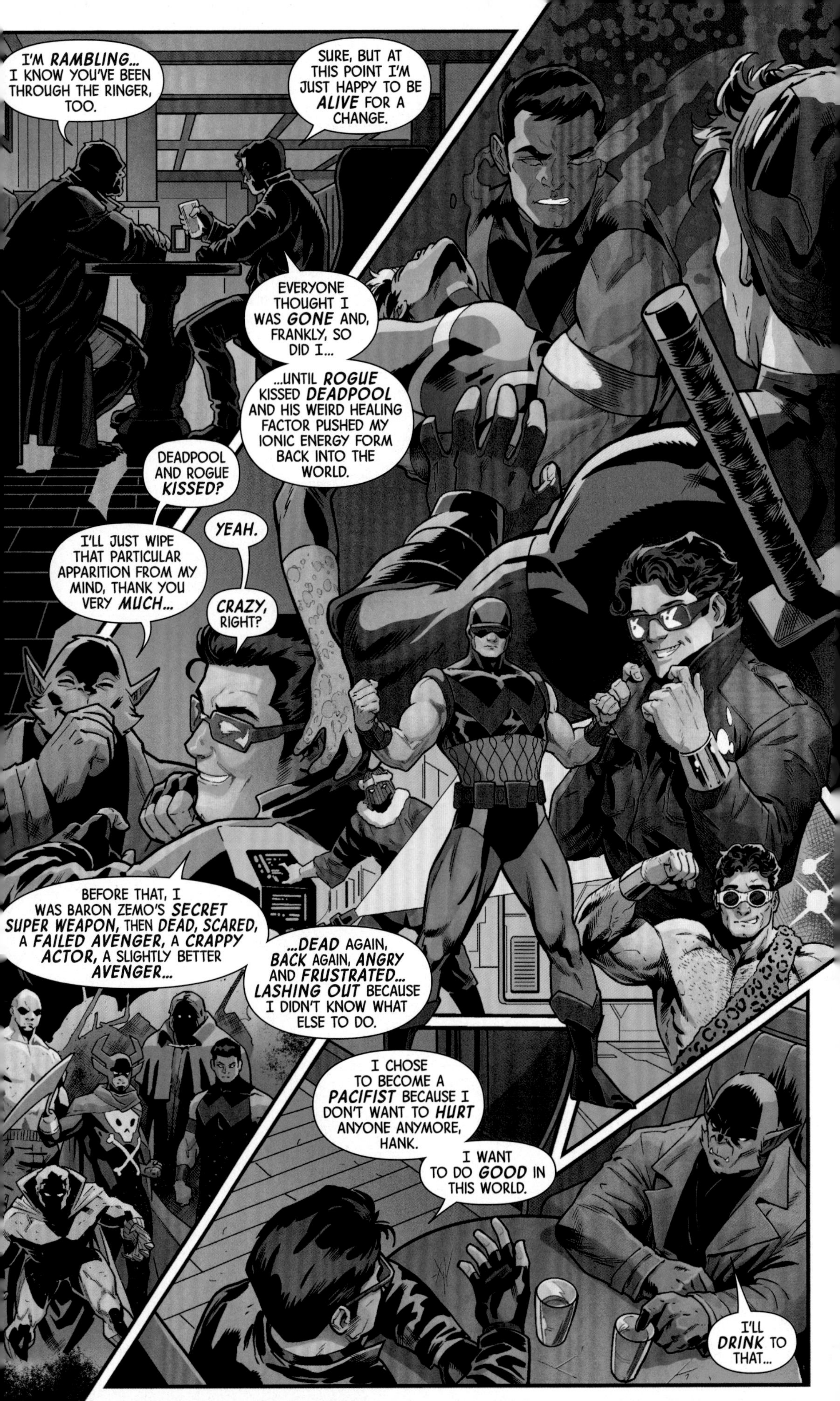
I'M RAMBLING... I KNOW YOU'VE BEEN THROUGH THE RINGER, TOO.
SURE, BUT AT THIS POINT I'M JUST HAPPY TO BE ALIVE FOR A CHANGE.
EVERYONE THOUGHT I WAS GONE AND, FRANKLY, SO DID I...
...UNTIL ROGUE KISSED DEADPOOL AND HIS WEIRD HEALING FACTOR PUSHED MY IONIC ENERGY FORM BACK INTO THE WORLD.
DEADPOOL AND ROGUE KISSED?
YEAH.
I'LL JUST WIPE THAT PARTICULAR APPARITION FROM MY MIND, THANK YOU VERY MUCH...
CRAZY, RIGHT?
BEFORE THAT, I WAS BARON ZEMO'S SECRET SUPER WEAPON, THEN DEAD, SCARED, A FAILED AVENGER, A CRAPPY ACTOR, A SLIGHTLY BETTER AVENGER...
...DEAD AGAIN, BACK AGAIN, ANGRY AND FRUSTRATED... LASHING OUT BECAUSE I DIDN'T KNOW WHAT ELSE TO DO.
I CHOSE TO BECOME A PACIFIST BECAUSE I DON'T WANT TO HURT ANYONE ANYMORE, HANK.
I WANT TO DO GOOD IN THIS WORLD.
I'LL DRINK TO THAT...

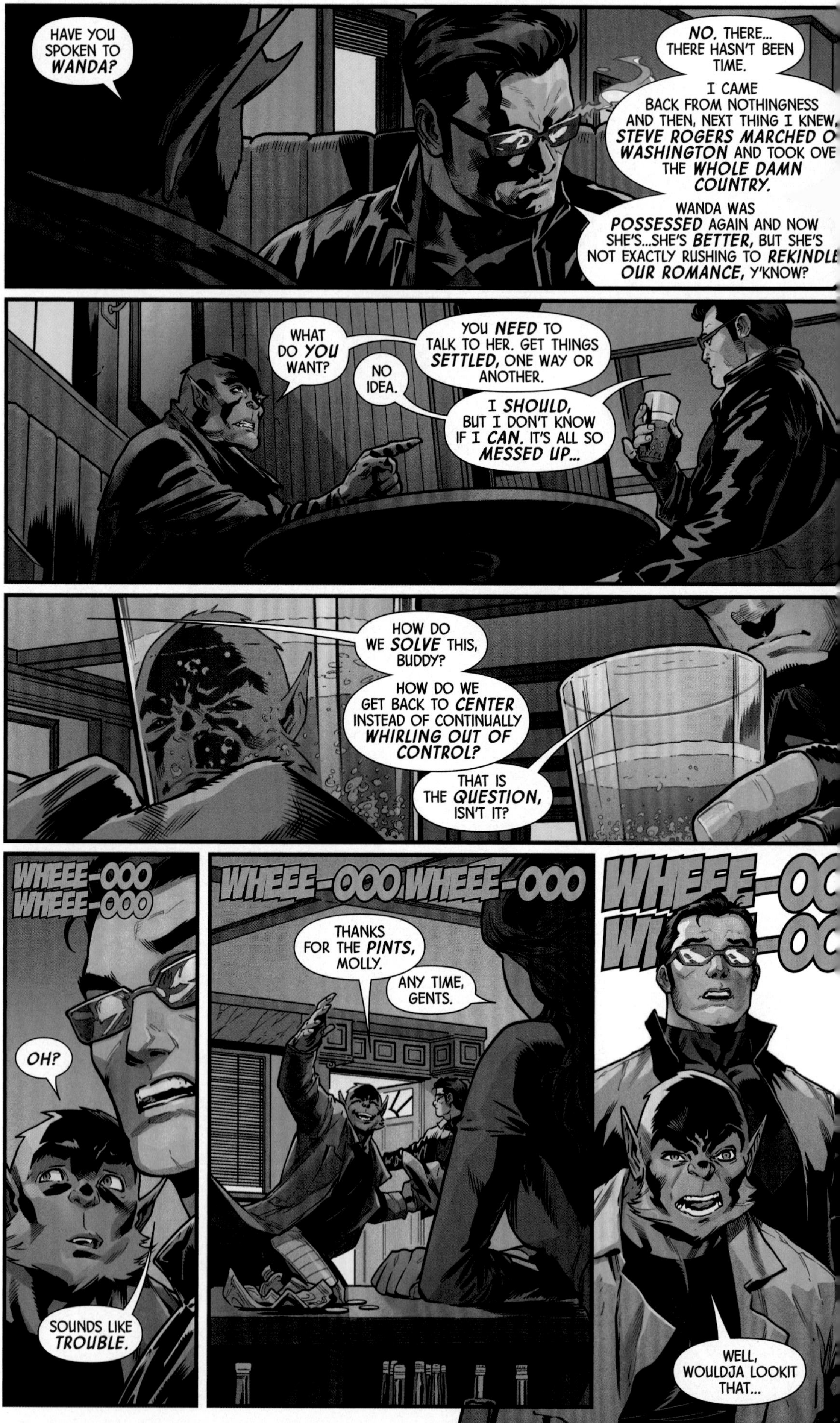
HAVE YOU SPOKEN TO WANDA?
NO. THERE... THERE HASN'T BEEN TIME.
I CAME BACK FROM NOTHINGNESS AND THEN, NEXT THING I KNEW, STEVE ROGERS MARCHED O WASHINGTON AND TOOK OVE THE WHOLE DAMN COUNTRY.
WANDA WAS POSSESSED AGAIN AND NOW SHE'S...SHE'S BETTER, BUT SHE'S NOT EXACTLY RUSHING TO REKINDLE OUR ROMANCE, Y'KNOW?
YOU NEED TO TALK TO HER. GET THINGS SETTLED, ONE WAY OR ANOTHER.
WHAT DO YOU WANT?
NO IDEA.
I SHOULD, BUT I DON'T KNOW IF I CAN. IT'S ALL SO MESSED UP...
HOW DO WE SOLVE THIS, BUDDY?
HOW DO WE GET BACK TO CENTER INSTEAD OF CONTINUALLY WHIRLING OUT OF CONTROL?
THAT IS THE QUESTION, ISN'T IT?
WHEEE-OOO WHEEE-OOO
OH?
SOUNDS LIKE TROUBLE.
WHEEE-OOO WHEEE-OOO
THANKS FOR THE PINTS, MOLLY.
ANY TIME, GENTS.
WELL, WOULDJA LOOKIT THAT...

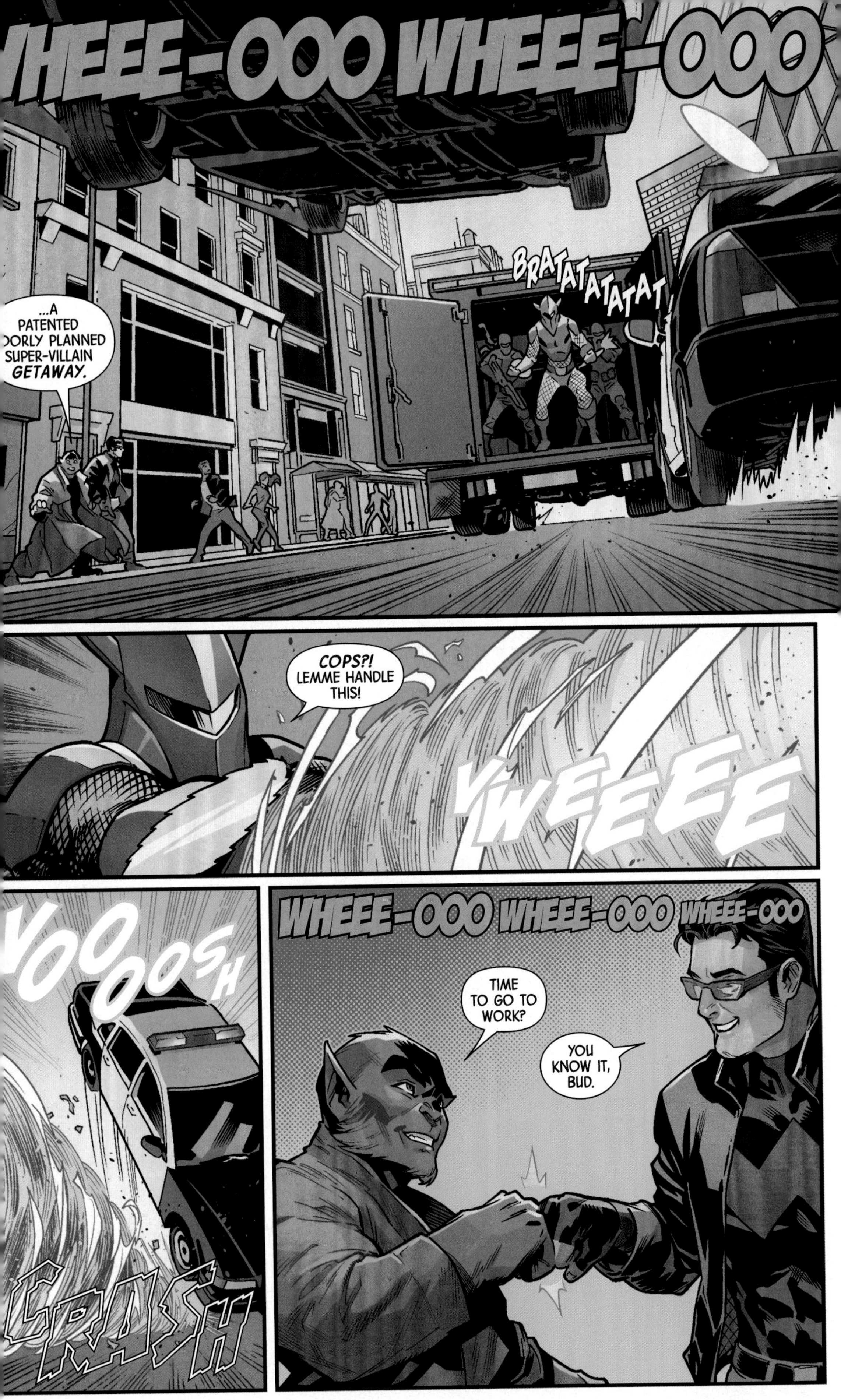
WHEEE-OOO WHEEE-OOO
...A PATENTED ...ORLY PLANNED SUPER-VILLAIN GETAWAY.
BRATATATATATAT
COPS?! LEMME HANDLE THIS!
VWEEEE
VOOOOOSH
CRASH
WHEEE-OOO WHEEE-OOO WHEEE-OOO
TIME TO GO TO WORK?
YOU KNOW IT, BUD.

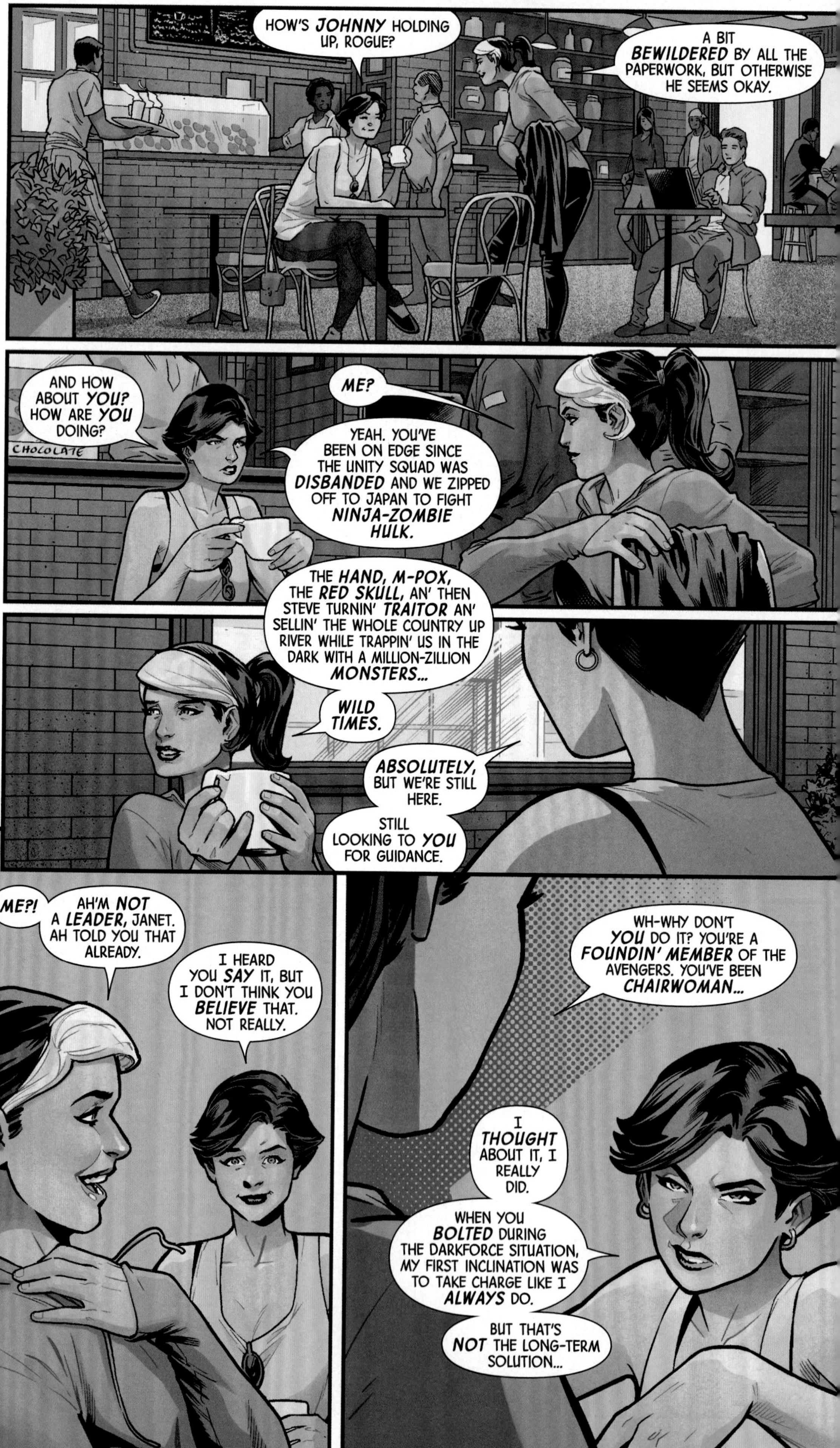
HOW'S JOHNNY HOLDING UP, ROGUE?
A BIT BEWILDERED BY ALL THE PAPERWORK, BUT OTHERWISE HE SEEMS OKAY.
AND HOW ABOUT YOU? HOW ARE YOU DOING?
CHOCOLATE
ME?
YEAH. YOU'VE BEEN ON EDGE SINCE THE UNITY SQUAD WAS DISBANDED AND WE ZIPPED OFF TO JAPAN TO FIGHT NINJA-ZOMBIE HULK.
THE HAND, M-POX, THE RED SKULL, AN' THEN STEVE TURNIN' TRAITOR AN' SELLIN' THE WHOLE COUNTRY UP RIVER WHILE TRAPPIN' US IN THE DARK WITH A MILLION-ZILLION MONSTERS...
WILD TIMES.
ABSOLUTELY, BUT WE'RE STILL HERE.
STILL LOOKING TO YOU FOR GUIDANCE.
ME?!
AH'M NOT A LEADER, JANET. AH TOLD YOU THAT ALREADY.
I HEARD YOU SAY IT, BUT I DON'T THINK YOU BELIEVE THAT. NOT REALLY.
WH-WHY DON'T YOU DO IT? YOU'RE A FOUNDIN' MEMBER OF THE AVENGERS. YOU'VE BEEN CHAIRWOMAN...
I THOUGHT ABOUT IT, I REALLY DID.
WHEN YOU BOLTED DURING THE DARKFORCE SITUATION, MY FIRST INCLINATION WAS TO TAKE CHARGE LIKE I ALWAYS DO.
BUT THAT'S NOT THE LONG-TERM SOLUTION...

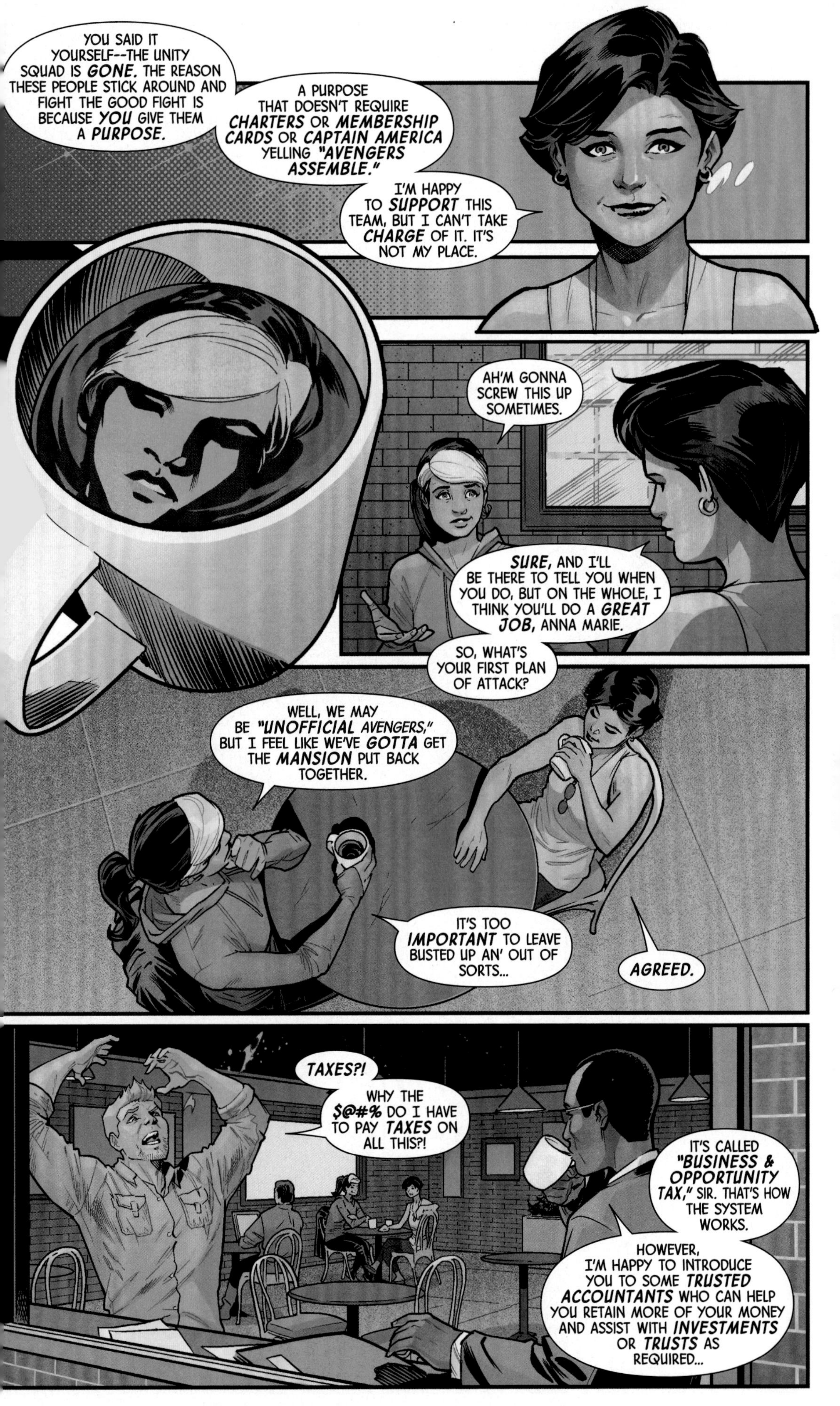
YOU SAID IT YOURSELF--THE UNITY SQUAD IS GONE. THE REASON THESE PEOPLE STICK AROUND AND FIGHT THE GOOD FIGHT IS BECAUSE YOU GIVE THEM A PURPOSE.
A PURPOSE THAT DOESN'T REQUIRE CHARTERS OR MEMBERSHIP CARDS OR CAPTAIN AMERICA YELLING "AVENGERS ASSEMBLE."
I'M HAPPY TO SUPPORT THIS TEAM, BUT I CAN'T TAKE CHARGE OF IT. IT'S NOT MY PLACE.
AH'M GONNA SCREW THIS UP SOMETIMES.
SURE, AND I'LL BE THERE TO TELL YOU WHEN YOU DO, BUT ON THE WHOLE, I THINK YOU'LL DO A GREAT JOB, ANNA MARIE.
SO, WHAT'S YOUR FIRST PLAN OF ATTACK?
WELL, WE MAY BE "UNOFFICIAL AVENGERS," BUT I FEEL LIKE WE'VE GOTTA GET THE MANSION PUT BACK TOGETHER.
IT'S TOO IMPORTANT TO LEAVE BUSTED UP AN' OUT OF SORTS...
AGREED.
TAXES?!
WHY THE $@#% DO I HAVE TO PAY TAXES ON ALL THIS?!
IT'S CALLED "BUSINESS & OPPORTUNITY TAX," SIR. THAT'S HOW THE SYSTEM WORKS.
HOWEVER, I'M HAPPY TO INTRODUCE YOU TO SOME TRUSTED ACCOUNTANTS WHO CAN HELP YOU RETAIN MORE OF YOUR MONEY AND ASSIST WITH INVESTMENTS OR TRUSTS AS REQUIRED...

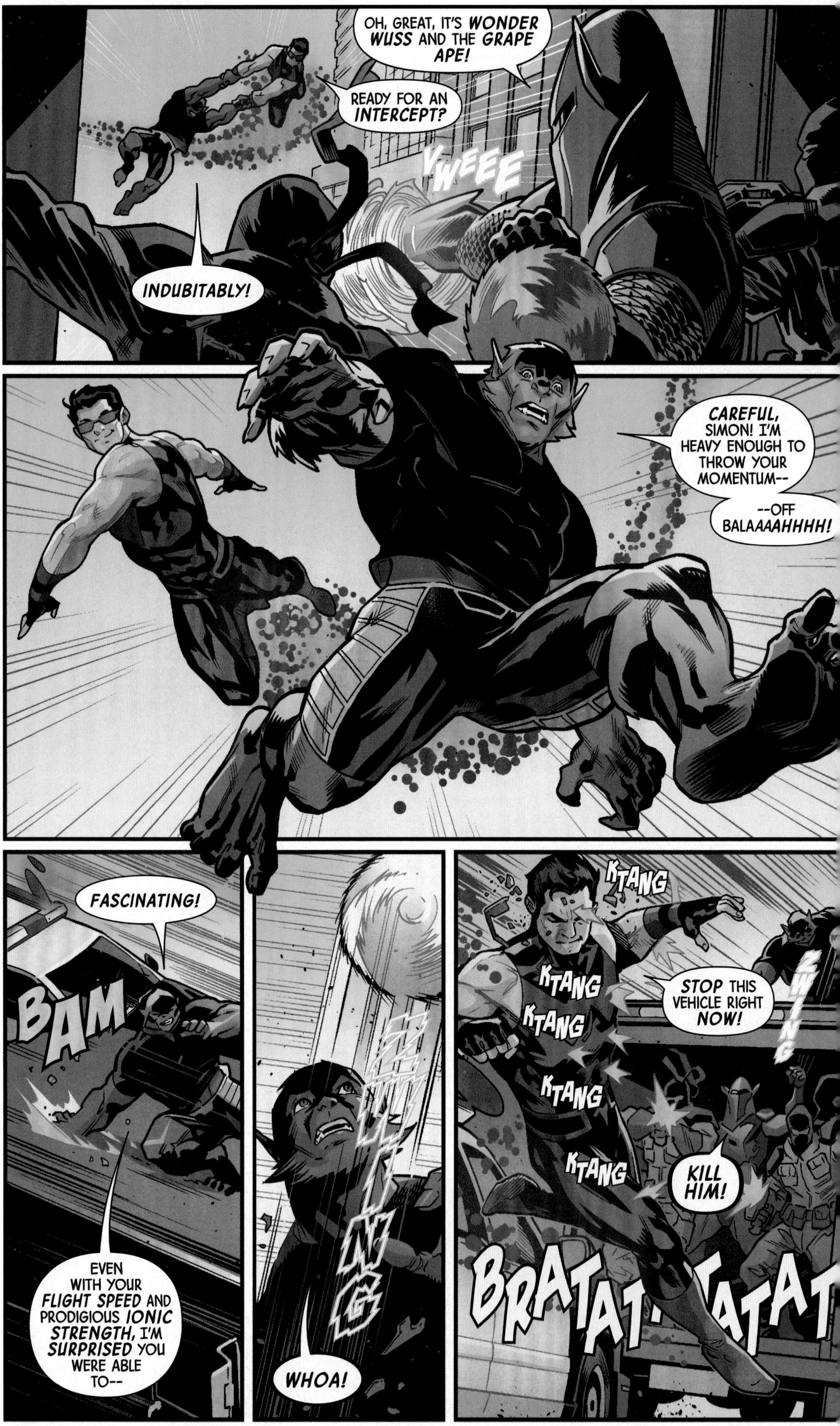
OH, GREAT, IT'S WONDER WUSS AND THE GRAPE APE!
READY FOR AN INTERCEPT?
VWEEE
INDUBITABLY!
CAREFUL, SIMON! I'M HEAVY ENOUGH TO THROW YOUR MOMENTUM--
--OFF BALAAAAHHHH!
FASCINATING!
BAM
EVEN WITH YOUR FLIGHT SPEED AND PRODIGIOUS IONIC STRENGTH, I'M SURPRISED YOU WERE ABLE TO--
WHOA!
KTANG
STOP THIS VEHICLE RIGHT NOW!
KTANG
KTANG
KTANG
KTANG
KILL HIM!
ZWING
BRATATATATAT

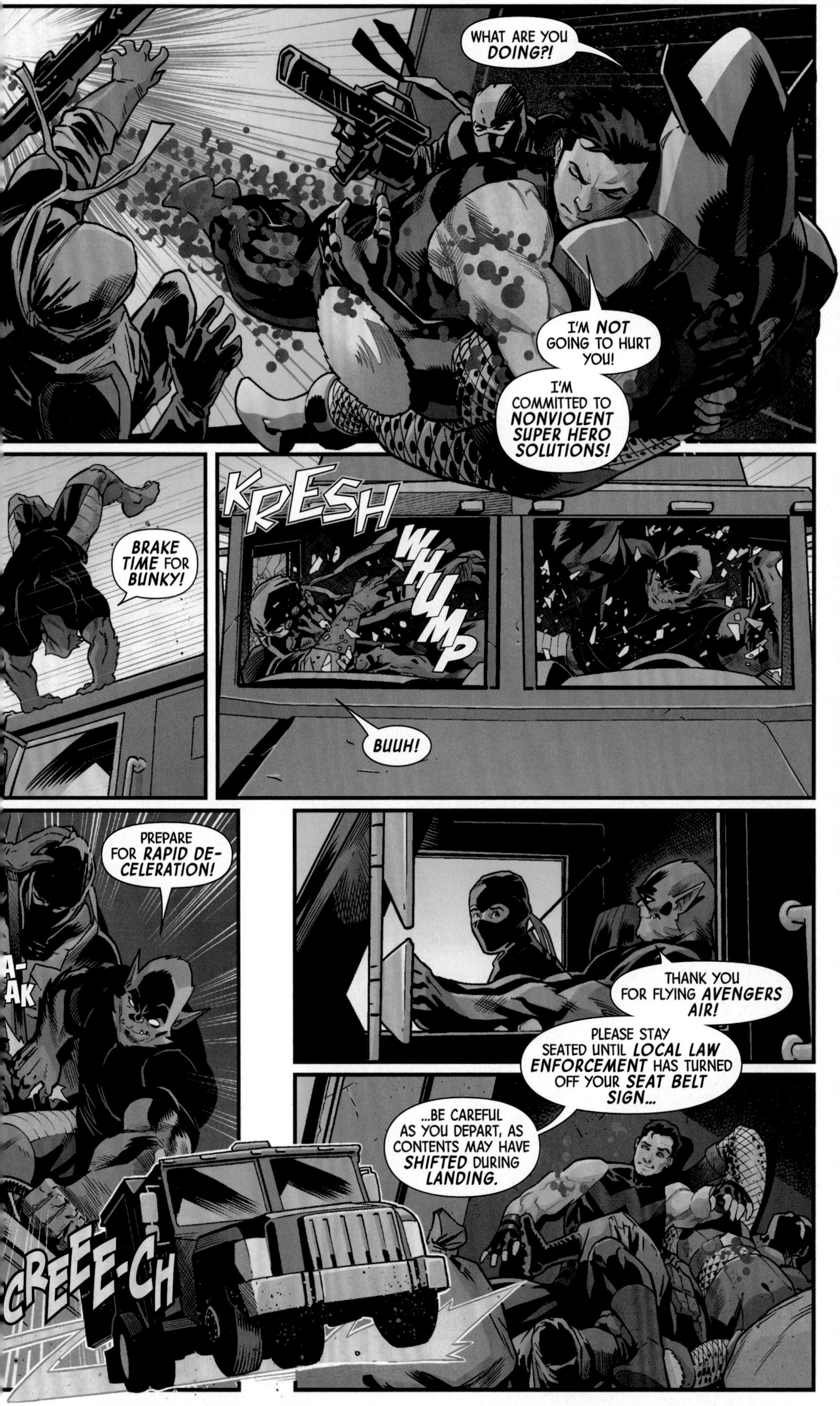
WHAT ARE YOU DOING?!
I'M NOT GOING TO HURT YOU!
I'M COMMITTED TO NONVIOLENT SUPER HERO SOLUTIONS!
BRAKE TIME FOR BUNKY!
KRESH
WHUMP
BUUH!
PREPARE FOR RAPID DE-CELERATION!
CREEE-CH
THANK YOU FOR FLYING AVENGERS AIR!
PLEASE STAY SEATED UNTIL LOCAL LAW ENFORCEMENT HAS TURNED OFF YOUR SEAT BELT SIGN...
...BE CAREFUL AS YOU DEPART, AS CONTENTS MAY HAVE SHIFTED DURING LANDING.

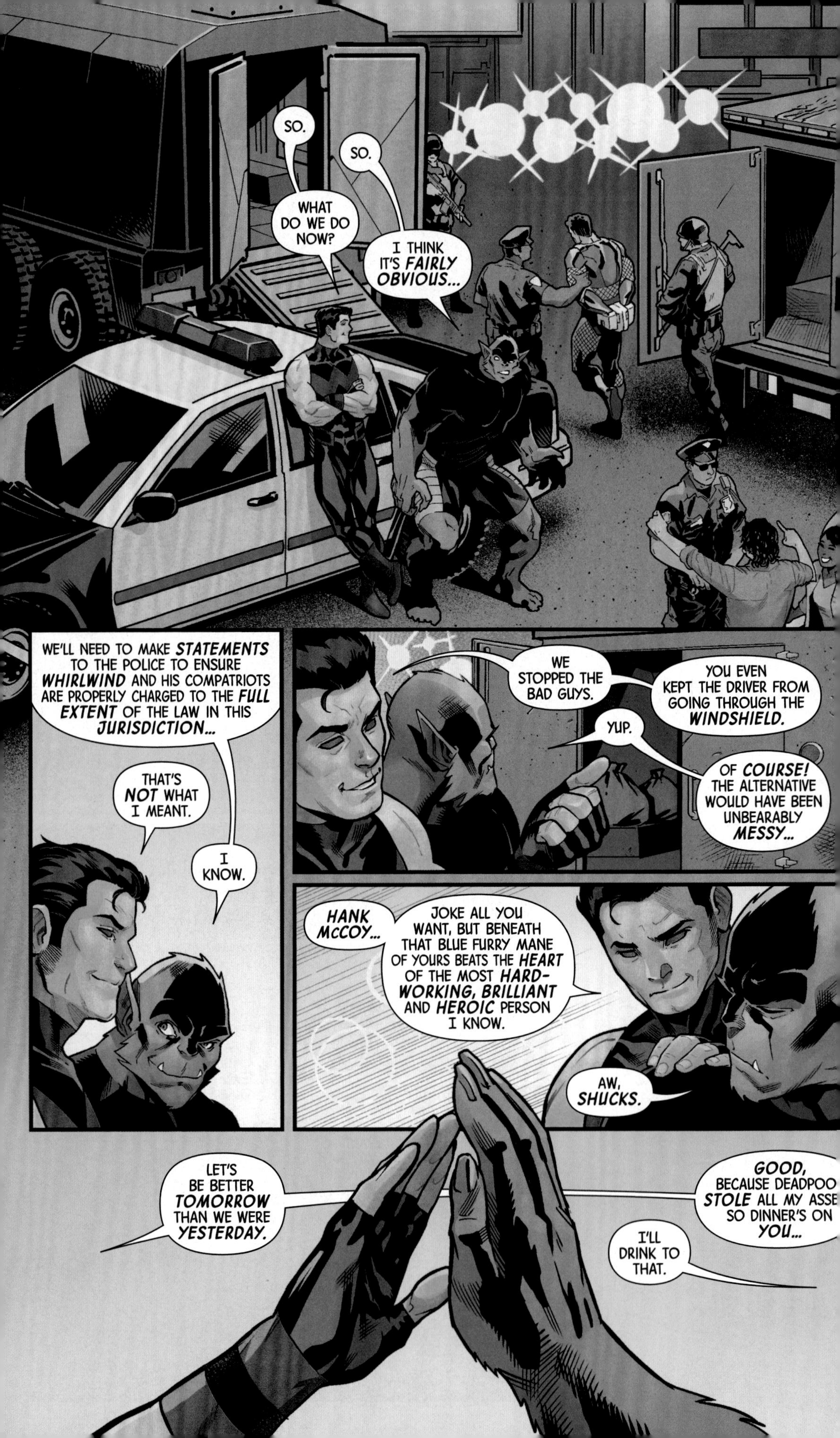
SO.
SO.
WHAT DO WE DO NOW?
I THINK IT'S FAIRLY OBVIOUS...
WE'LL NEED TO MAKE STATEMENTS TO THE POLICE TO ENSURE WHIRLWIND AND HIS COMPATRIOTS ARE PROPERLY CHARGED TO THE FULL EXTENT OF THE LAW IN THIS JURISDICTION...
THAT'S NOT WHAT I MEANT.
I KNOW.
WE STOPPED THE BAD GUYS.
YOU EVEN KEPT THE DRIVER FROM GOING THROUGH THE WINDSHIELD.
YUP.
OF COURSE! THE ALTERNATIVE WOULD HAVE BEEN UNBEARABLY MESSY...
HANK McCOY...
JOKE ALL YOU WANT, BUT BENEATH THAT BLUE FURRY MANE OF YOURS BEATS THE HEART OF THE MOST HARD-WORKING, BRILLIANT AND HEROIC PERSON I KNOW.
AW, SHUCKS.
LET'S BE BETTER TOMORROW THAN WE WERE YESTERDAY.
GOOD, BECAUSE DEADPOO STOLE ALL MY ASSE SO DINNER'S ON YOU...
I'LL DRINK TO THAT.

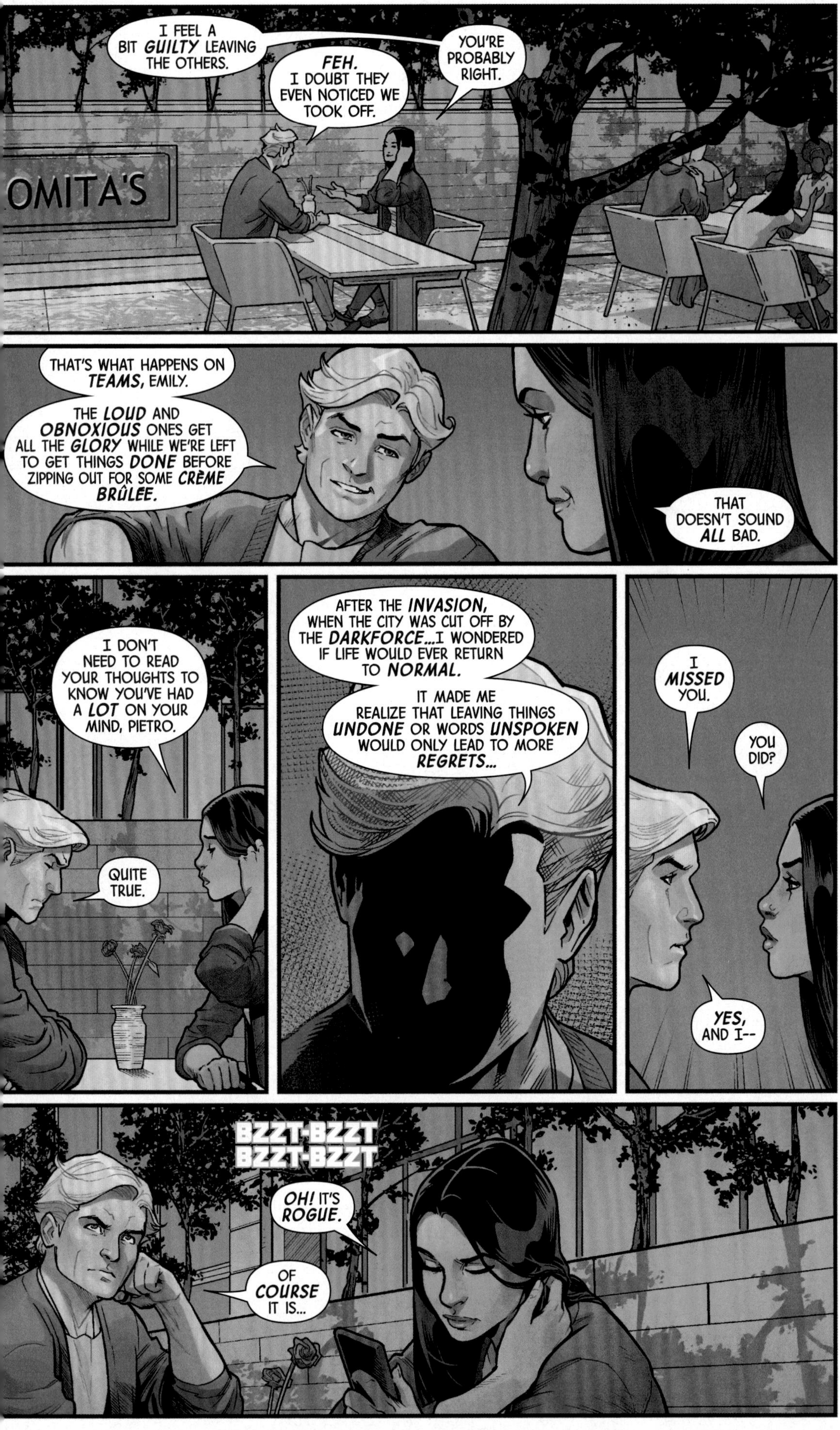

OMITA'S
I FEEL A BIT GUILTY LEAVING THE OTHERS.
FEH. I DOUBT THEY EVEN NOTICED WE TOOK OFF.
YOU'RE PROBABLY RIGHT.
THAT'S WHAT HAPPENS ON TEAMS, EMILY.
THE LOUD AND OBNOXIOUS ONES GET ALL THE GLORY WHILE WE'RE LEFT TO GET THINGS DONE BEFORE ZIPPING OUT FOR SOME CRÈME BRÛLEE.
THAT DOESN'T SOUND ALL BAD.
I DON'T NEED TO READ YOUR THOUGHTS TO KNOW YOU'VE HAD A LOT ON YOUR MIND, PIETRO.
QUITE TRUE.
AFTER THE INVASION, WHEN THE CITY WAS CUT OFF BY THE DARKFORCE...I WONDERED IF LIFE WOULD EVER RETURN TO NORMAL.
IT MADE ME REALIZE THAT LEAVING THINGS UNDONE OR WORDS UNSPOKEN WOULD ONLY LEAD TO MORE REGRETS...
I MISSED YOU.
YOU DID?
YES, AND I--
BZZT-BZZT BZZT-BZZT
OH! IT'S ROGUE.
OF COURSE IT IS...

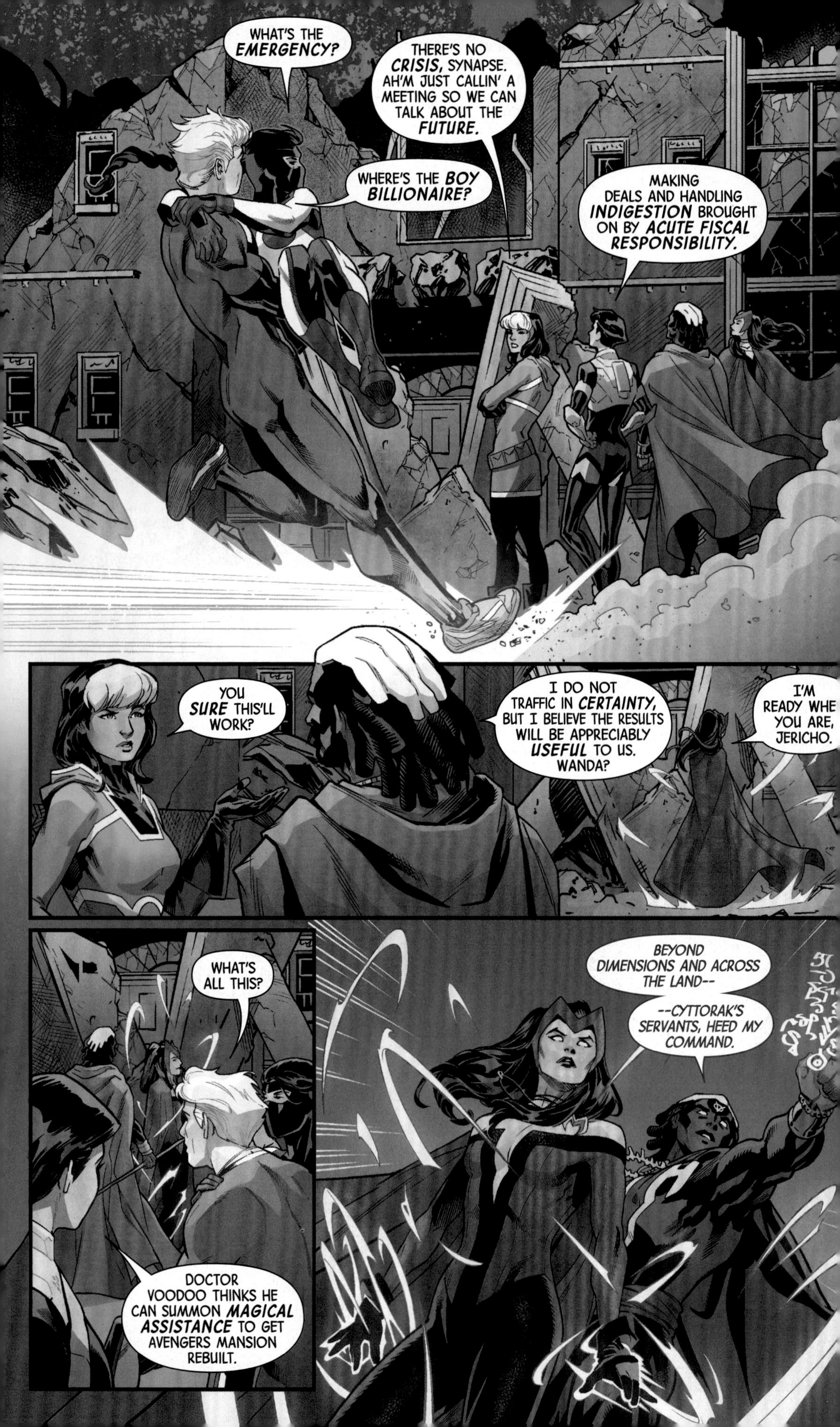
WHAT'S THE EMERGENCY?
THERE'S NO CRISIS, SYNAPSE. AH'M JUST CALLIN' A MEETING SO WE CAN TALK ABOUT THE FUTURE.
WHERE'S THE BOY BILLIONAIRE?
MAKING DEALS AND HANDLING INDIGESTION BROUGHT ON BY ACUTE FISCAL RESPONSIBILITY.
YOU SURE THIS'LL WORK?
I DO NOT TRAFFIC IN CERTAINTY, BUT I BELIEVE THE RESULTS WILL BE APPRECIABLY USEFUL TO US. WANDA?
I'M READY WHE YOU ARE, JERICHO.
WHAT'S ALL THIS?
DOCTOR VOODOO THINKS HE CAN SUMMON MAGICAL ASSISTANCE TO GET AVENGERS MANSION REBUILT.
BEYOND DIMENSIONS AND ACROSS THE LAND--
--CYTTORAK'S SERVANTS, HEED MY COMMAND.

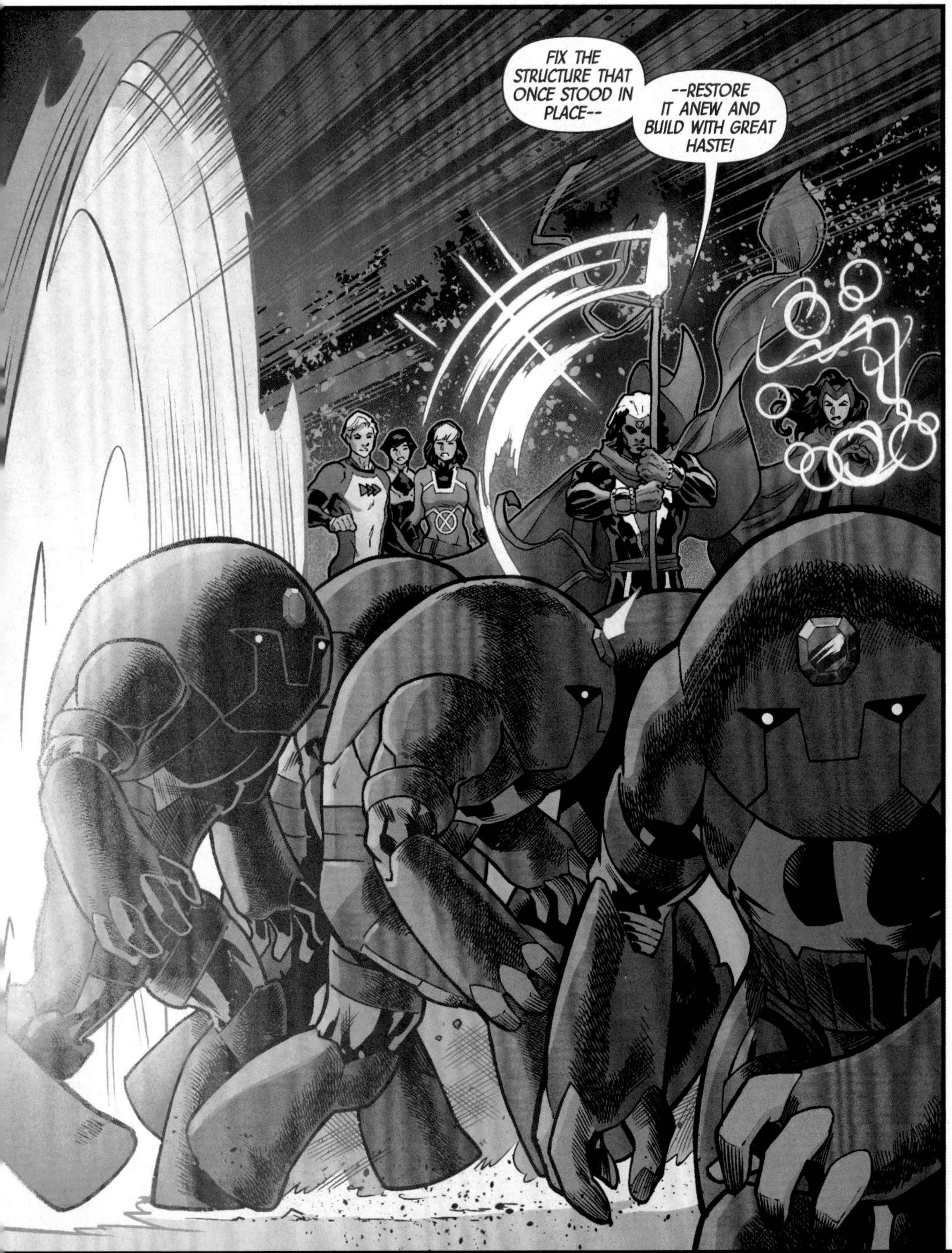
FIX THE STRUCTURE THAT ONCE STOOD IN PLACE--
--RESTORE IT ANEW AND BUILD WITH GREAT HASTE!

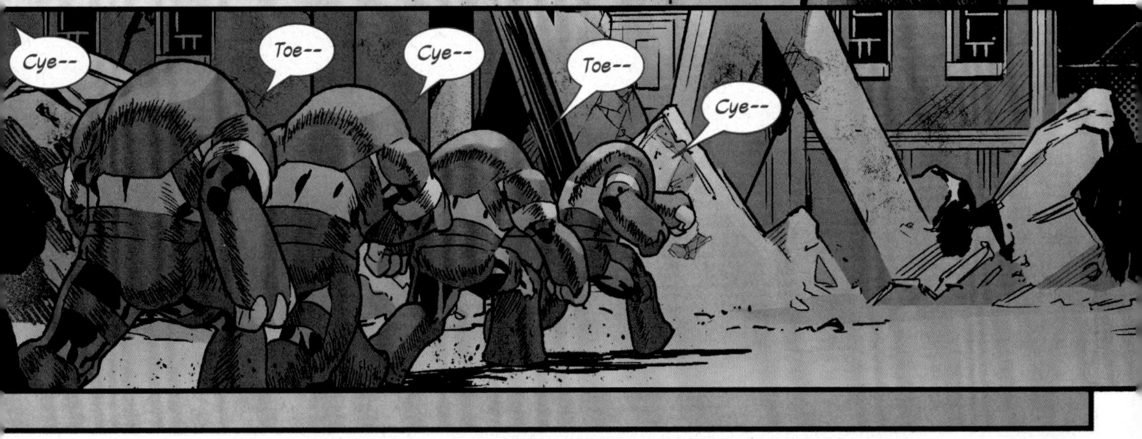
Cye--
Toe--
Cye--
Toe--
Cye--

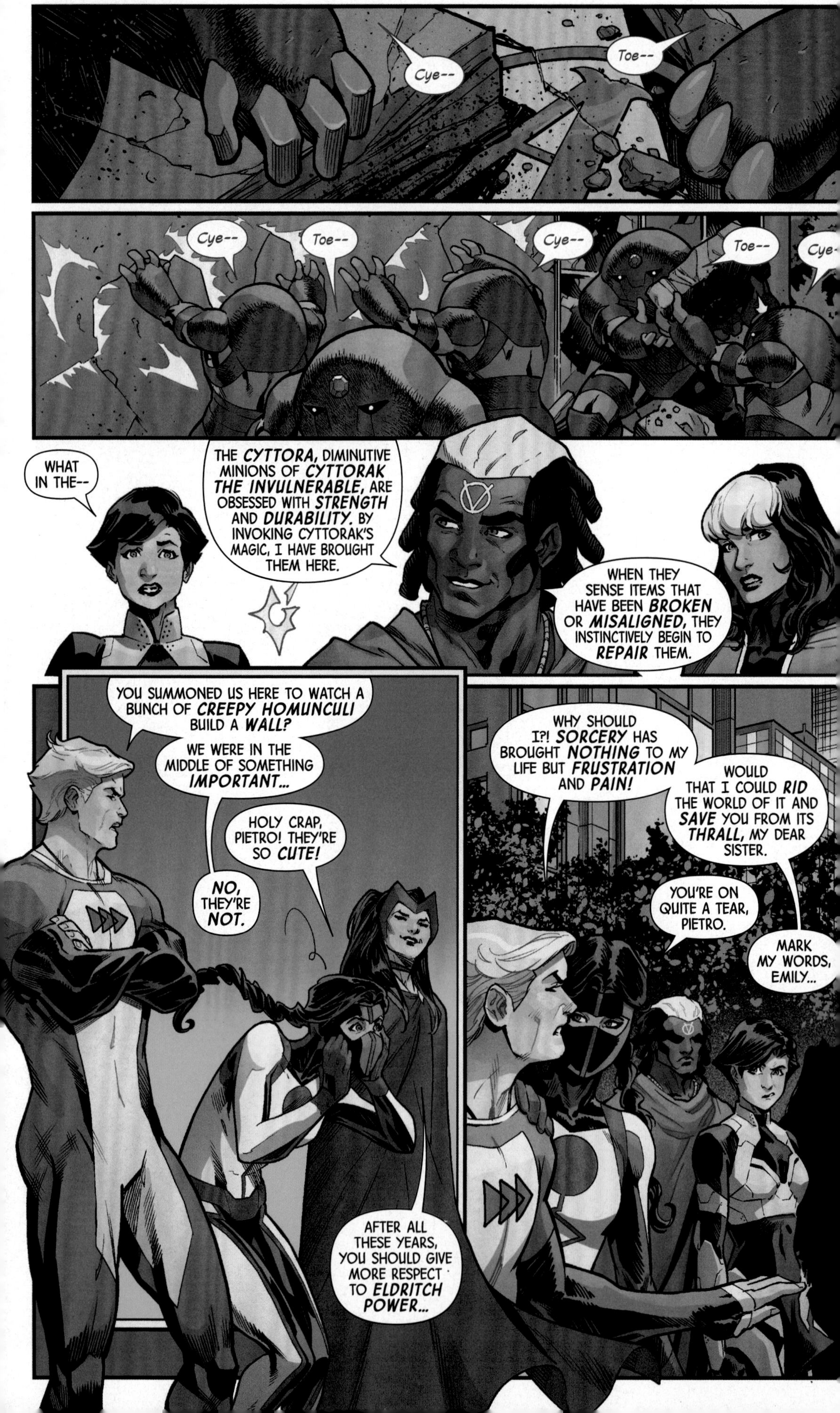
Cye--
Toe--
Cye--
Toe--
Cye--
Toe--
Cye-
WHAT IN THE--
THE CYTTORA, DIMINUTIVE MINIONS OF CYTTORAK THE INVULNERABLE, ARE OBSESSED WITH STRENGTH AND DURABILITY. BY INVOKING CYTTORAK'S MAGIC, I HAVE BROUGHT THEM HERE.
WHEN THEY SENSE ITEMS THAT HAVE BEEN BROKEN OR MISALIGNED, THEY INSTINCTIVELY BEGIN TO REPAIR THEM.
YOU SUMMONED US HERE TO WATCH A BUNCH OF CREEPY HOMUNCULI BUILD A WALL?
WE WERE IN THE MIDDLE OF SOMETHING IMPORTANT...
HOLY CRAP, PIETRO! THEY'RE SO CUTE!
NO, THEY'RE NOT.
AFTER ALL THESE YEARS, YOU SHOULD GIVE MORE RESPECT TO ELDRITCH POWER...
WHY SHOULD I?! SORCERY HAS BROUGHT NOTHING TO MY LIFE BUT FRUSTRATION AND PAIN!
WOULD THAT I COULD RID THE WORLD OF IT AND SAVE YOU FROM ITS THRALL, MY DEAR SISTER.
YOU'RE ON QUITE A TEAR, PIETRO.
MARK MY WORDS, EMILY...

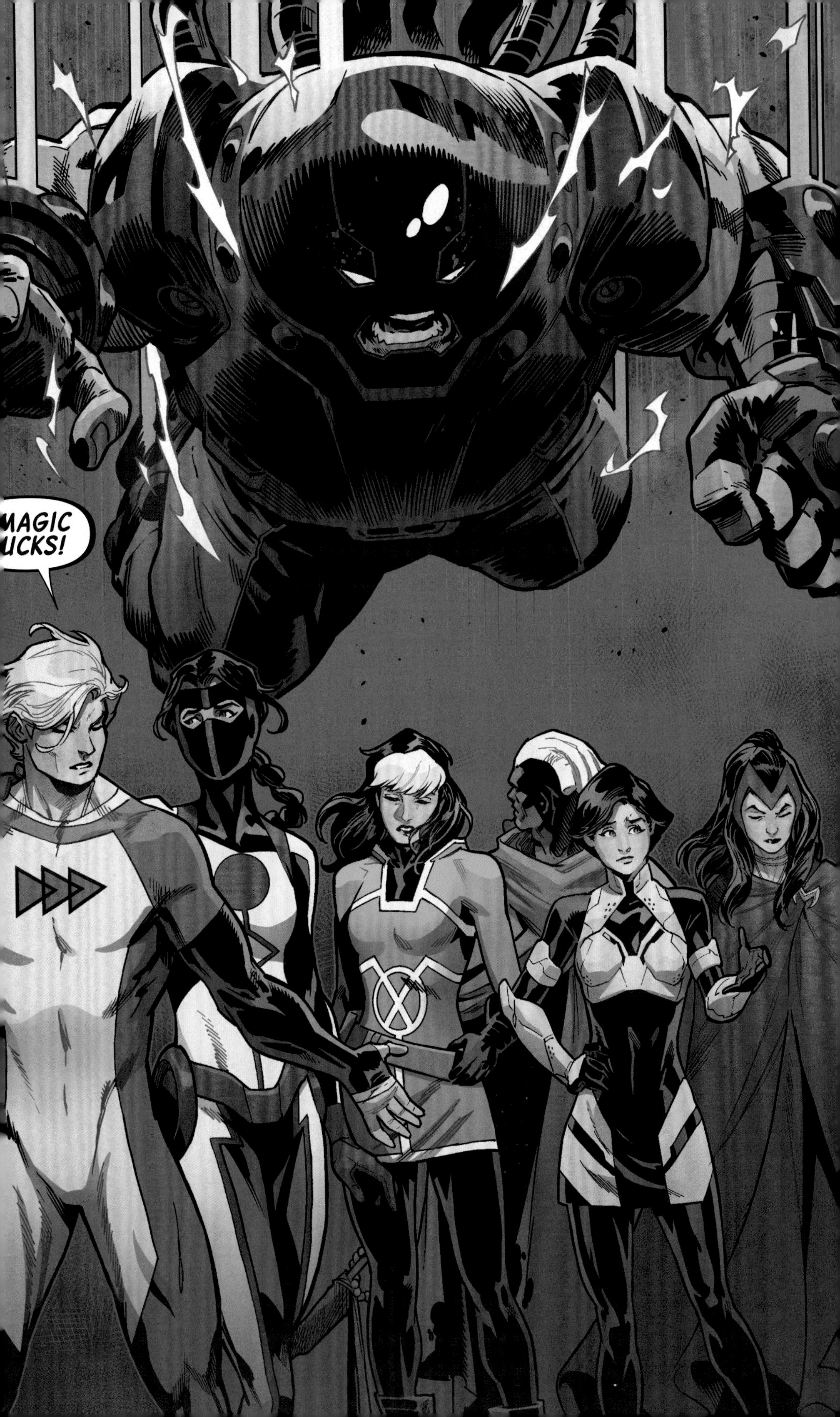
MAGIC
UCKS!

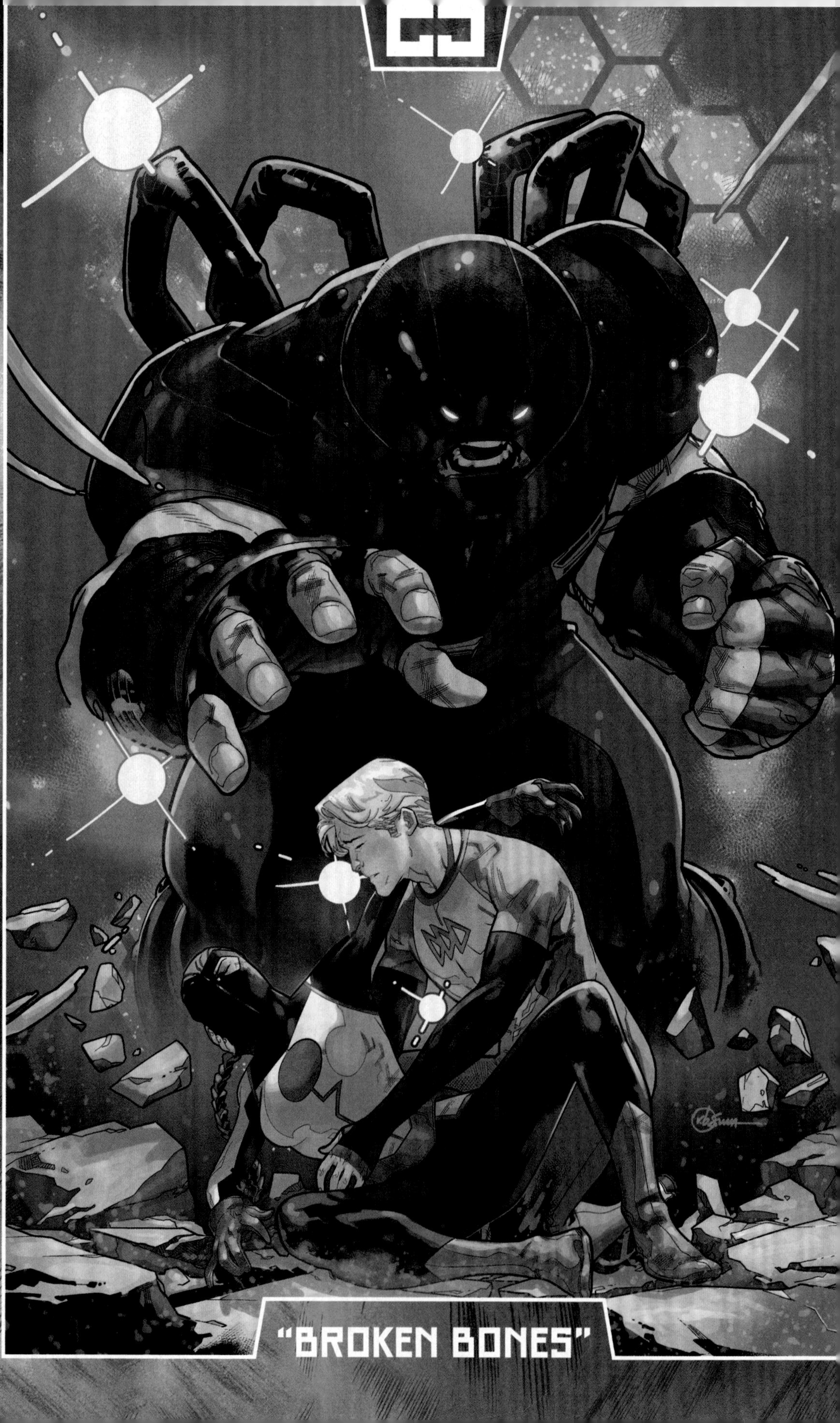
"BROKEN BONES"

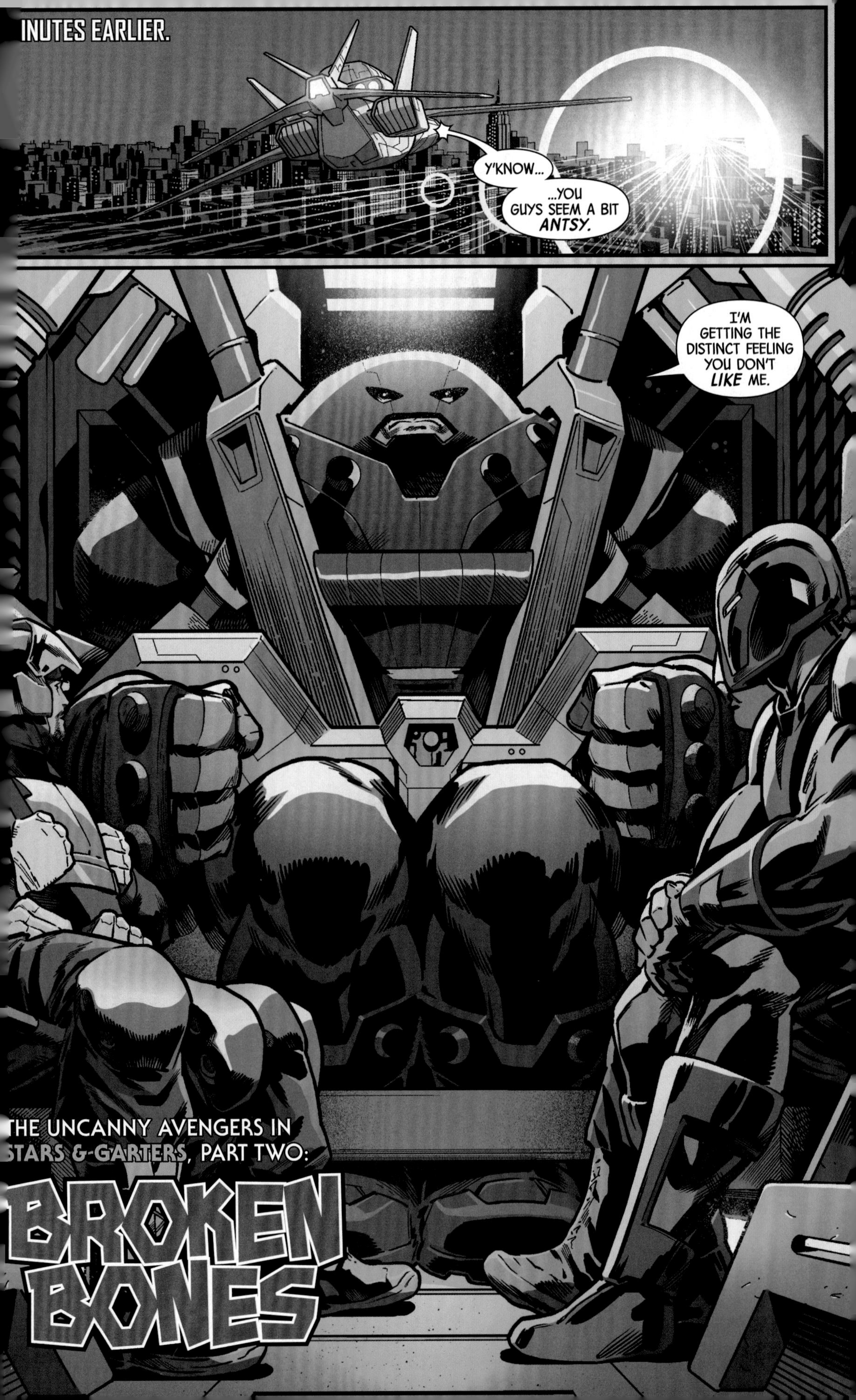
INUTES EARLIER.
Y'KNOW...
...YOU GUYS SEEM A BIT ANTSY.
I'M GETTING THE DISTINCT FEELING YOU DON'T LIKE ME.
THE UNCANNY AVENGERS IN STARS & GARTERS, PART TWO:
BROKEN BONES

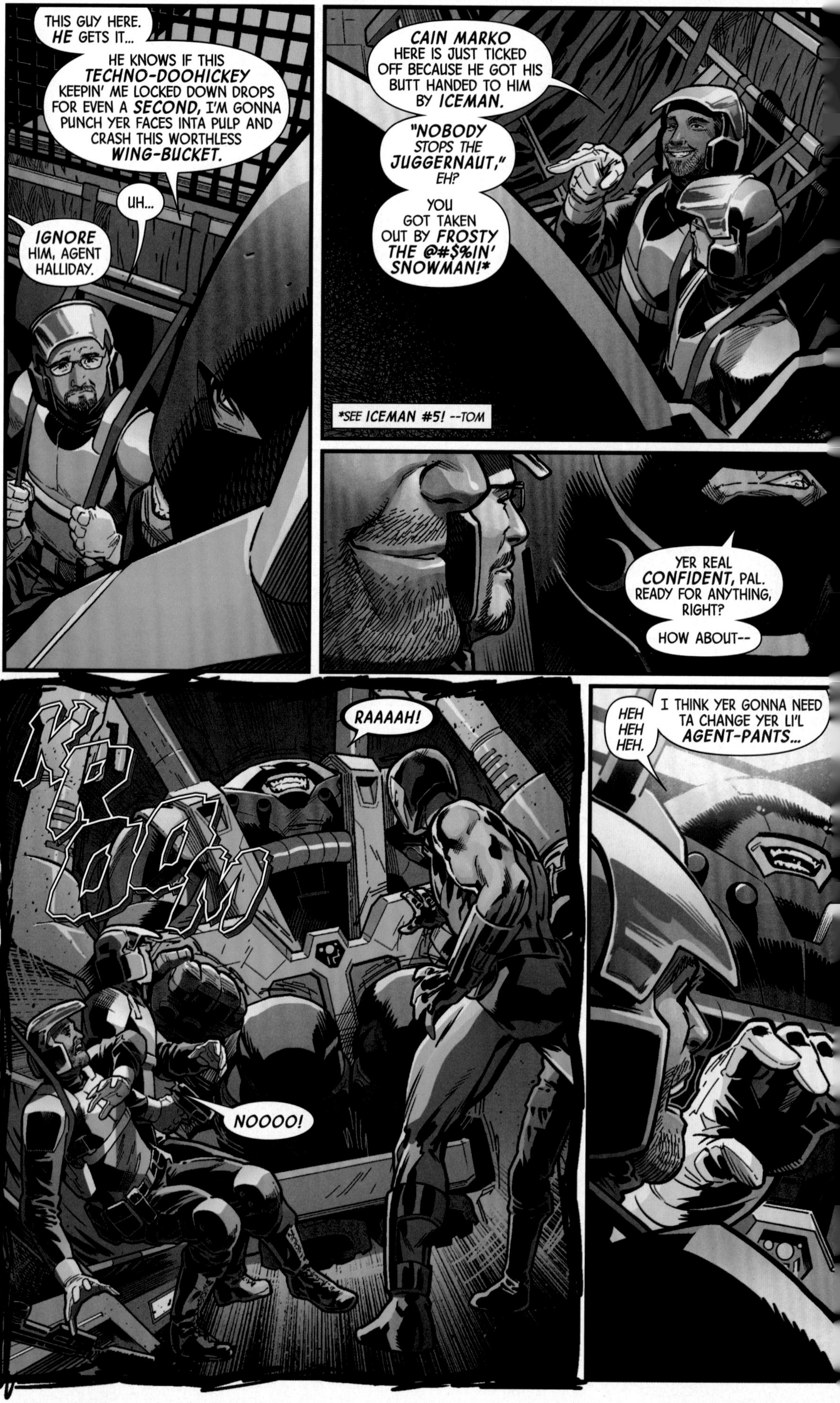

THIS GUY HERE. HE GETS IT...
HE KNOWS IF THIS TECHNO-DOOHICKEY KEEPIN' ME LOCKED DOWN DROPS FOR EVEN A SECOND, I'M GONNA PUNCH YER FACES INTA PULP AND CRASH THIS WORTHLESS WING-BUCKET.
UH...
IGNORE HIM, AGENT HALLIDAY.
CAIN MARKO HERE IS JUST TICKED OFF BECAUSE HE GOT HIS BUTT HANDED TO HIM BY ICEMAN.
"NOBODY STOPS THE JUGGERNAUT," EH?
YOU GOT TAKEN OUT BY FROSTY THE @#$%IN' SNOWMAN!*
*SEE ICEMAN #5! --TOM
YER REAL CONFIDENT, PAL. READY FOR ANYTHING, RIGHT?
HOW ABOUT--
KA-BOOOM
RAAAAH!
NOOOO!
HEH HEH HEH.
I THINK YER GONNA NEED TA CHANGE YER LI'L AGENT-PANTS...

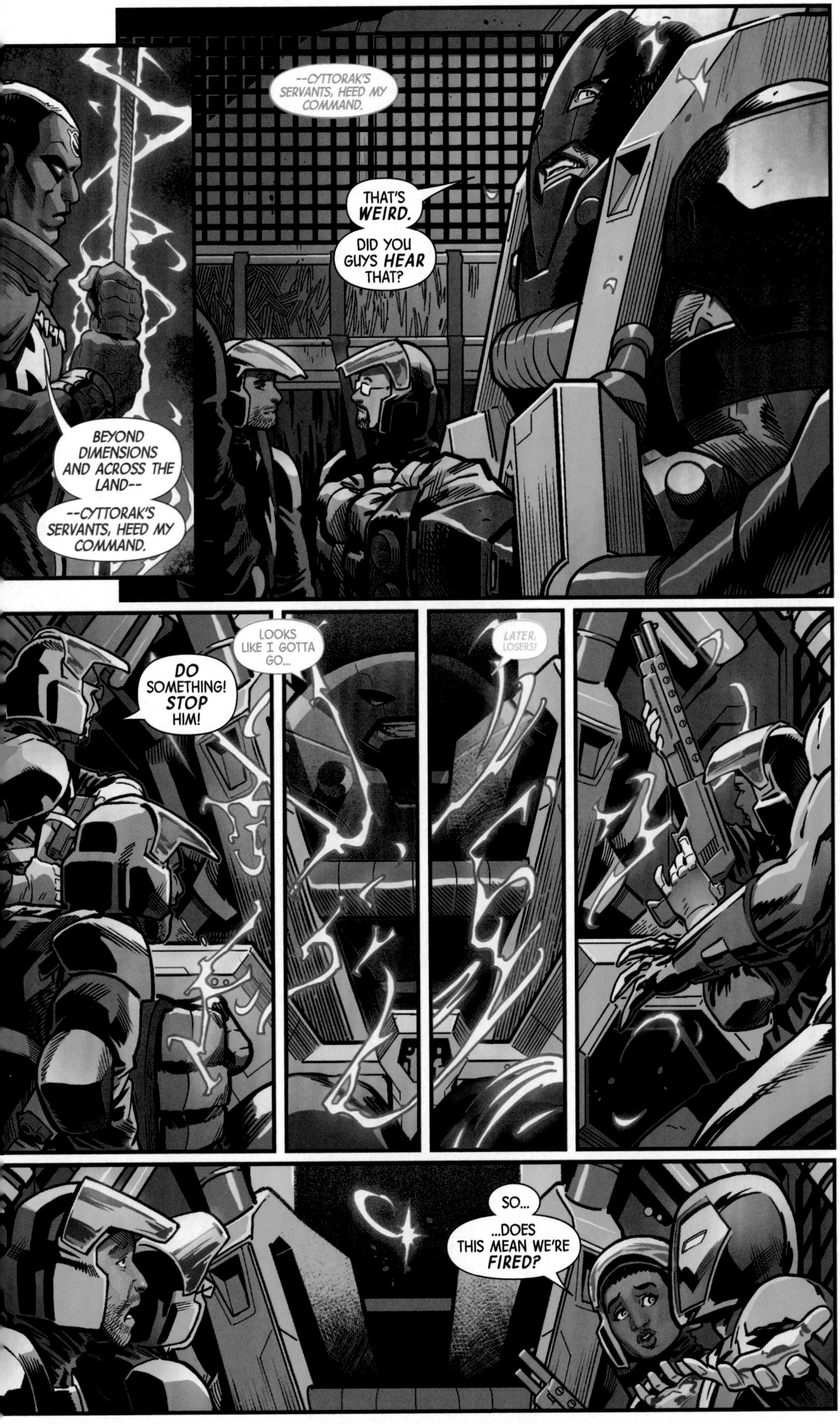
BEYOND DIMENSIONS AND ACROSS THE LAND--
--CYTTORAK'S SERVANTS, HEED MY COMMAND.
--CYTTORAK'S SERVANTS, HEED MY COMMAND.
THAT'S WEIRD.
DID YOU GUYS HEAR THAT?
DO SOMETHING! STOP HIM!
LOOKS LIKE I GOTTA GO...
LATER, LOSERS!
SO...
...DOES THIS MEAN WE'RE FIRED?

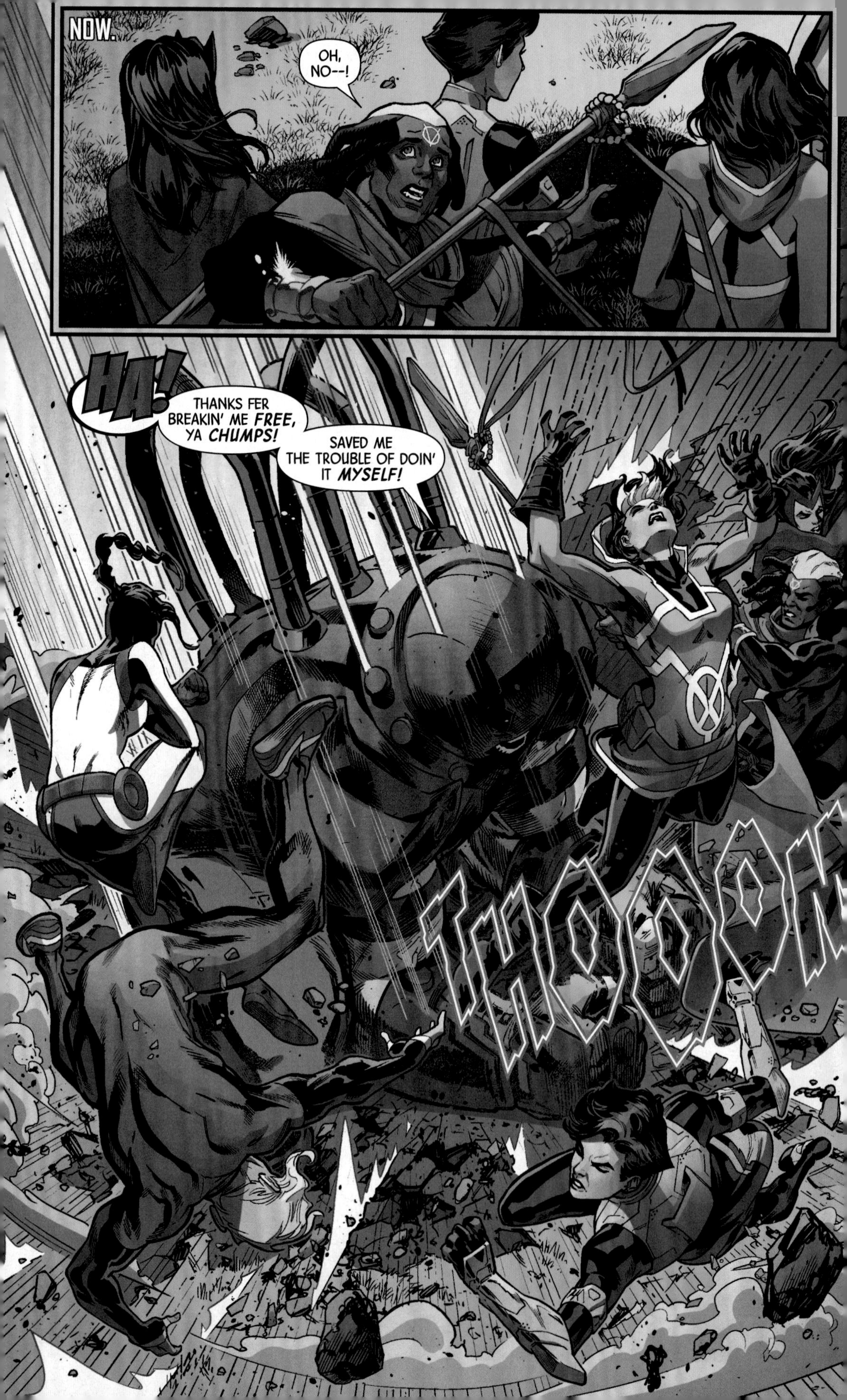
NOW.
OH, NO--!
HA!
THANKS FER BREAKIN' ME FREE, YA CHUMPS!
SAVED ME THE TROUBLE OF DOIN' IT MYSELF!
THOOOM

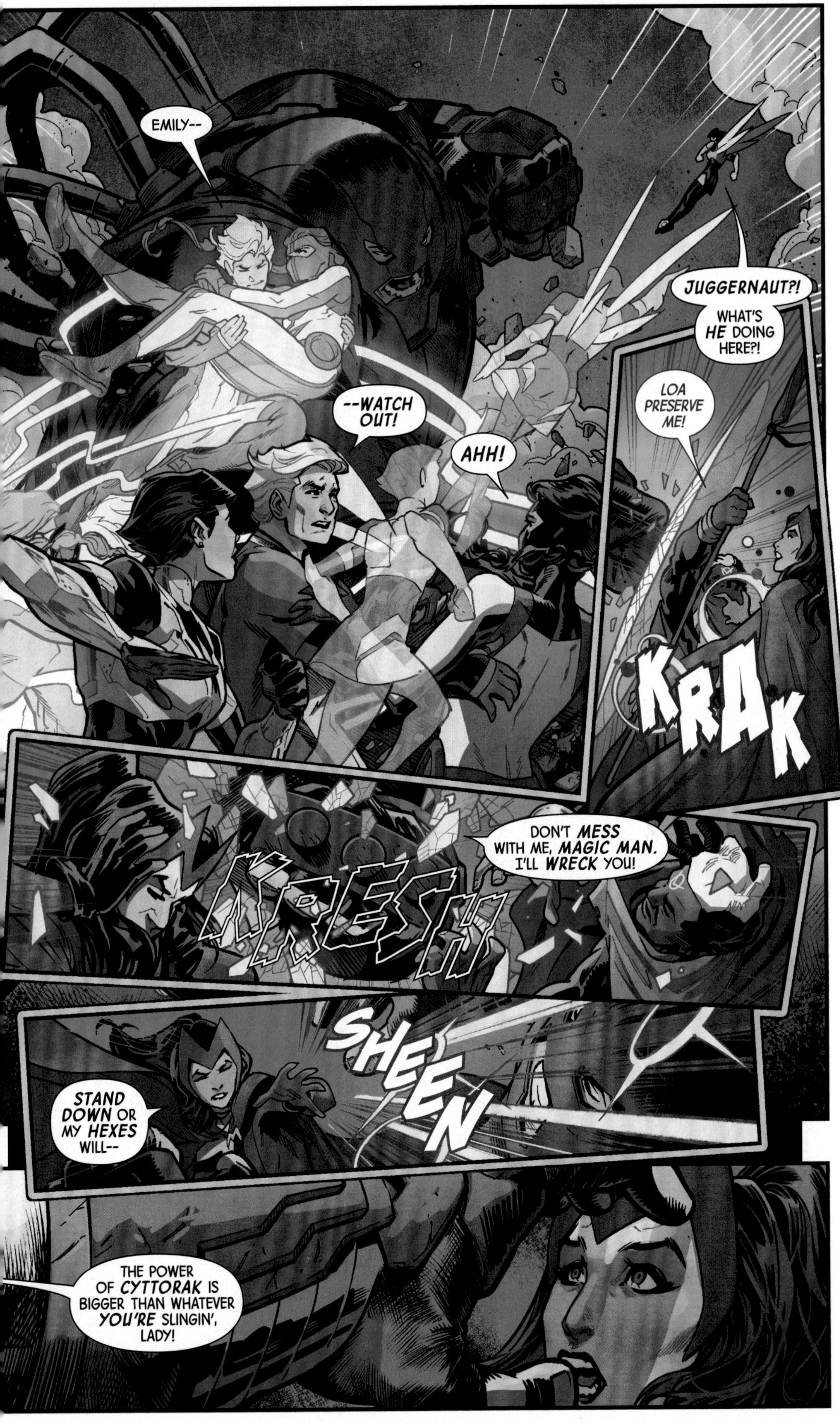
EMILY--
JUGGERNAUT?!
WHAT'S HE DOING HERE?!
--WATCH OUT!
AHH!
LOA PRESERVE ME!
KRAK
KRESH
DON'T MESS WITH ME, MAGIC MAN. I'LL WRECK YOU!
SHEEN
STAND DOWN OR MY HEXES WILL--
THE POWER OF CYTTORAK IS BIGGER THAN WHATEVER YOU'RE SLINGIN', LADY!

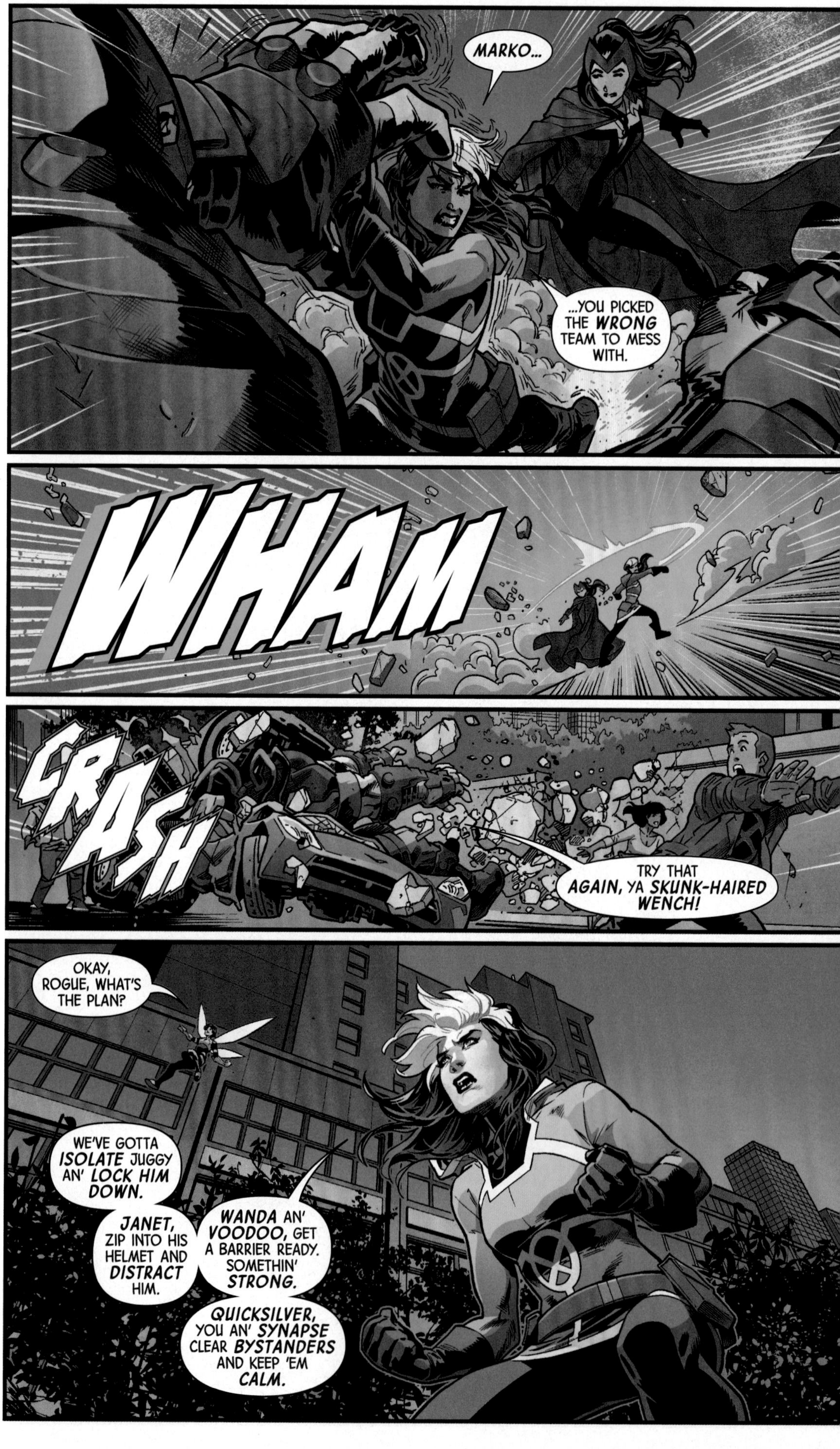

MARKO...
...YOU PICKED THE WRONG TEAM TO MESS WITH.
WHAM
CRASH
TRY THAT AGAIN, YA SKUNK-HAIRED WENCH!
OKAY, ROGUE, WHAT'S THE PLAN?
WE'VE GOTTA ISOLATE JUGGY AN' LOCK HIM DOWN.
JANET, ZIP INTO HIS HELMET AND DISTRACT HIM.
WANDA AN' VOODOO, GET A BARRIER READY. SOMETHIN' STRONG.
QUICKSILVER, YOU AN' SYNAPSE CLEAR BYSTANDERS AND KEEP 'EM CALM.

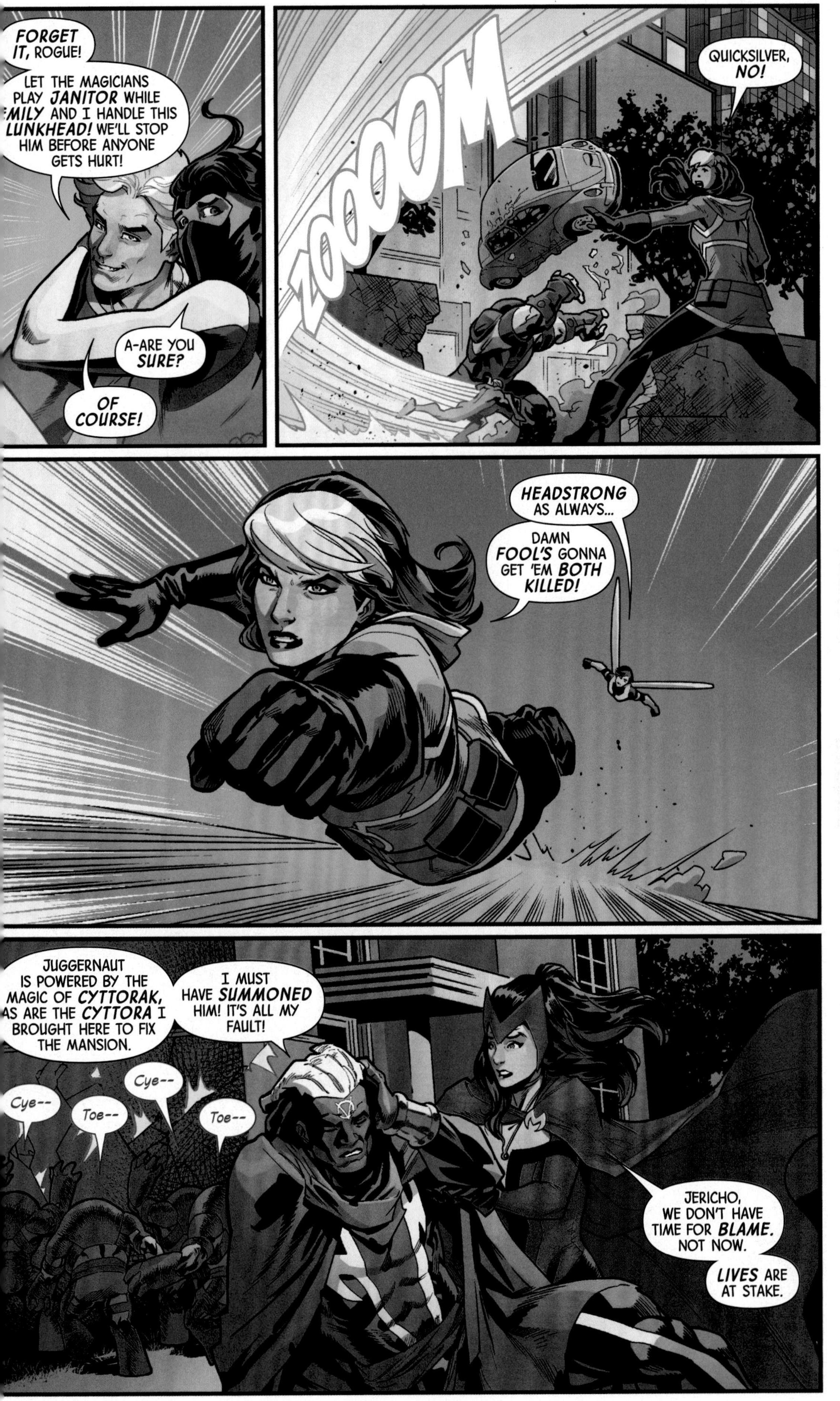

FORGET IT, ROGUE!
LET THE MAGICIANS PLAY JANITOR WHILE EMILY AND I HANDLE THIS LUNKHEAD! WE'LL STOP HIM BEFORE ANYONE GETS HURT!
A-ARE YOU SURE?
OF COURSE!
ZOOOOOM
QUICKSILVER, NO!
HEADSTRONG AS ALWAYS...
DAMN FOOL'S GONNA GET 'EM BOTH KILLED!
JUGGERNAUT IS POWERED BY THE MAGIC OF CYTTORAK, AS ARE THE CYTTORA I BROUGHT HERE TO FIX THE MANSION.
I MUST HAVE SUMMONED HIM! IT'S ALL MY FAULT!
Cye--
Toe--
Cye--
Toe--
JERICHO, WE DON'T HAVE TIME FOR BLAME. NOT NOW.
LIVES ARE AT STAKE.

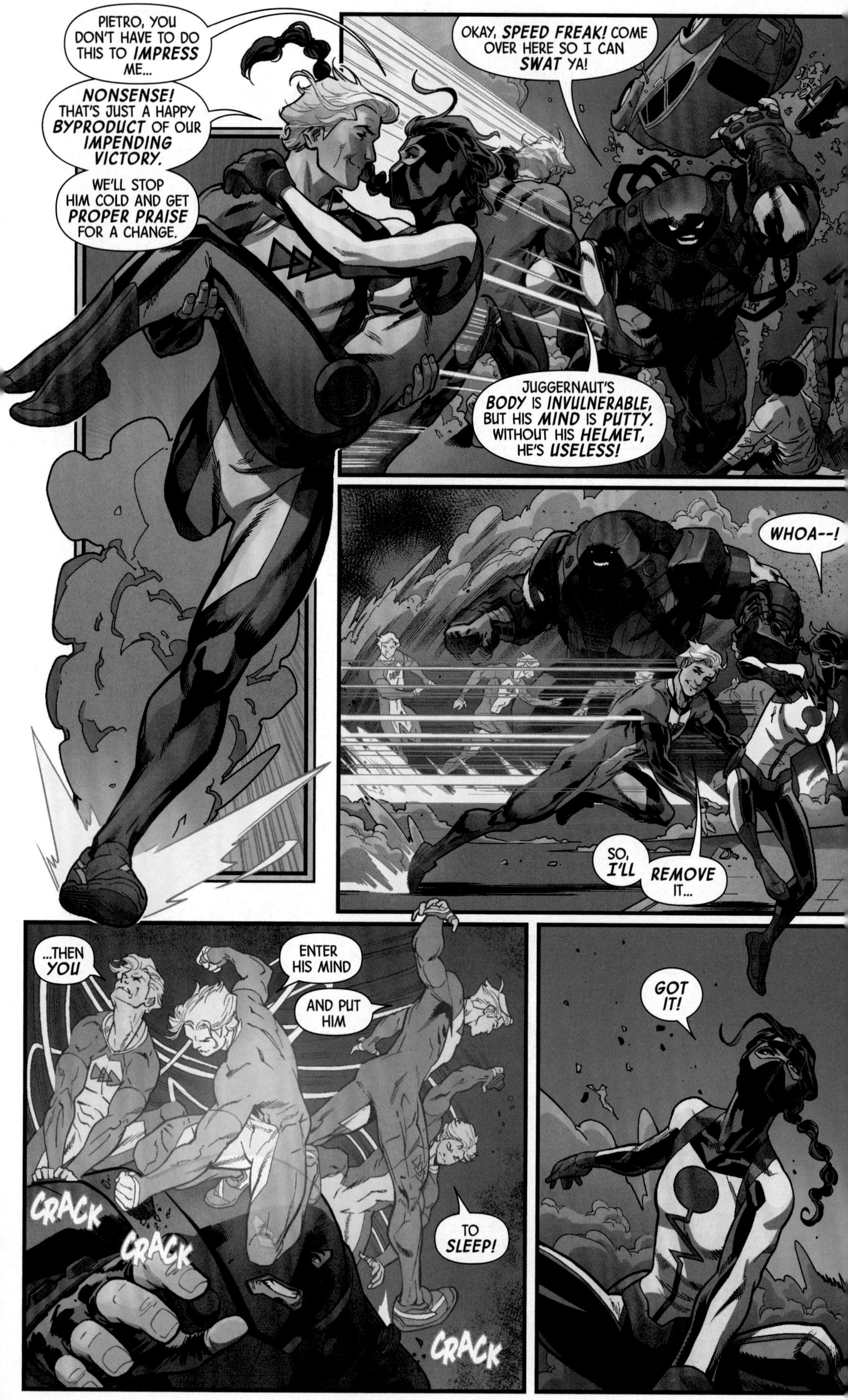
PIETRO, YOU DON'T HAVE TO DO THIS TO IMPRESS ME...
NONSENSE! THAT'S JUST A HAPPY BYPRODUCT OF OUR IMPENDING VICTORY.
WE'LL STOP HIM COLD AND GET PROPER PRAISE FOR A CHANGE.
OKAY, SPEED FREAK! COME OVER HERE SO I CAN SWAT YA!
JUGGERNAUT'S BODY IS INVULNERABLE, BUT HIS MIND IS PUTTY. WITHOUT HIS HELMET, HE'S USELESS!
WHOA--!
SO, I'LL
REMOVE IT...
...THEN YOU
ENTER HIS MIND
AND PUT HIM
TO SLEEP!
CRACK
CRACK
CRACK
GOT IT!

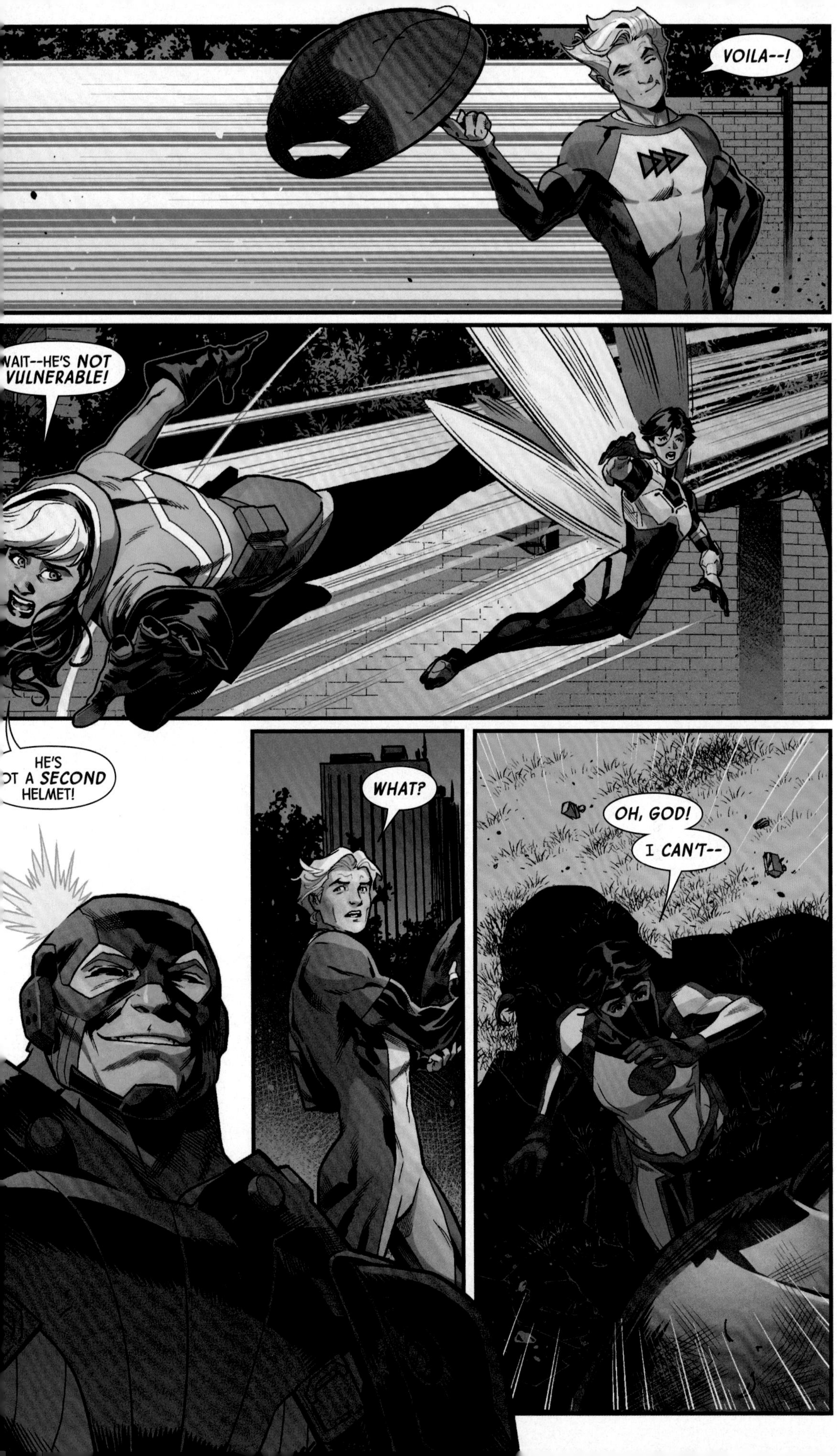
VOILA--!
WAIT--HE'S NOT VULNERABLE!
HE'S OT A SECOND HELMET!
WHAT?
OH, GOD!
I CAN'T--

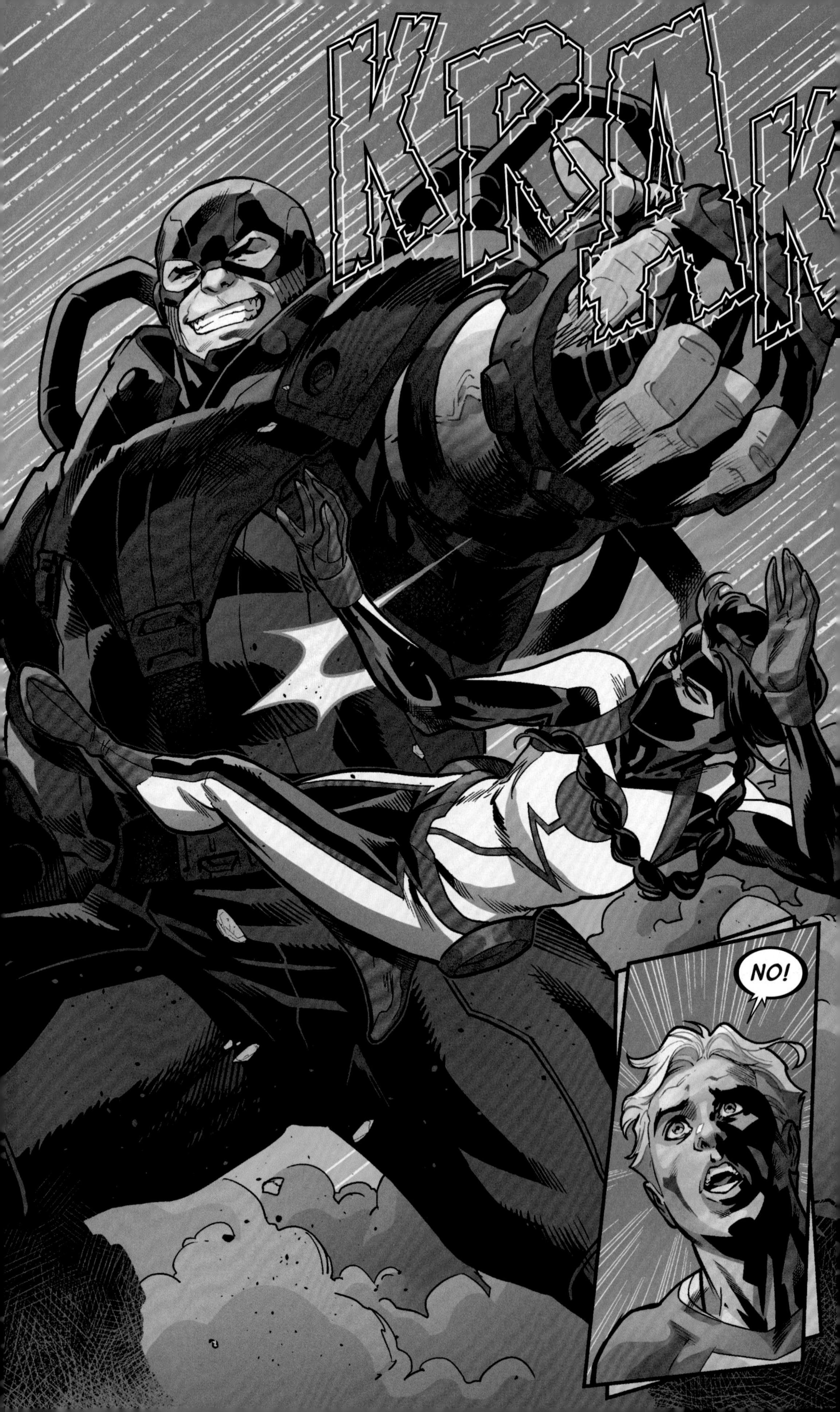
KRAAK
NO!

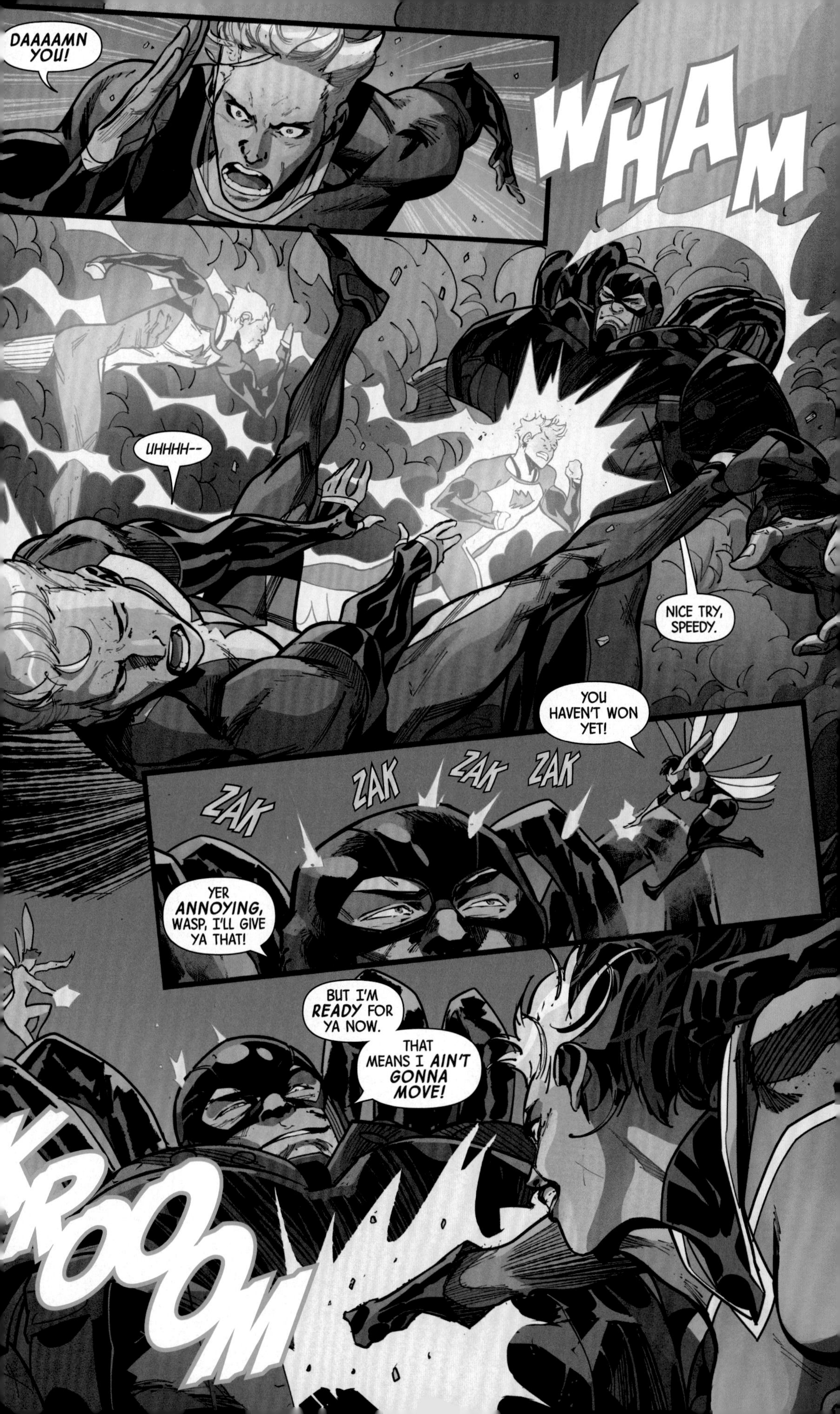
DAAAAMN YOU!
WHAM
UHHHH--
NICE TRY, SPEEDY.
YOU HAVEN'T WON YET!
ZAK
ZAK
ZAK
ZAK
YER ANNOYING, WASP, I'LL GIVE YA THAT!
BUT I'M READY FOR YA NOW.
THAT MEANS I AIN'T GONNA MOVE!
KROOOM

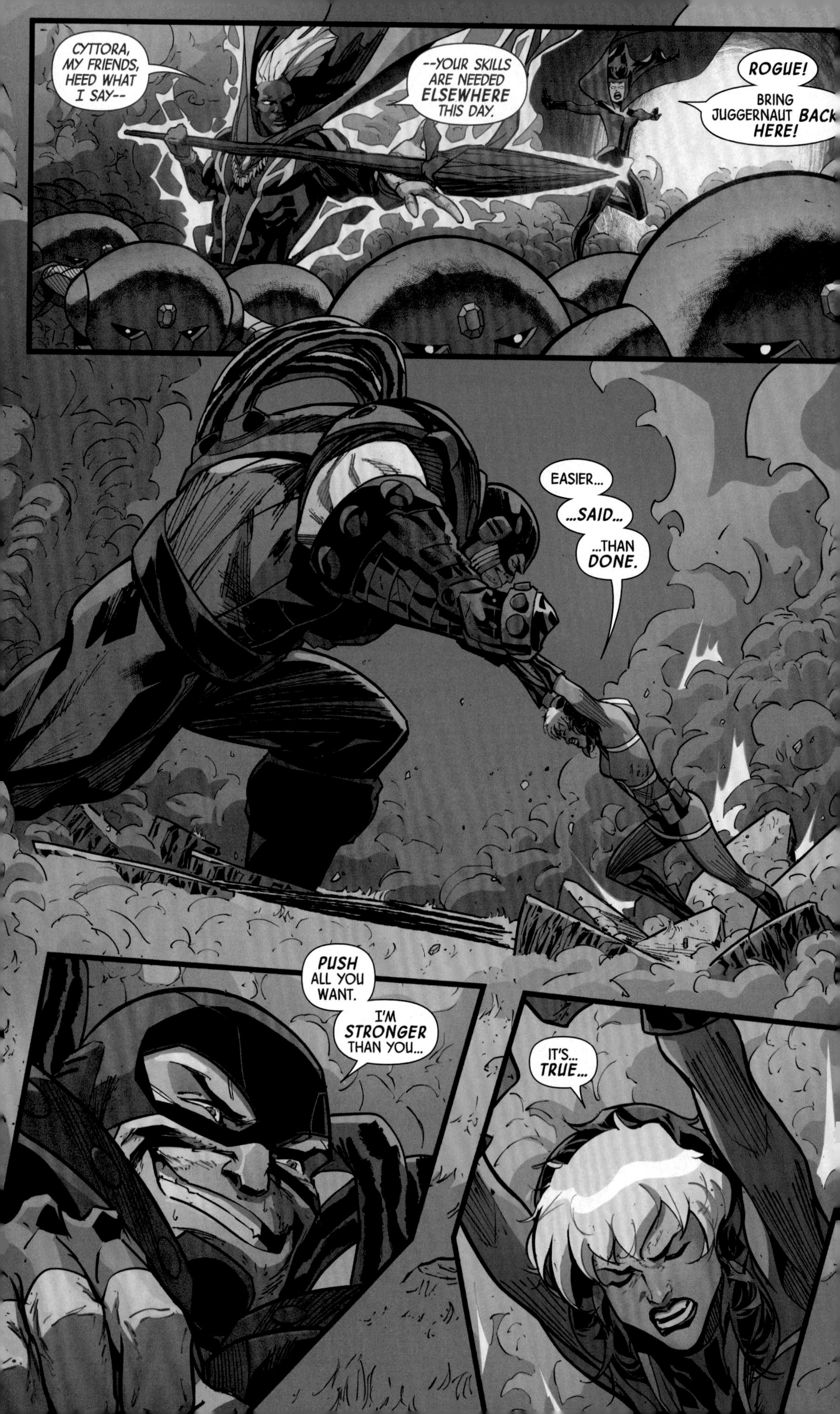
CYTTORA, MY FRIENDS, HEED WHAT I SAY--
--YOUR SKILLS ARE NEEDED ELSEWHERE THIS DAY.
ROGUE!
BRING JUGGERNAUT BACK HERE!
EASIER...
...SAID...
...THAN DONE.
PUSH ALL YOU WANT.
I'M STRONGER THAN YOU...
IT'S... TRUE...

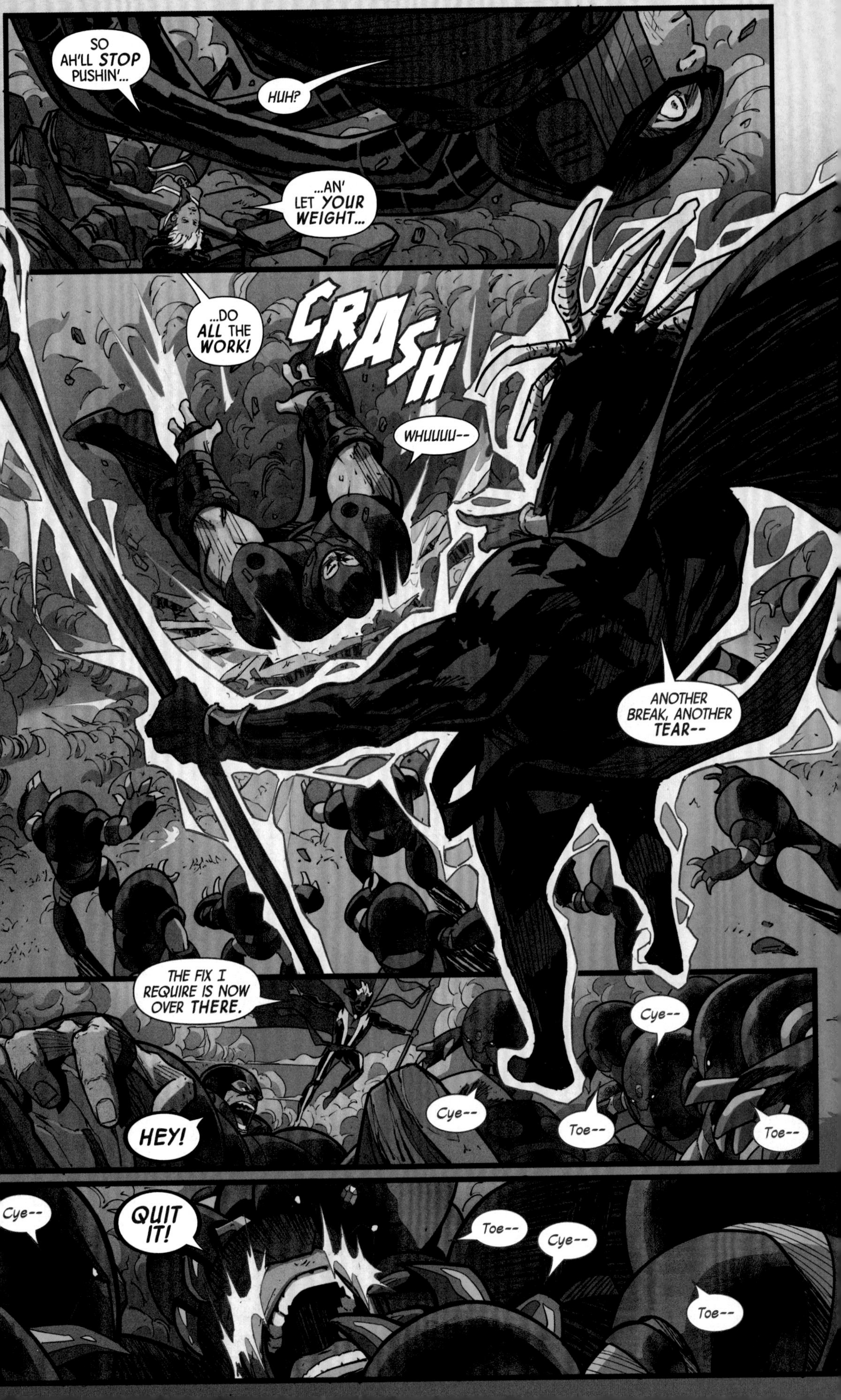

SO AH'LL STOP PUSHIN'...
HUH?
...AN' LET YOUR WEIGHT...
...DO ALL THE WORK!
CRASH
WHUUUU--
ANOTHER BREAK, ANOTHER TEAR--
THE FIX I REQUIRE IS NOW OVER THERE.
Cye--
HEY!
Cye--
Toe--
Toe--
Cye--
QUIT IT!
Toe--
Cye--
Toe--

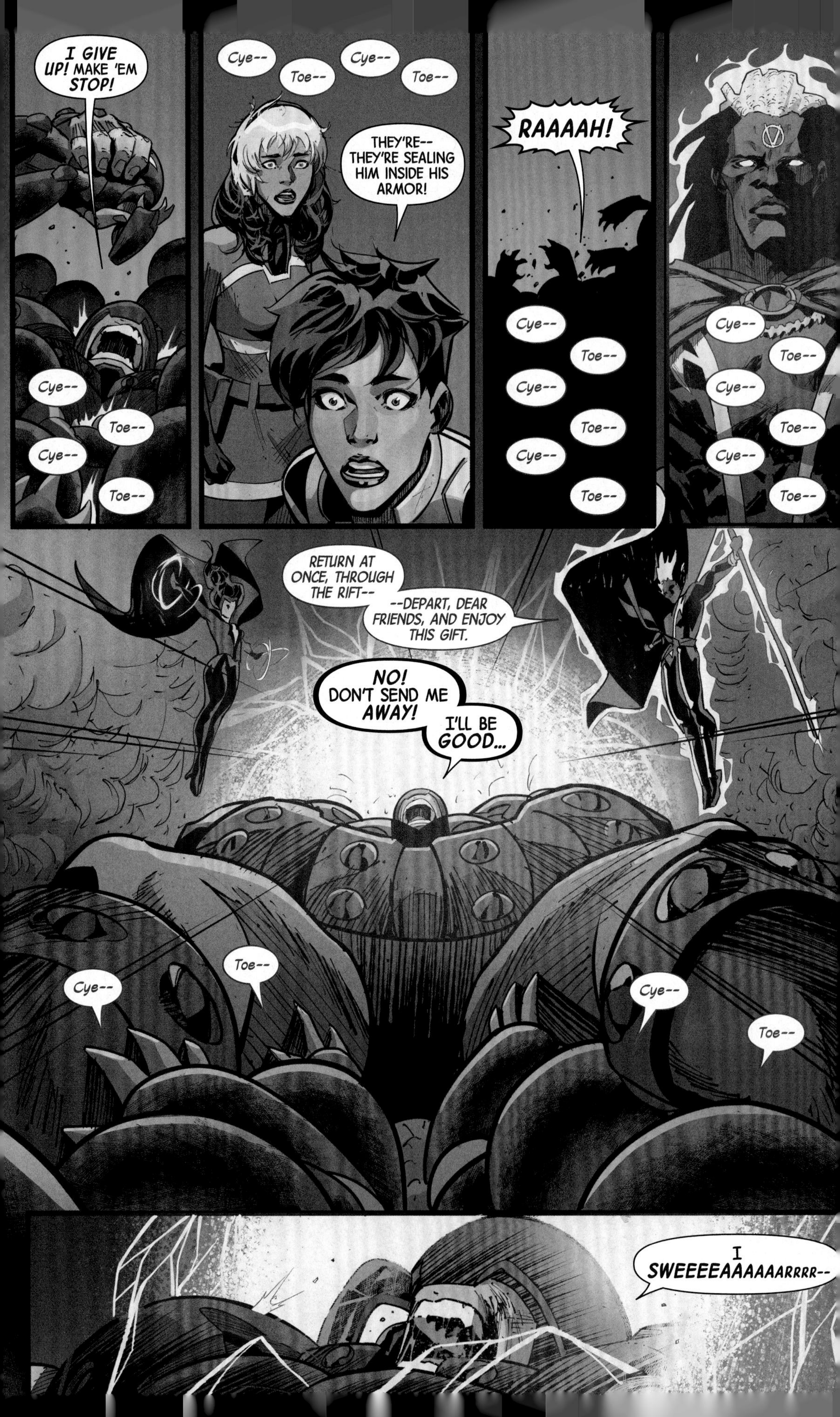
I GIVE UP! MAKE 'EM STOP!
Cye--
Toe--
Cye--
Toe--
Cye--
Toe--
Cye--
Toe--
THEY'RE-- THEY'RE SEALING HIM INSIDE HIS ARMOR!
RAAAAH!
Cye--
Toe--
Cye--
Toe--
Cye--
Toe--
Cye--
Toe--
Cye--
Toe--
Cye--
Toe--
RETURN AT ONCE, THROUGH THE RIFT--
--DEPART, DEAR FRIENDS, AND ENJOY THIS GIFT.
NO! DON'T SEND ME AWAY!
I'LL BE GOOD...
Cye--
Toe--
Cye--
Toe--
I SWEEEEAAAAAARRRR--

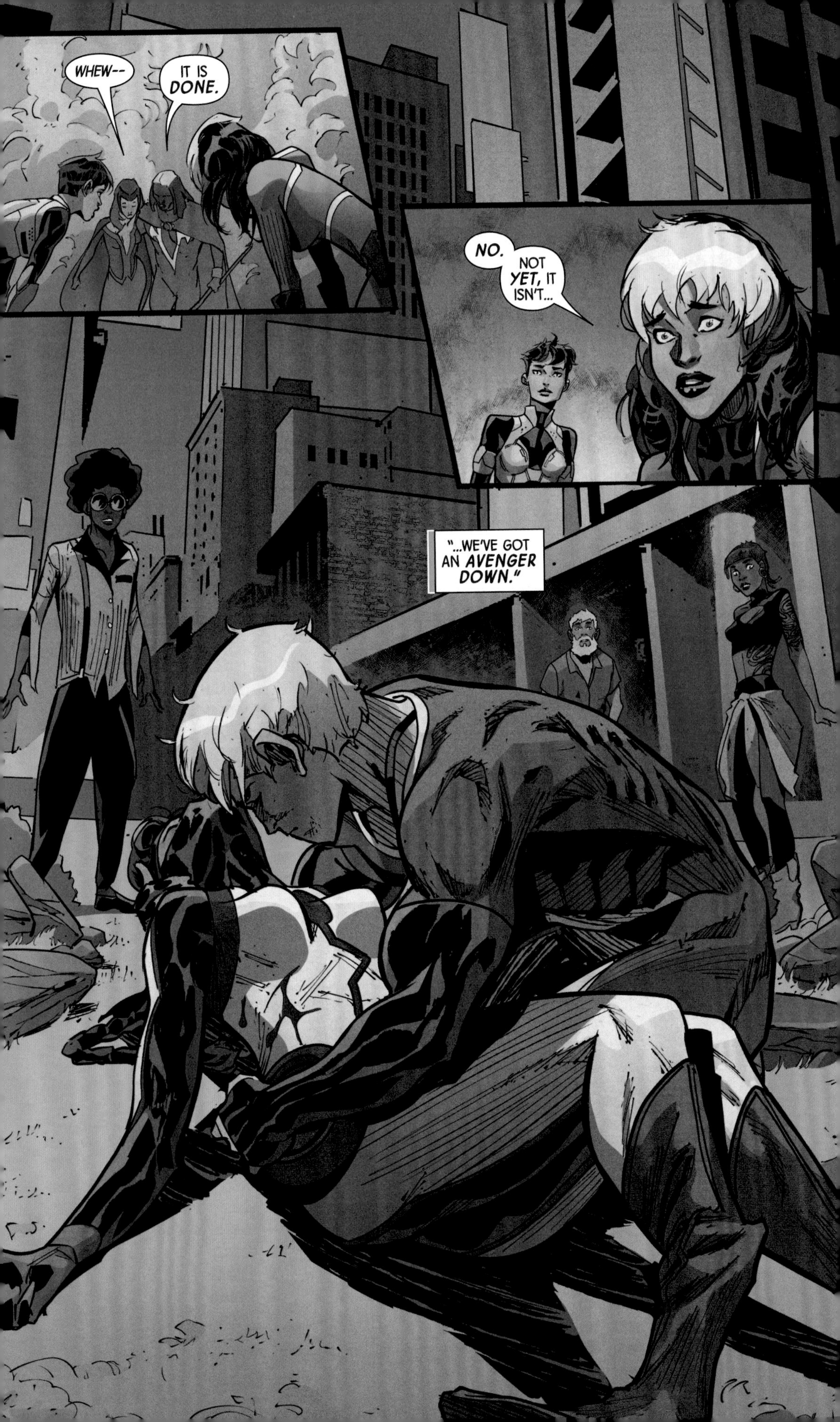
WHEW--
IT IS DONE.
NO.
NOT YET, IT ISN'T...
"...WE'VE GOT AN AVENGER DOWN."

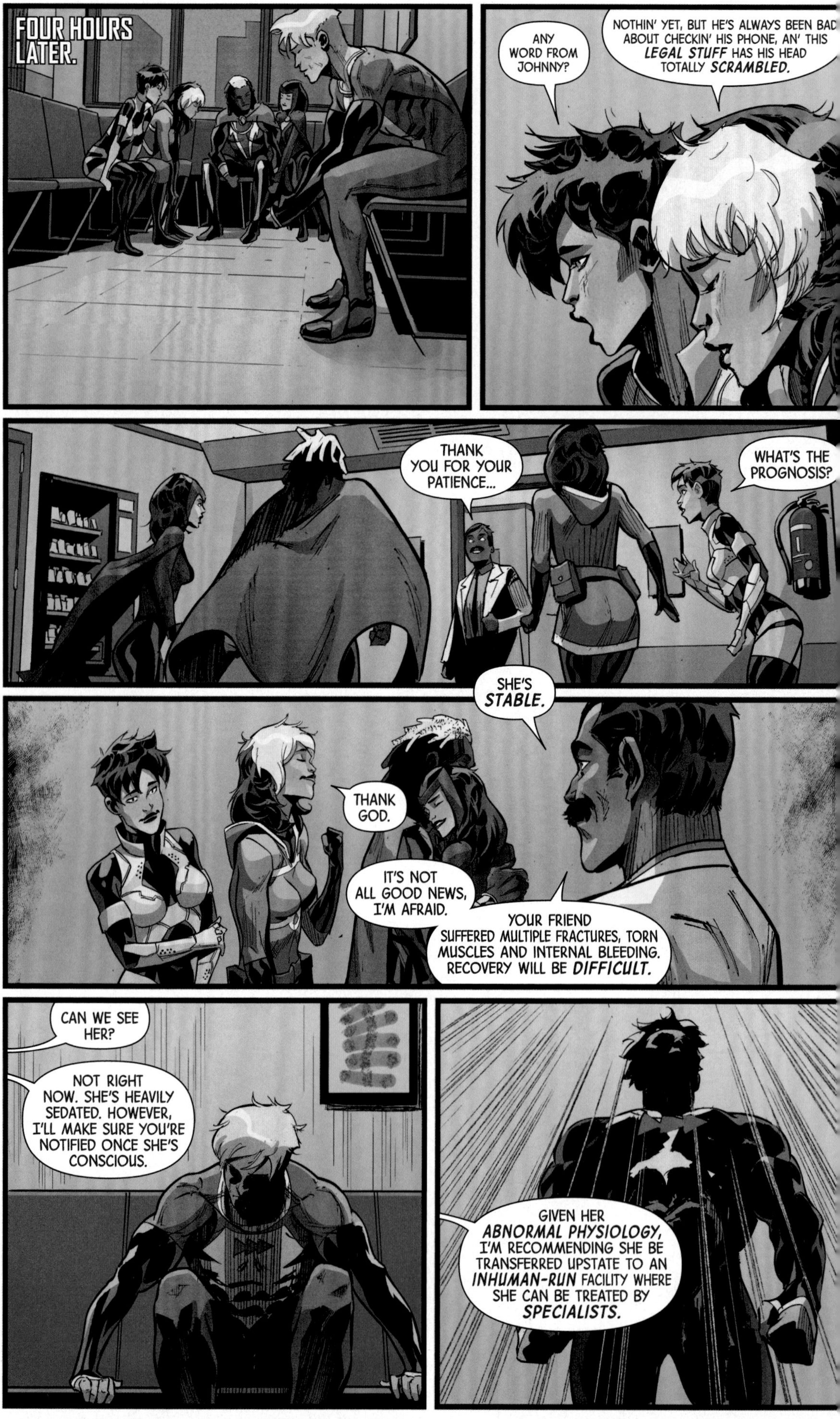
FOUR HOURS LATER.
ANY WORD FROM JOHNNY?
NOTHIN' YET, BUT HE'S ALWAYS BEEN BAD ABOUT CHECKIN' HIS PHONE, AN' THIS LEGAL STUFF HAS HIS HEAD TOTALLY SCRAMBLED.
THANK YOU FOR YOUR PATIENCE...
WHAT'S THE PROGNOSIS?
SHE'S STABLE.
THANK GOD.
IT'S NOT ALL GOOD NEWS, I'M AFRAID.
YOUR FRIEND SUFFERED MULTIPLE FRACTURES, TORN MUSCLES AND INTERNAL BLEEDING. RECOVERY WILL BE DIFFICULT.
CAN WE SEE HER?
NOT RIGHT NOW. SHE'S HEAVILY SEDATED. HOWEVER, I'LL MAKE SURE YOU'RE NOTIFIED ONCE SHE'S CONSCIOUS.
GIVEN HER ABNORMAL PHYSIOLOGY, I'M RECOMMENDING SHE BE TRANSFERRED UPSTATE TO AN INHUMAN-RUN FACILITY WHERE SHE CAN BE TREATED BY SPECIALISTS.

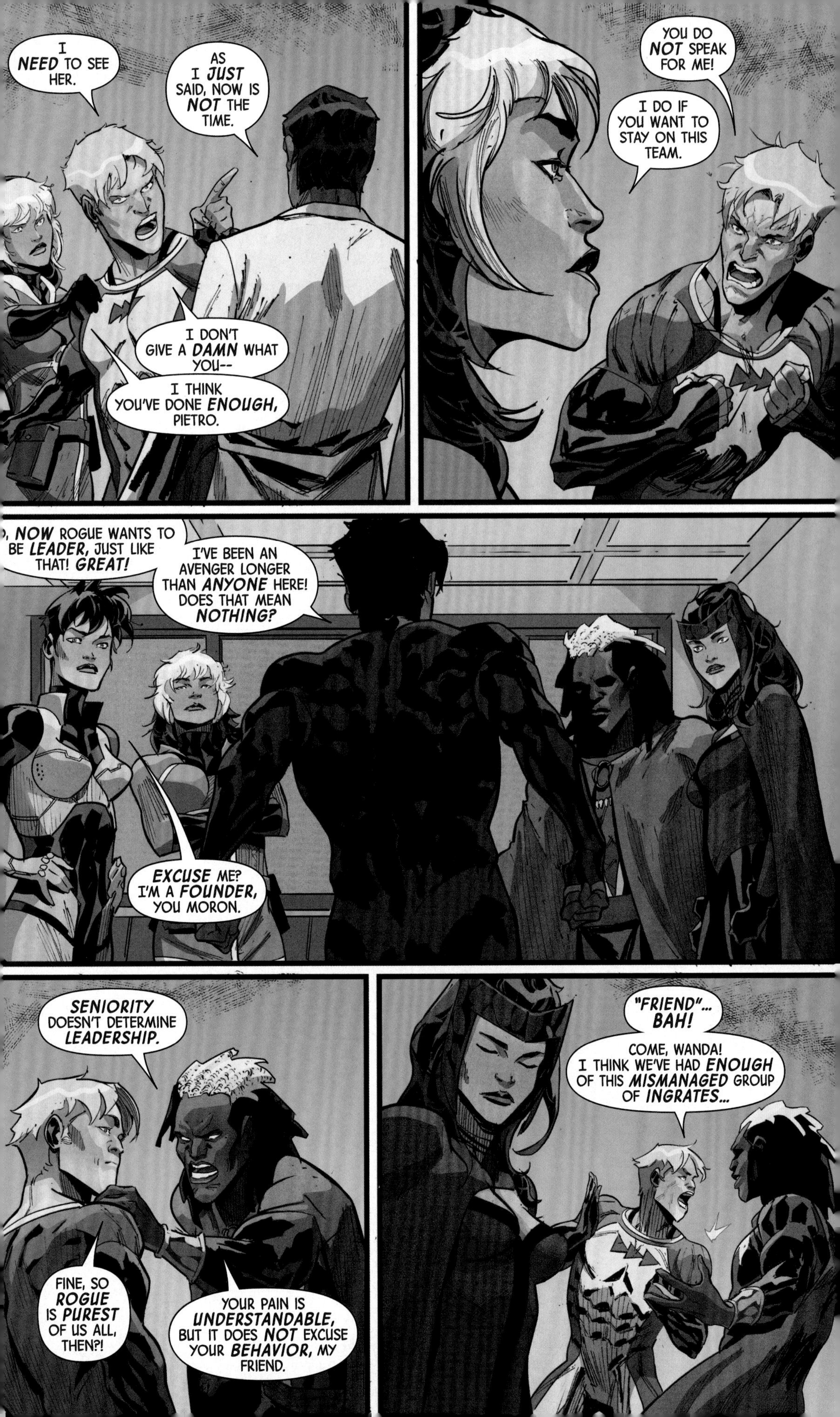

I NEED TO SEE HER.
AS I JUST SAID, NOW IS NOT THE TIME.
I DON'T GIVE A DAMN WHAT YOU--
I THINK YOU'VE DONE ENOUGH, PIETRO.
YOU DO NOT SPEAK FOR ME!
I DO IF YOU WANT TO STAY ON THIS TEAM.
, NOW ROGUE WANTS TO BE LEADER, JUST LIKE THAT! GREAT!
I'VE BEEN AN AVENGER LONGER THAN ANYONE HERE! DOES THAT MEAN NOTHING?
EXCUSE ME? I'M A FOUNDER, YOU MORON.
SENIORITY DOESN'T DETERMINE LEADERSHIP.
FINE, SO ROGUE IS PUREST OF US ALL, THEN?!
YOUR PAIN IS UNDERSTANDABLE, BUT IT DOES NOT EXCUSE YOUR BEHAVIOR, MY FRIEND.
"FRIEND"... BAH!
COME, WANDA! I THINK WE'VE HAD ENOUGH OF THIS MISMANAGED GROUP OF INGRATES...

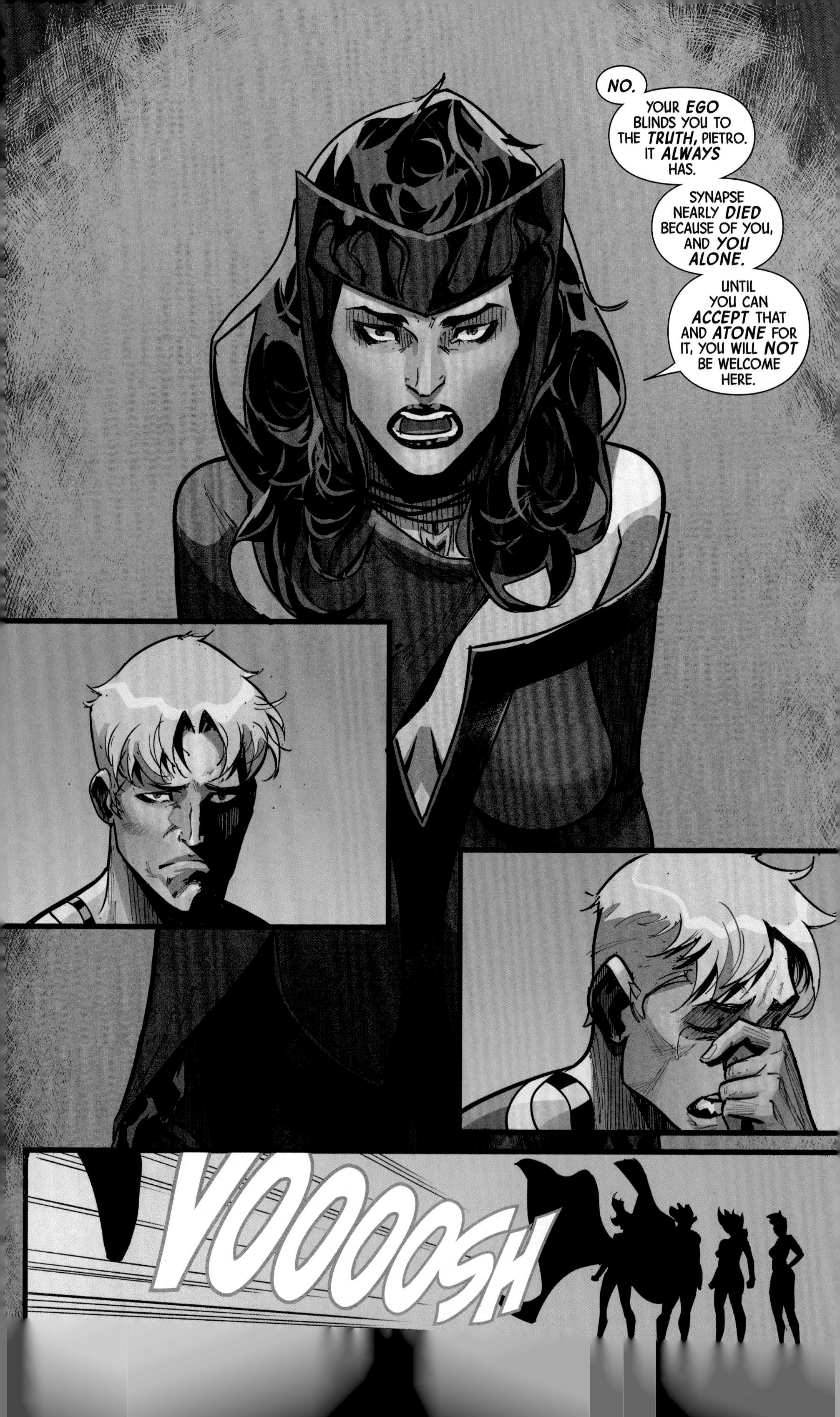
NO.
YOUR EGO BLINDS YOU TO THE TRUTH, PIETRO. IT ALWAYS HAS.
SYNAPSE NEARLY DIED BECAUSE OF YOU, AND YOU ALONE.
UNTIL YOU CAN ACCEPT THAT AND ATONE FOR IT, YOU WILL NOT BE WELCOME HERE.
VOOOOSH

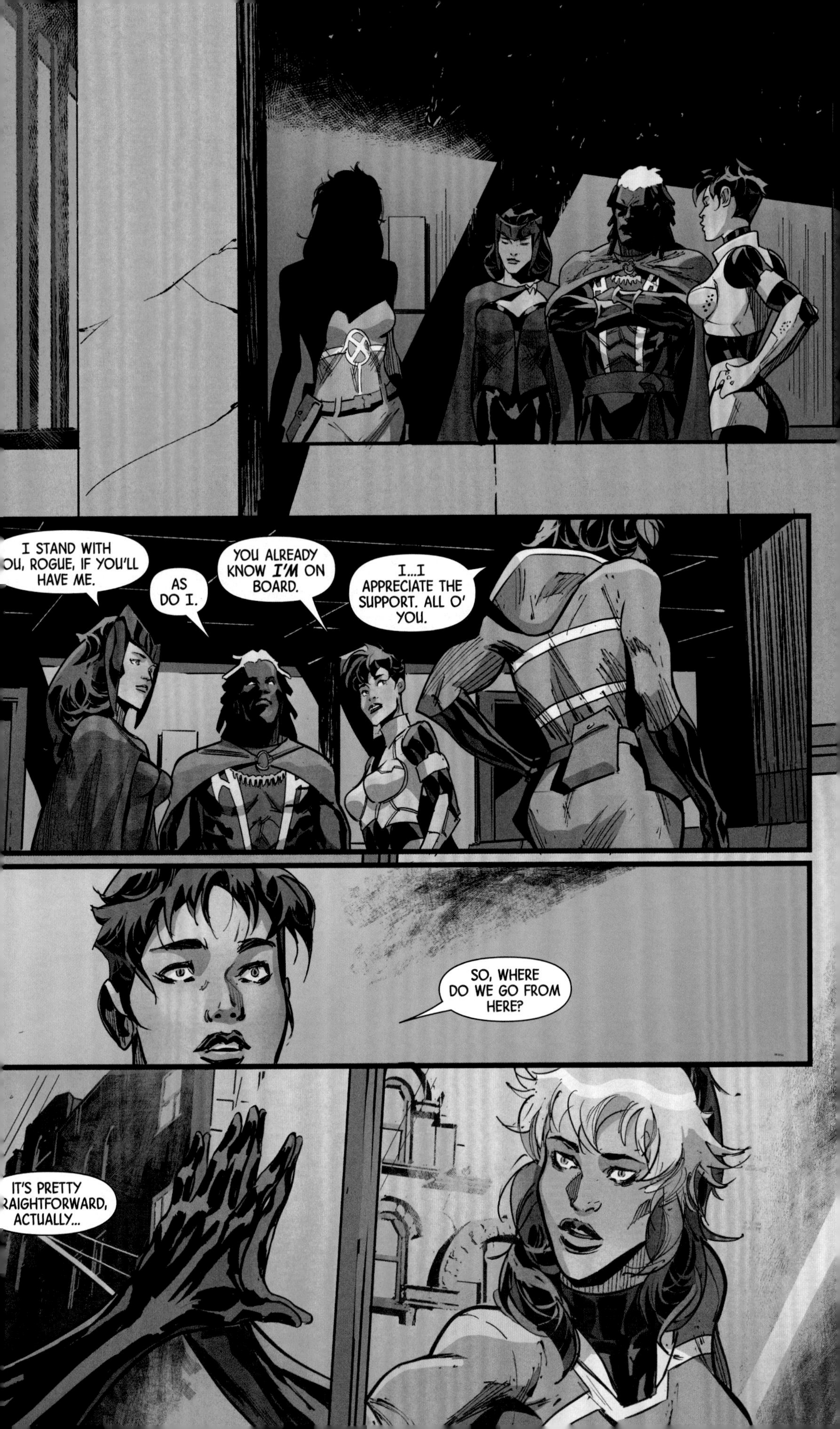

I STAND WITH OU, ROGUE, IF YOU'LL HAVE ME.
AS DO I.
YOU ALREADY KNOW *I'M* ON BOARD.
I...I APPRECIATE THE SUPPORT. ALL O' YOU.
SO, WHERE DO WE GO FROM HERE?
IT'S PRETTY RAIGHTFORWARD, ACTUALLY...

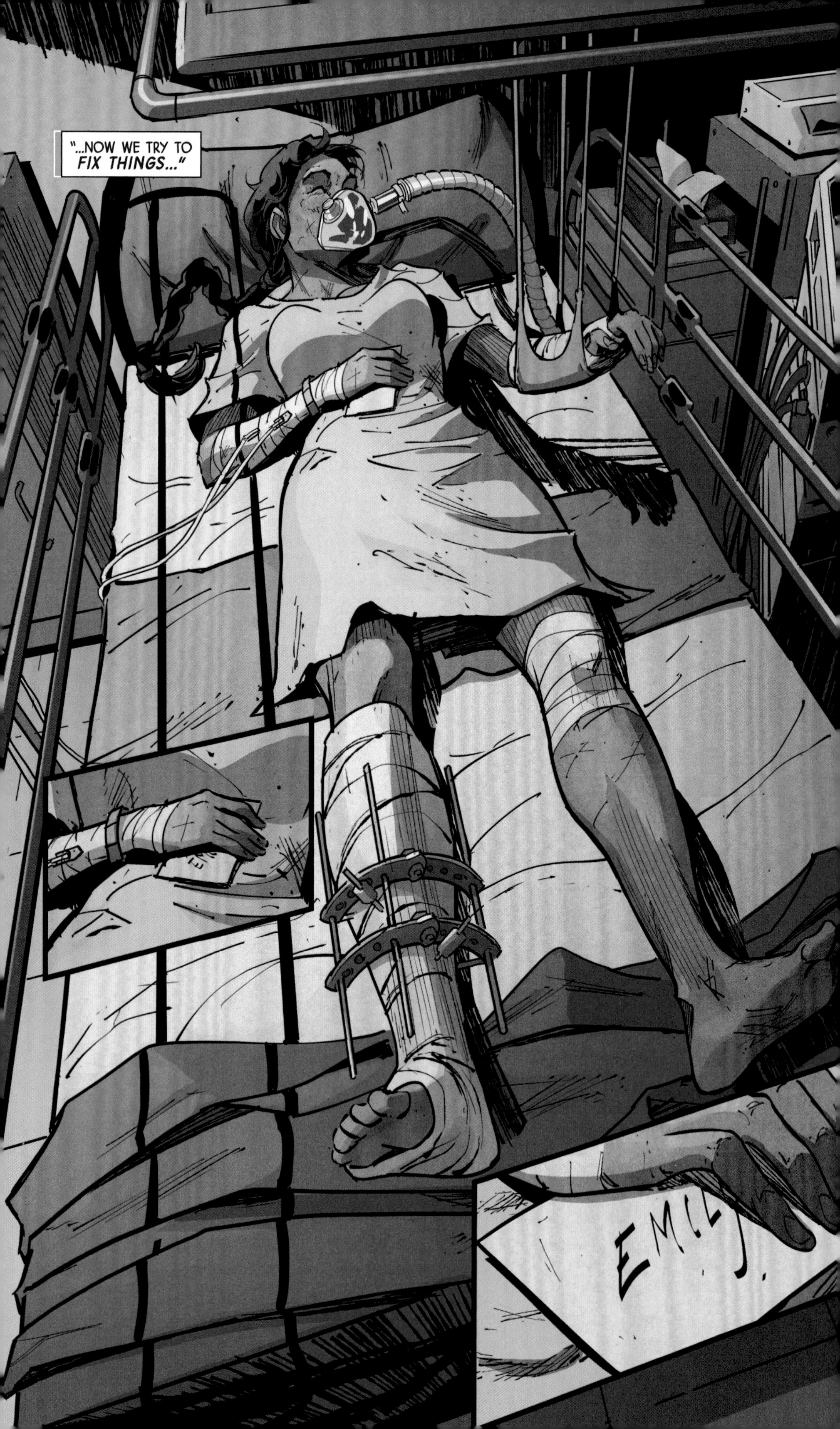
"...NOW WE TRY TO FIX THINGS..."

30

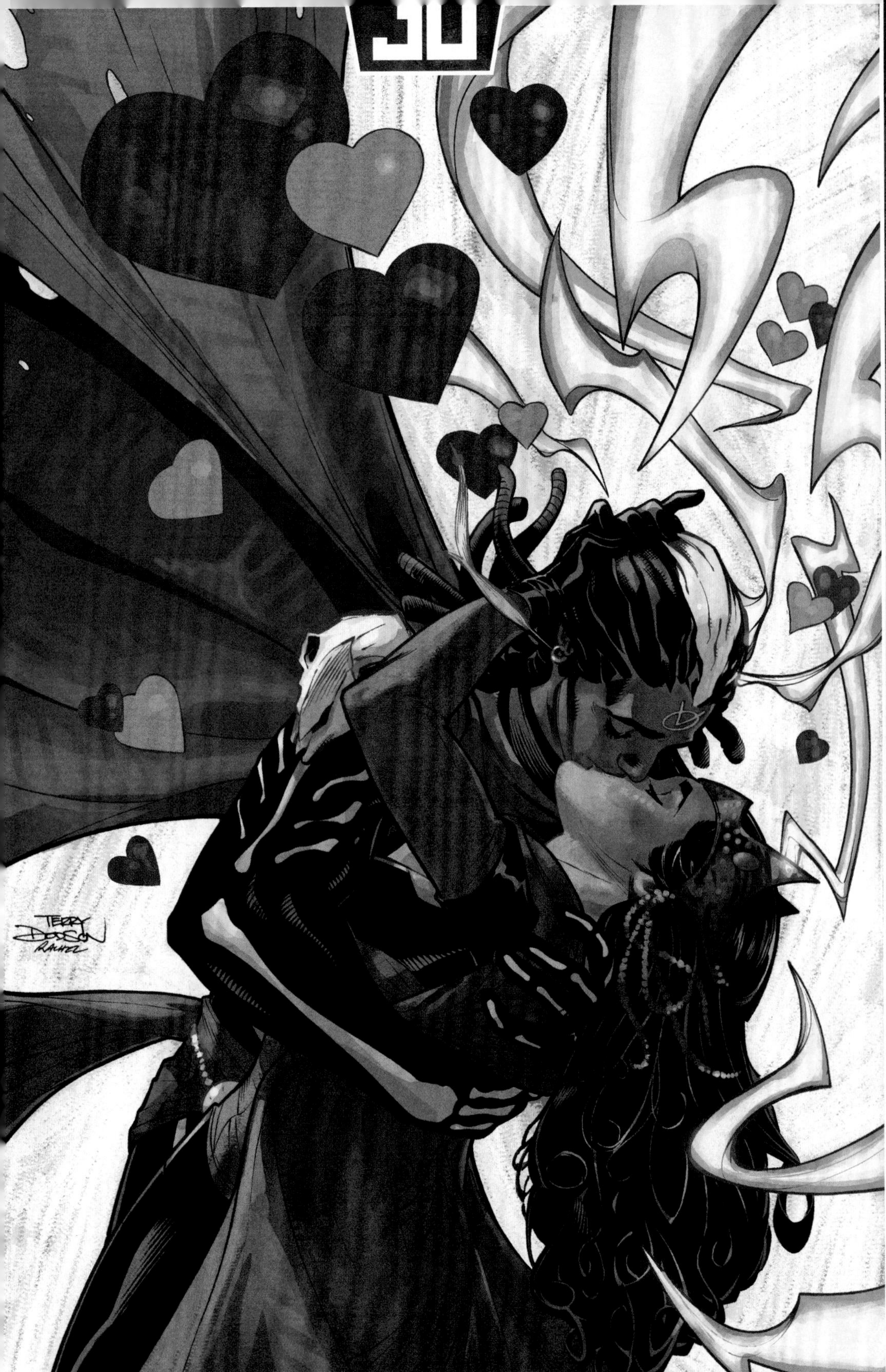

"FINDING THE FUTURE"

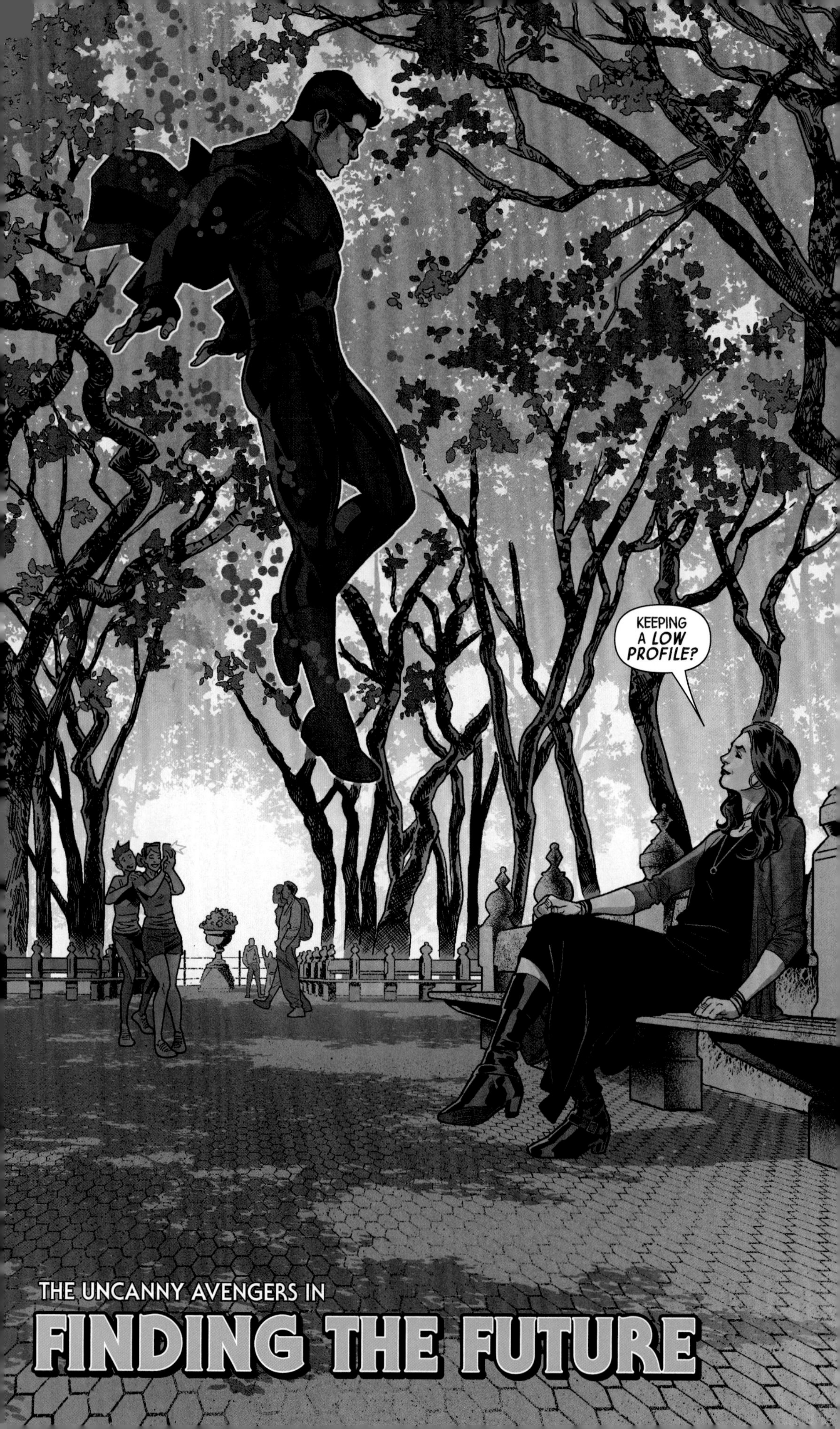
KEEPING A LOW PROFILE?
THE UNCANNY AVENGERS IN
FINDING THE FUTURE

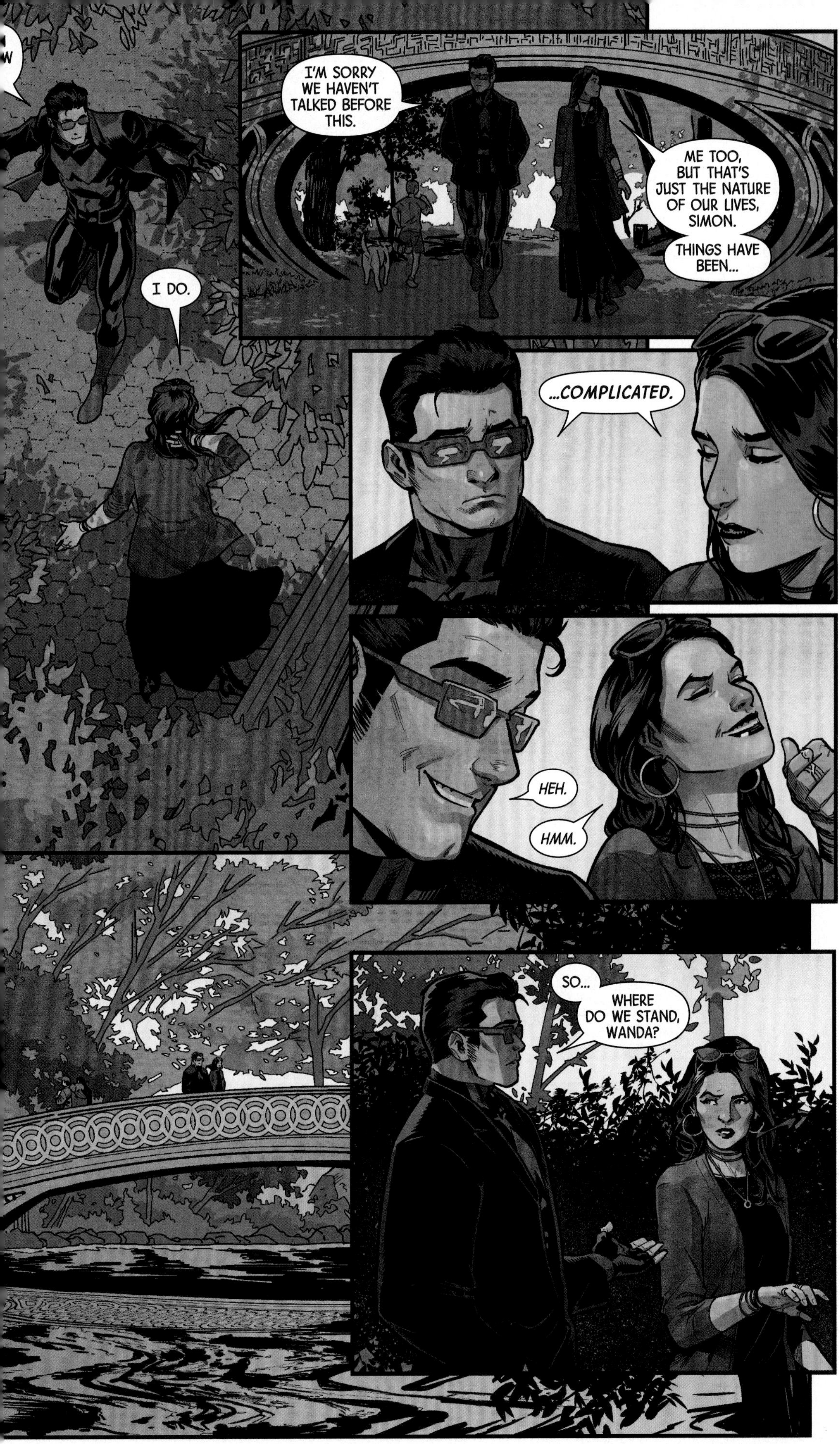
I DO.
I'M SORRY WE HAVEN'T TALKED BEFORE THIS.
ME TOO, BUT THAT'S JUST THE NATURE OF OUR LIVES, SIMON.
THINGS HAVE BEEN...
...COMPLICATED.
HEH.
HMM.
SO...
WHERE DO WE STAND, WANDA?

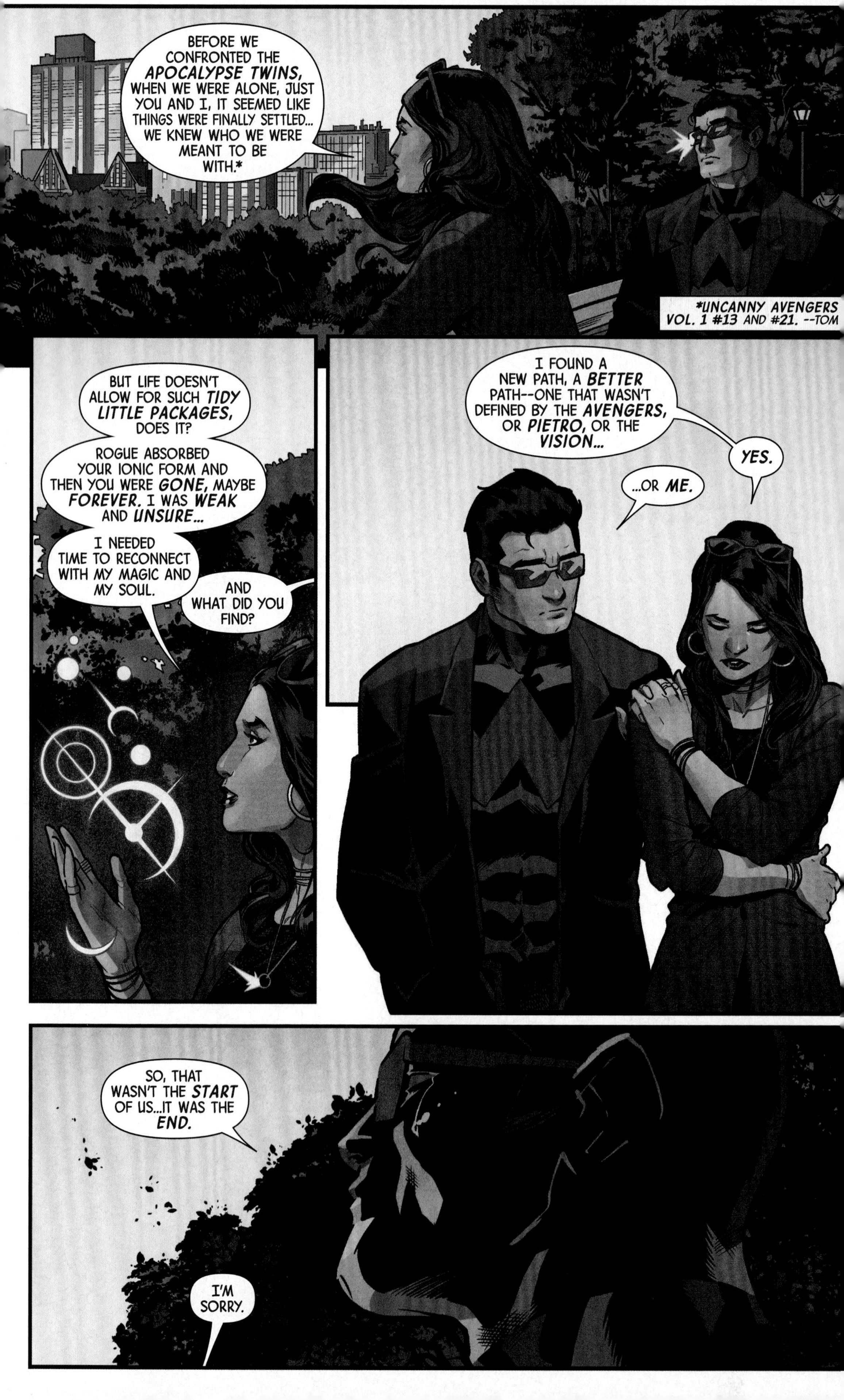

BEFORE WE CONFRONTED THE APOCALYPSE TWINS, WHEN WE WERE ALONE, JUST YOU AND I, IT SEEMED LIKE THINGS WERE FINALLY SETTLED... WE KNEW WHO WE WERE MEANT TO BE WITH.*
*UNCANNY AVENGERS VOL. 1 #13 AND #21. --TOM
BUT LIFE DOESN'T ALLOW FOR SUCH TIDY LITTLE PACKAGES, DOES IT?
ROGUE ABSORBED YOUR IONIC FORM AND THEN YOU WERE GONE, MAYBE FOREVER. I WAS WEAK AND UNSURE...
I NEEDED TIME TO RECONNECT WITH MY MAGIC AND MY SOUL.
AND WHAT DID YOU FIND?
I FOUND A NEW PATH, A BETTER PATH--ONE THAT WASN'T DEFINED BY THE AVENGERS, OR PIETRO, OR THE VISION...
...OR ME.
YES.
SO, THAT WASN'T THE START OF US...IT WAS THE END.
I'M SORRY.

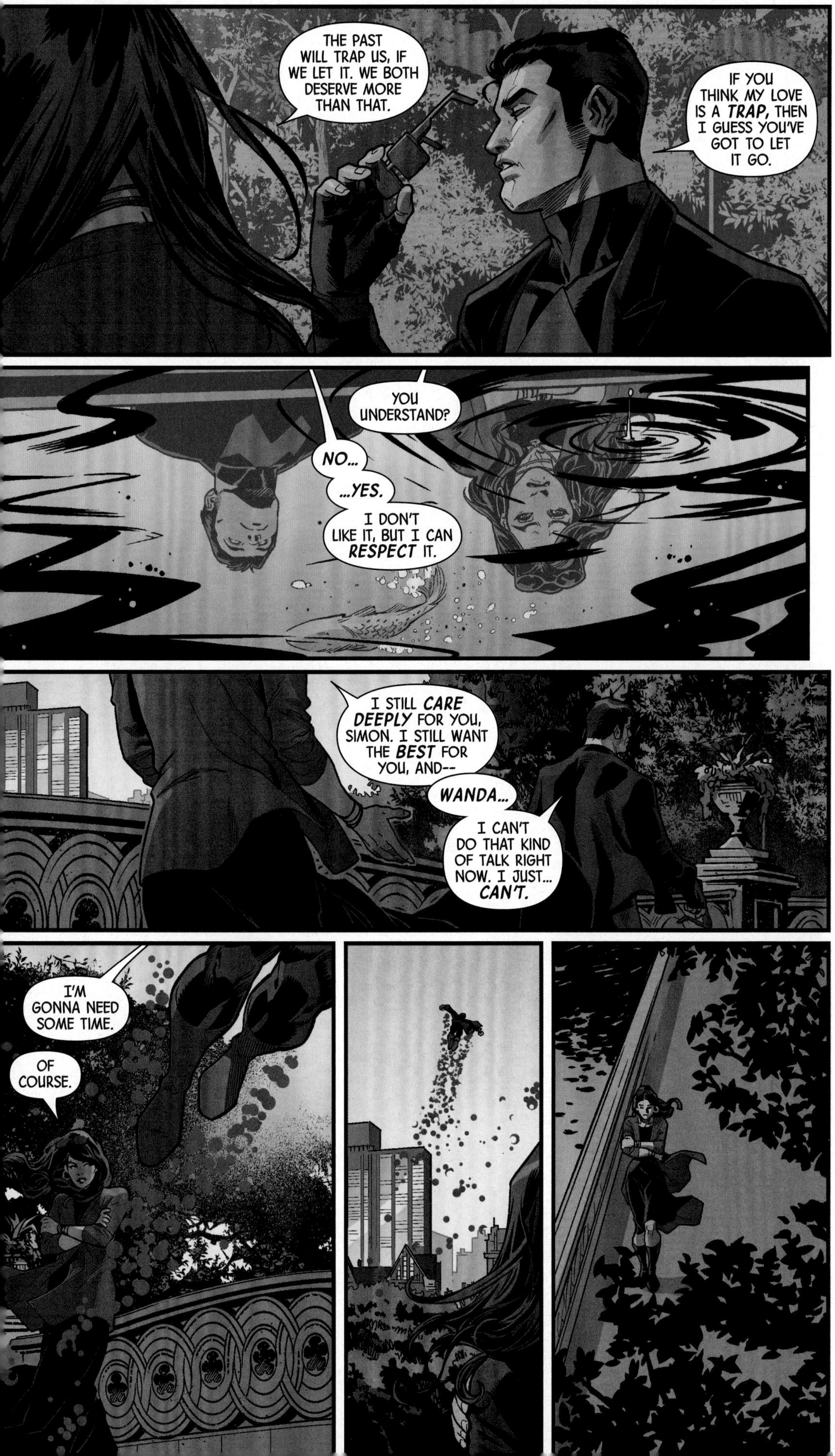
THE PAST WILL TRAP US, IF WE LET IT. WE BOTH DESERVE MORE THAN THAT.
IF YOU THINK MY LOVE IS A TRAP, THEN I GUESS YOU'VE GOT TO LET IT GO.
YOU UNDERSTAND?
NO...
...YES.
I DON'T LIKE IT, BUT I CAN RESPECT IT.
I STILL CARE DEEPLY FOR YOU, SIMON. I STILL WANT THE BEST FOR YOU, AND--
WANDA...
I CAN'T DO THAT KIND OF TALK RIGHT NOW. I JUST... CAN'T.
I'M GONNA NEED SOME TIME.
OF COURSE.

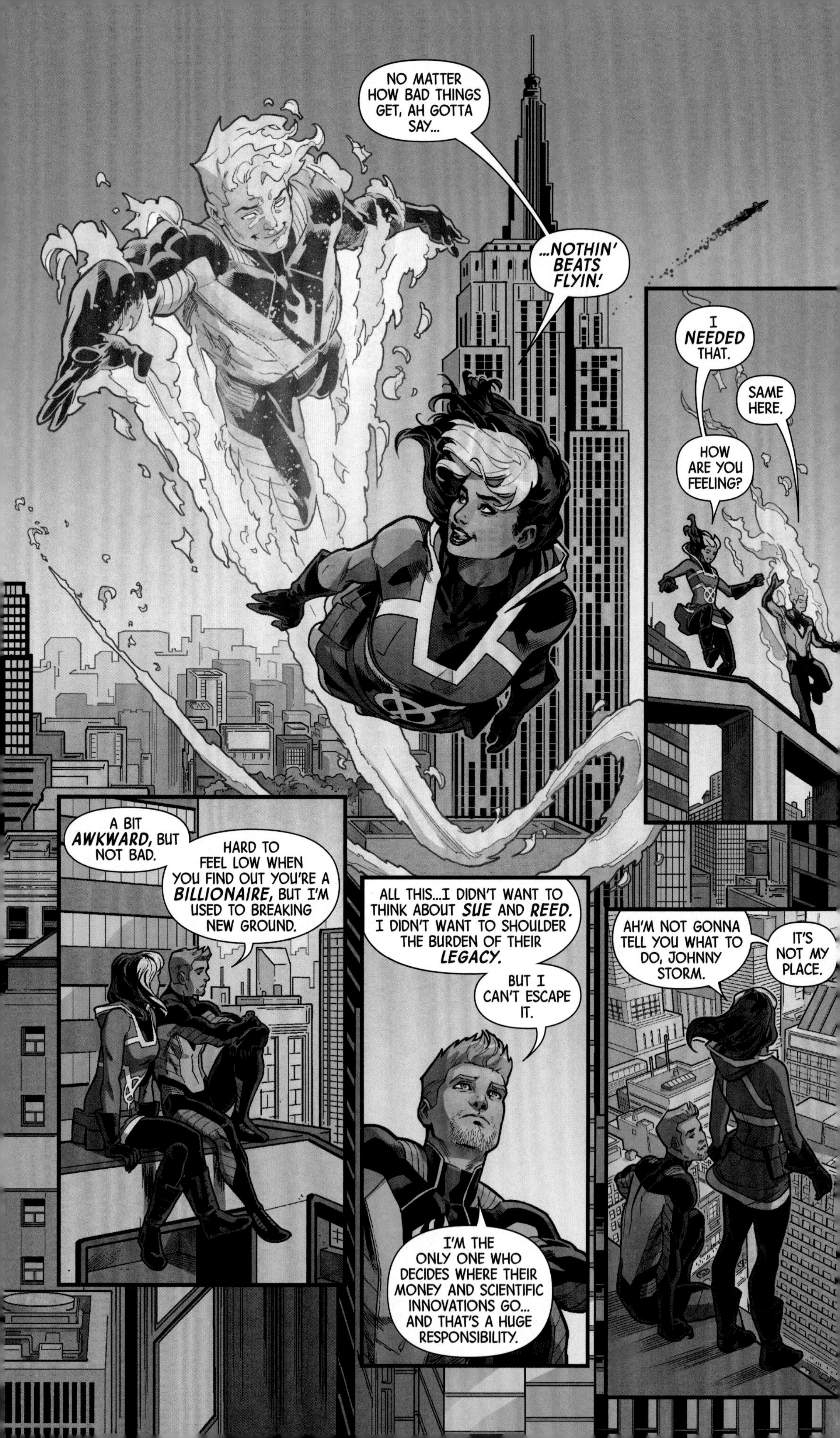
NO MATTER HOW BAD THINGS GET, AH GOTTA SAY...
...NOTHIN' BEATS FLYIN.'
I NEEDED THAT.
SAME HERE.
HOW ARE YOU FEELING?
A BIT AWKWARD, BUT NOT BAD.
HARD TO FEEL LOW WHEN YOU FIND OUT YOU'RE A BILLIONAIRE, BUT I'M USED TO BREAKING NEW GROUND.
ALL THIS...I DIDN'T WANT TO THINK ABOUT SUE AND REED. I DIDN'T WANT TO SHOULDER THE BURDEN OF THEIR LEGACY.
BUT I CAN'T ESCAPE IT.
I'M THE ONLY ONE WHO DECIDES WHERE THEIR MONEY AND SCIENTIFIC INNOVATIONS GO... AND THAT'S A HUGE RESPONSIBILITY.
AH'M NOT GONNA TELL YOU WHAT TO DO, JOHNNY STORM.
IT'S NOT MY PLACE.

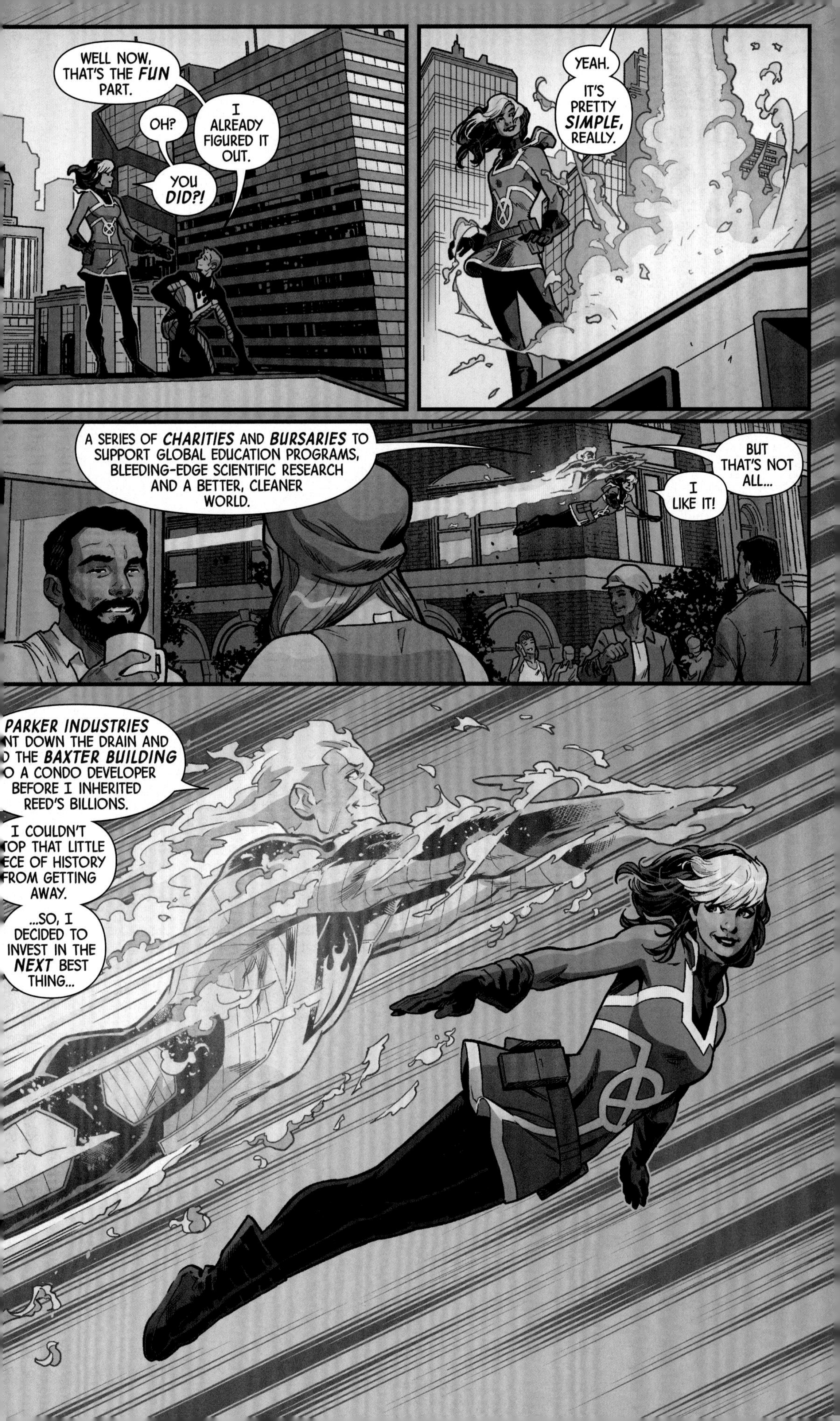
WELL NOW, THAT'S THE FUN PART.
OH?
I ALREADY FIGURED IT OUT.
YOU DID?!
YEAH.
IT'S PRETTY SIMPLE, REALLY.
A SERIES OF CHARITIES AND BURSARIES TO SUPPORT GLOBAL EDUCATION PROGRAMS, BLEEDING-EDGE SCIENTIFIC RESEARCH AND A BETTER, CLEANER WORLD.
I LIKE IT!
BUT THAT'S NOT ALL...
PARKER INDUSTRIES
NT DOWN THE DRAIN AND
D THE BAXTER BUILDING
O A CONDO DEVELOPER
BEFORE I INHERITED REED'S BILLIONS.
I COULDN'T
OP THAT LITTLE
ECE OF HISTORY
FROM GETTING AWAY.
...SO, I DECIDED TO INVEST IN THE NEXT BEST THING...

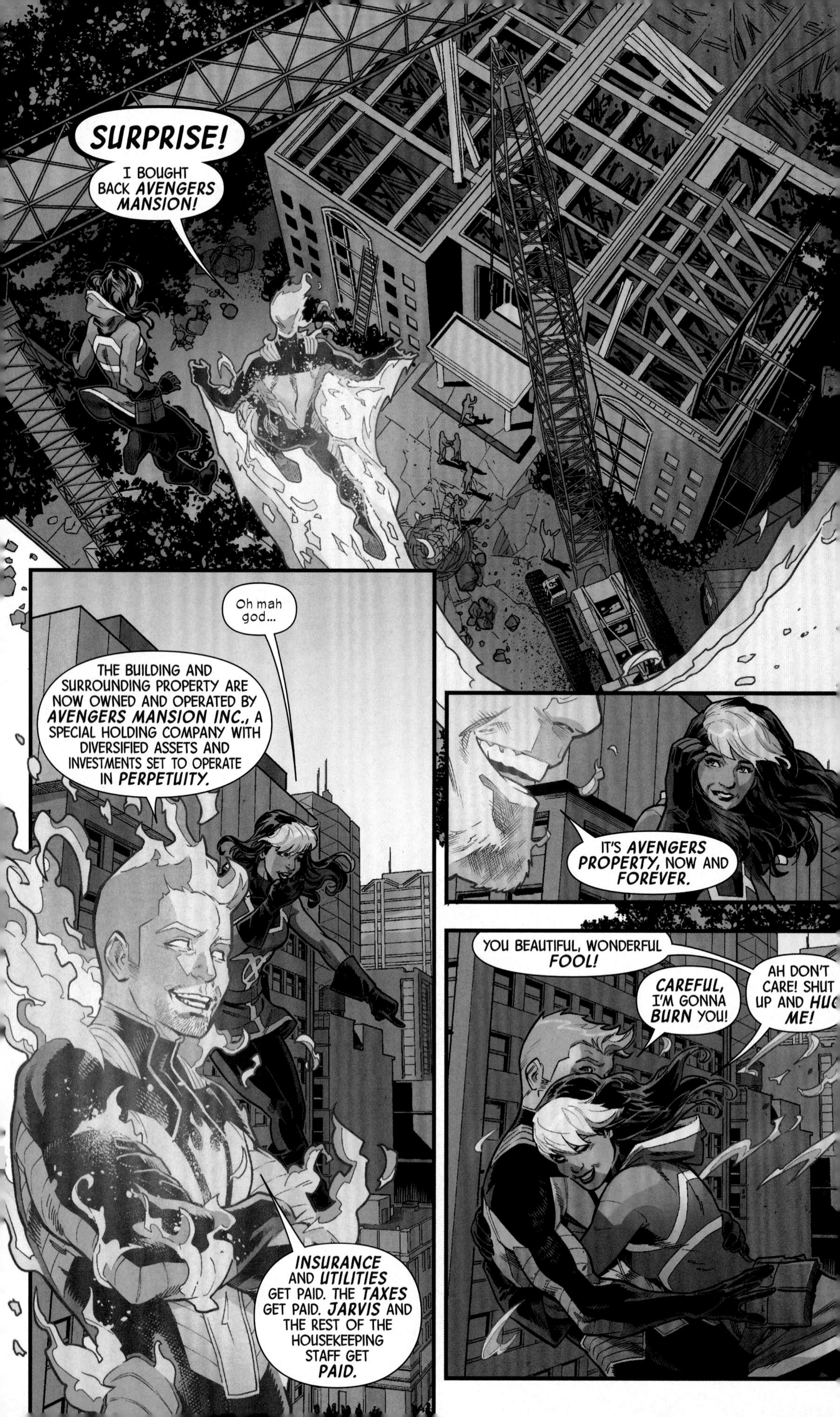
SURPRISE!
I BOUGHT BACK AVENGERS MANSION!
Oh mah god...
THE BUILDING AND SURROUNDING PROPERTY ARE NOW OWNED AND OPERATED BY AVENGERS MANSION INC., A SPECIAL HOLDING COMPANY WITH DIVERSIFIED ASSETS AND INVESTMENTS SET TO OPERATE IN PERPETUITY.
INSURANCE AND UTILITIES GET PAID. THE TAXES GET PAID. JARVIS AND THE REST OF THE HOUSEKEEPING STAFF GET PAID.
IT'S AVENGERS PROPERTY, NOW AND FOREVER.
YOU BEAUTIFUL, WONDERFUL FOOL!
CAREFUL, I'M GONNA BURN YOU!
AH DON'T CARE! SHUT UP AND HUG ME!

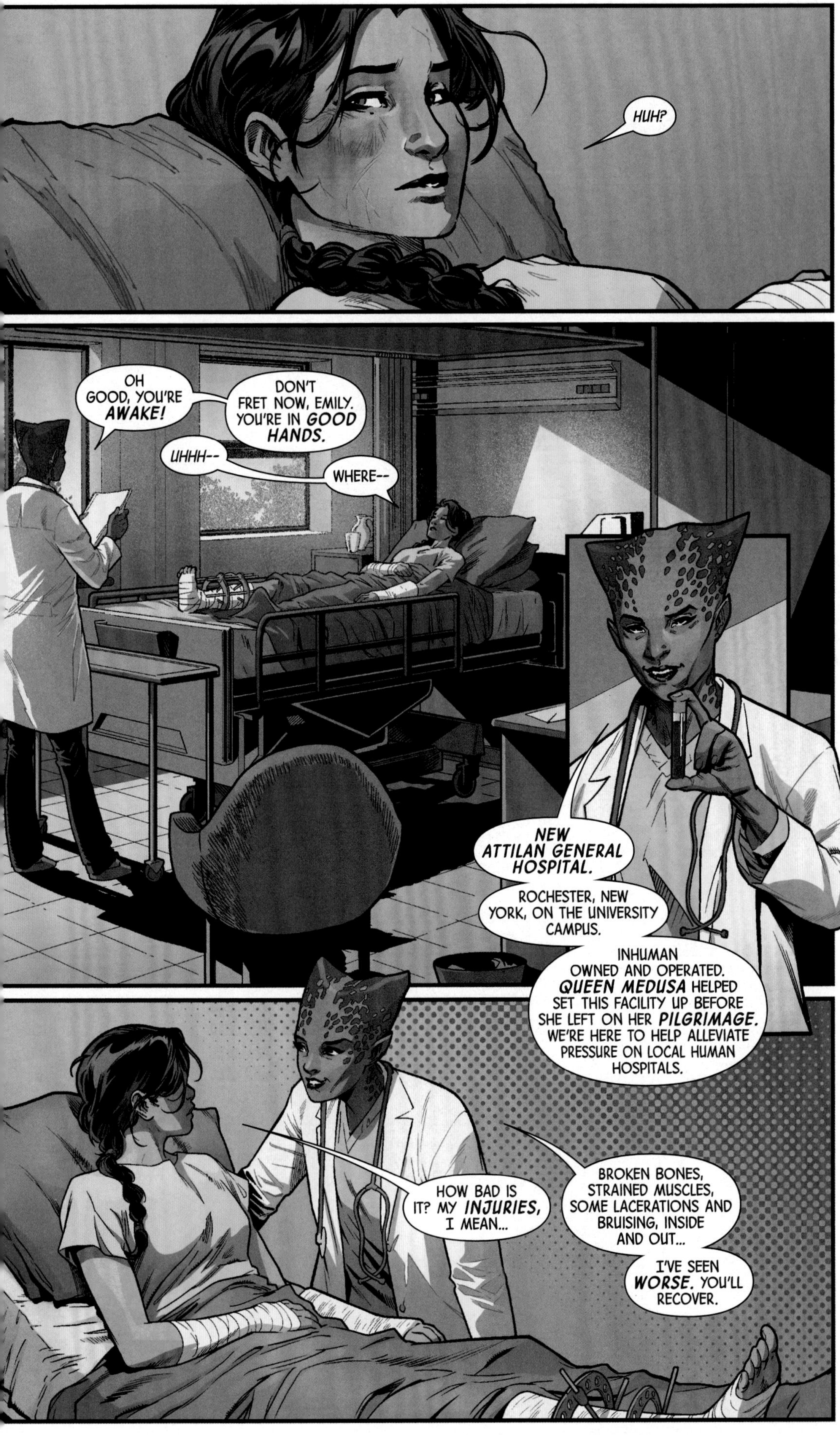
HUH?
OH GOOD, YOU'RE AWAKE!
DON'T FRET NOW, EMILY. YOU'RE IN GOOD HANDS.
UHHH--
WHERE--
NEW ATTILAN GENERAL HOSPITAL.
ROCHESTER, NEW YORK, ON THE UNIVERSITY CAMPUS.
INHUMAN OWNED AND OPERATED. QUEEN MEDUSA HELPED SET THIS FACILITY UP BEFORE SHE LEFT ON HER PILGRIMAGE. WE'RE HERE TO HELP ALLEVIATE PRESSURE ON LOCAL HUMAN HOSPITALS.
HOW BAD IS IT? MY INJURIES, I MEAN...
BROKEN BONES, STRAINED MUSCLES, SOME LACERATIONS AND BRUISING, INSIDE AND OUT...
I'VE SEEN WORSE. YOU'LL RECOVER.

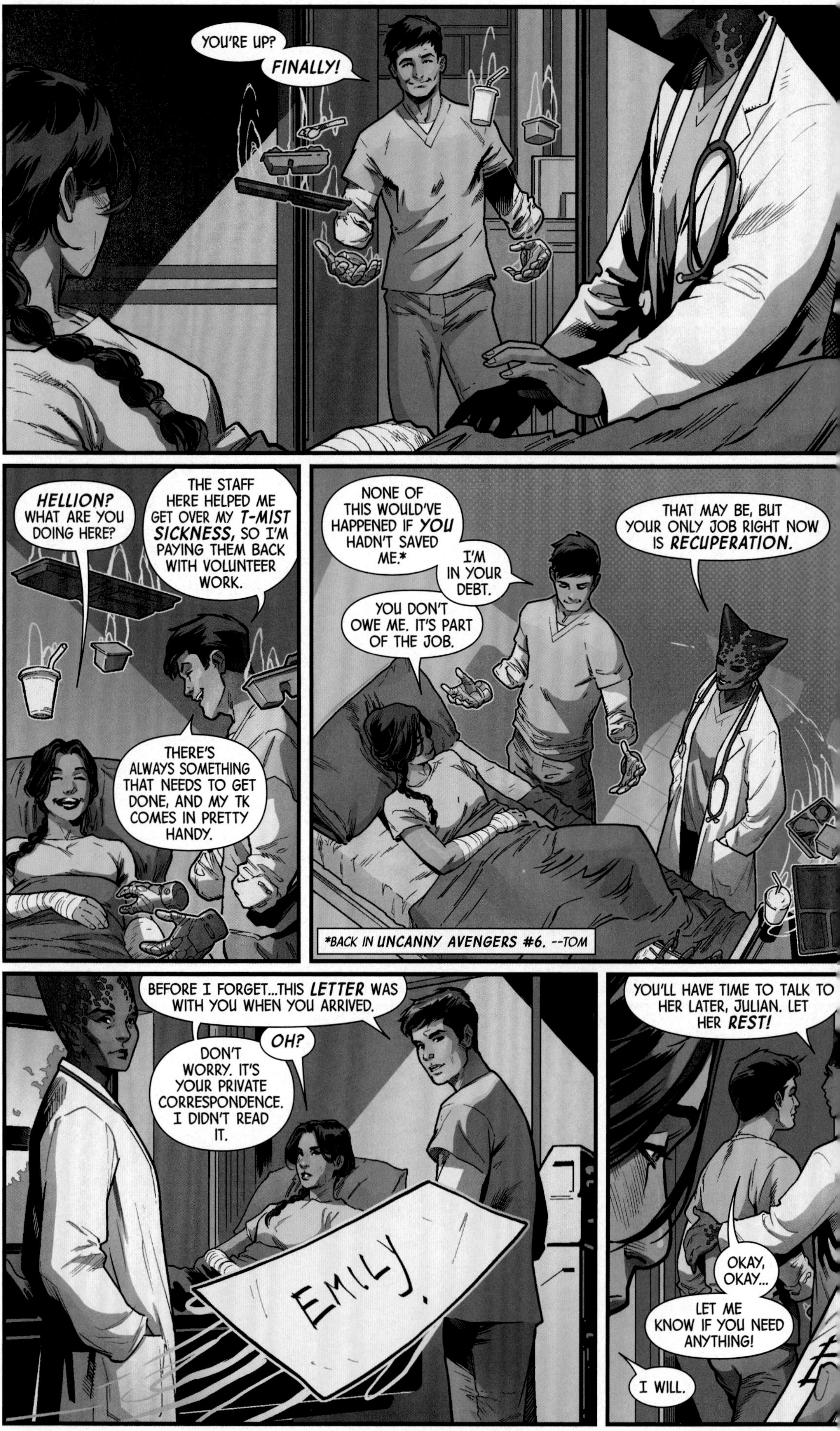

YOU'RE UP? FINALLY!
HELLION? WHAT ARE YOU DOING HERE?
THE STAFF HERE HELPED ME GET OVER MY T-MIST SICKNESS, SO I'M PAYING THEM BACK WITH VOLUNTEER WORK.
THERE'S ALWAYS SOMETHING THAT NEEDS TO GET DONE, AND MY TK COMES IN PRETTY HANDY.
NONE OF THIS WOULD'VE HAPPENED IF YOU HADN'T SAVED ME.*
I'M IN YOUR DEBT.
YOU DON'T OWE ME. IT'S PART OF THE JOB.
THAT MAY BE, BUT YOUR ONLY JOB RIGHT NOW IS RECUPERATION.
*BACK IN UNCANNY AVENGERS #6. --TOM
BEFORE I FORGET...THIS LETTER WAS WITH YOU WHEN YOU ARRIVED.
OH?
DON'T WORRY. IT'S YOUR PRIVATE CORRESPONDENCE. I DIDN'T READ IT.
EMILY.
YOU'LL HAVE TIME TO TALK TO HER LATER, JULIAN. LET HER REST!
OKAY, OKAY...
LET ME KNOW IF YOU NEED ANYTHING!
I WILL.

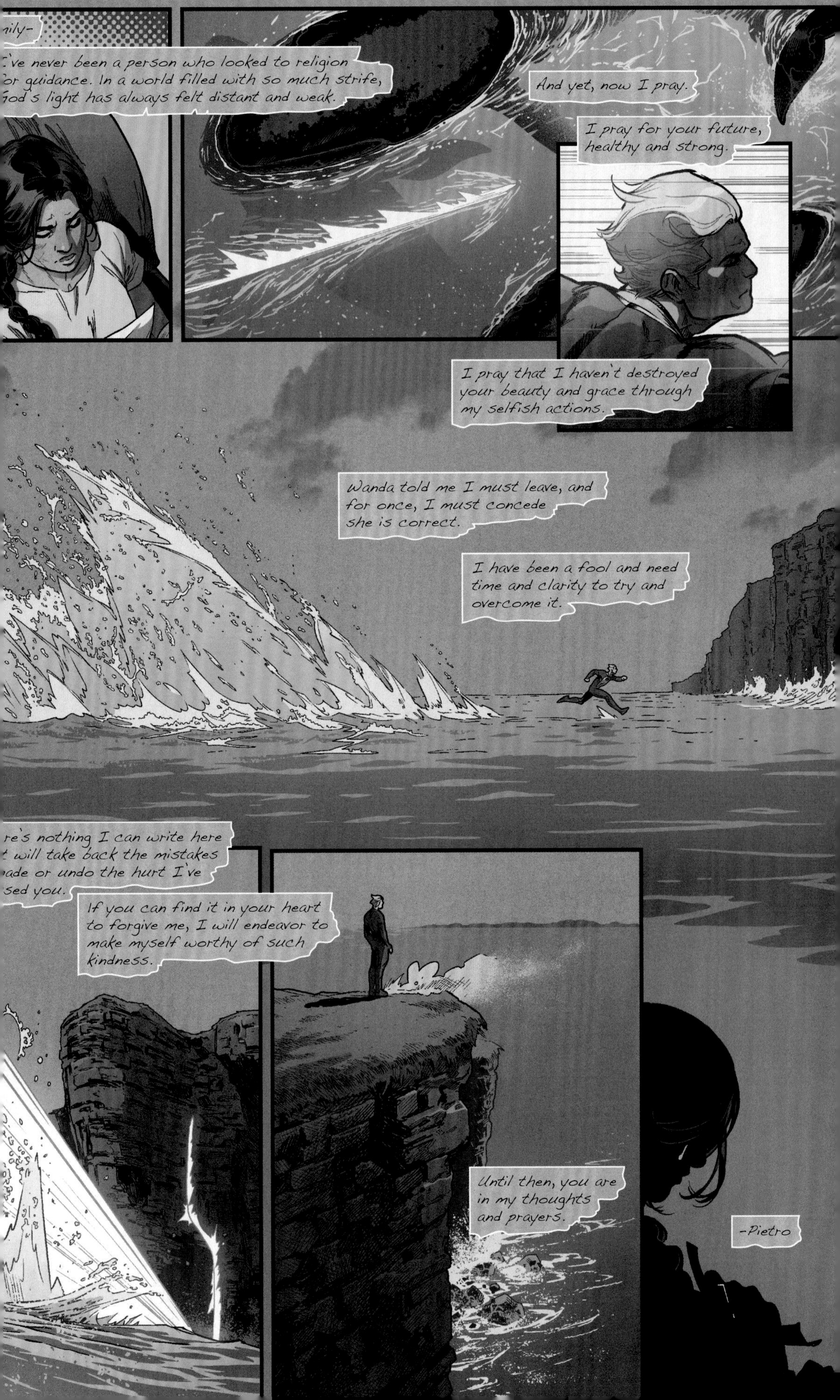
nily-
've never been a person who looked to religion or guidance. In a world filled with so much strife, od's light has always felt distant and weak.
And yet, now I pray.
I pray for your future, healthy and strong.
I pray that I haven't destroyed your beauty and grace through my selfish actions.
Wanda told me I must leave, and for once, I must concede she is correct.
I have been a fool and need time and clarity to try and overcome it.
re's nothing I can write here t will take back the mistakes ade or undo the hurt I've sed you.
If you can find it in your heart to forgive me, I will endeavor to make myself worthy of such kindness.
Until then, you are in my thoughts and prayers.
-Pietro

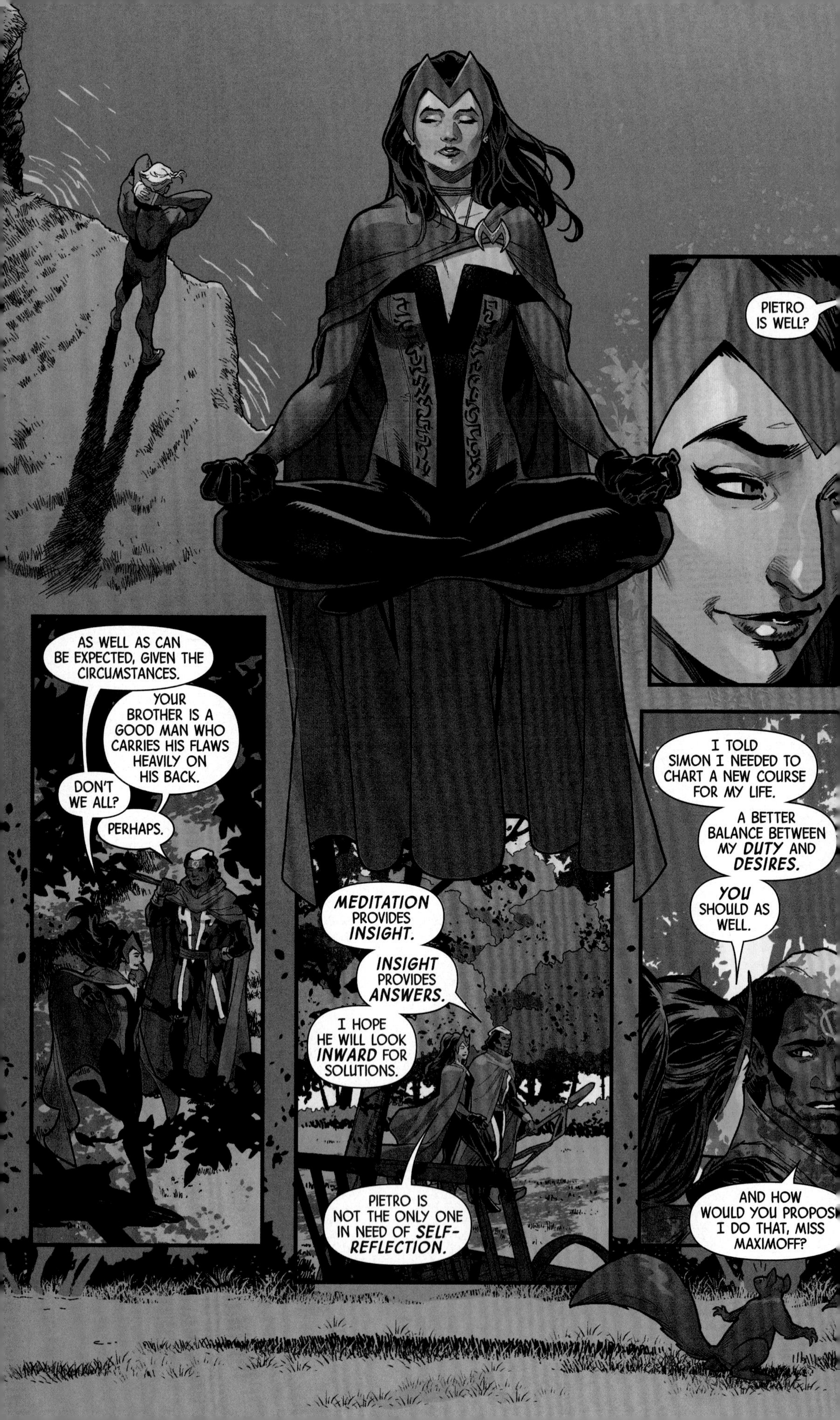
PIETRO IS WELL?
AS WELL AS CAN BE EXPECTED, GIVEN THE CIRCUMSTANCES.
YOUR BROTHER IS A GOOD MAN WHO CARRIES HIS FLAWS HEAVILY ON HIS BACK.
DON'T WE ALL?
PERHAPS.
MEDITATION PROVIDES INSIGHT.
INSIGHT PROVIDES ANSWERS.
I HOPE HE WILL LOOK INWARD FOR SOLUTIONS.
PIETRO IS NOT THE ONLY ONE IN NEED OF SELF-REFLECTION.
I TOLD SIMON I NEEDED TO CHART A NEW COURSE FOR MY LIFE.
A BETTER BALANCE BETWEEN MY DUTY AND DESIRES.
YOU SHOULD AS WELL.
AND HOW WOULD YOU PROPOS I DO THAT, MISS MAXIMOFF?

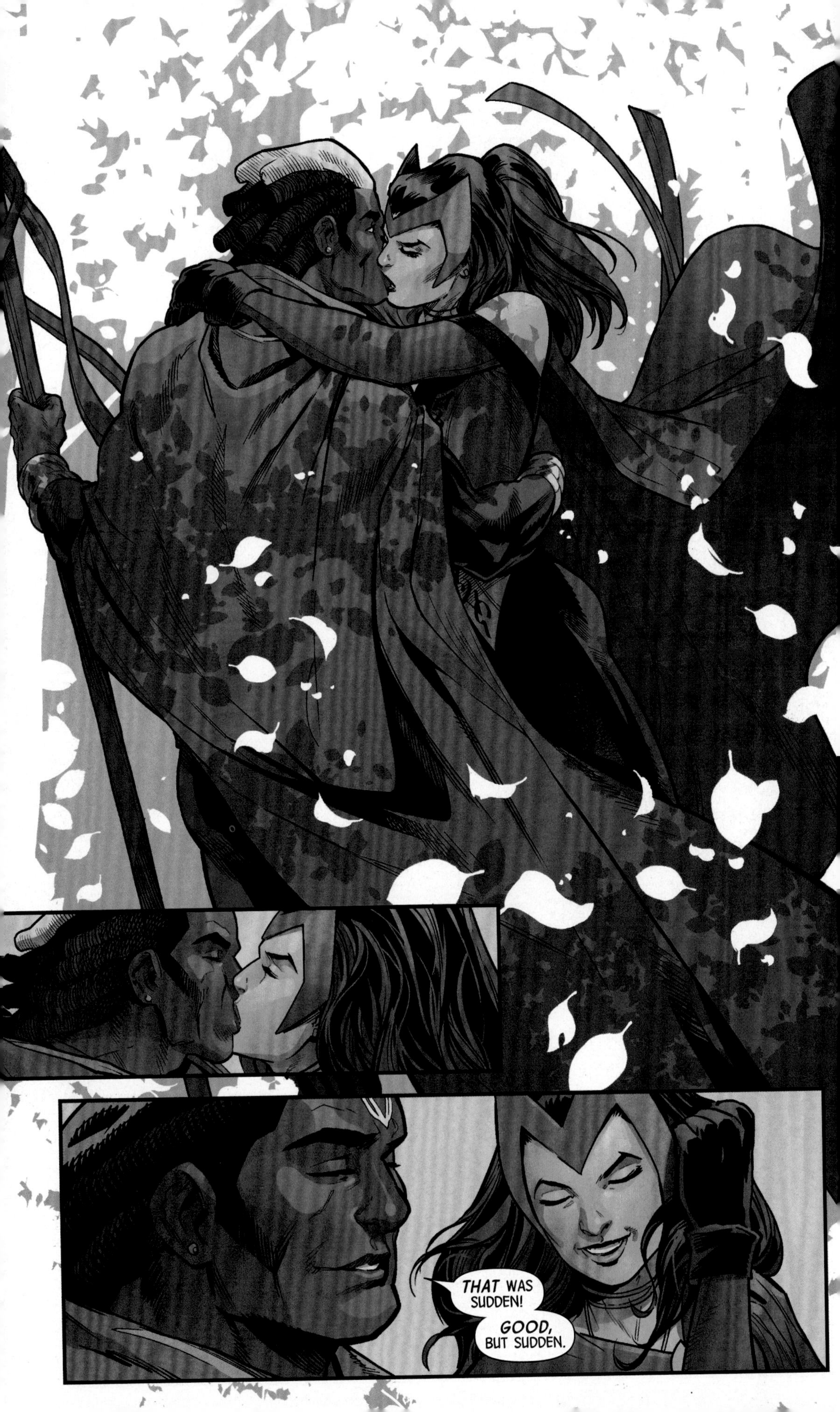
THAT WAS SUDDEN!
GOOD, BUT SUDDEN.

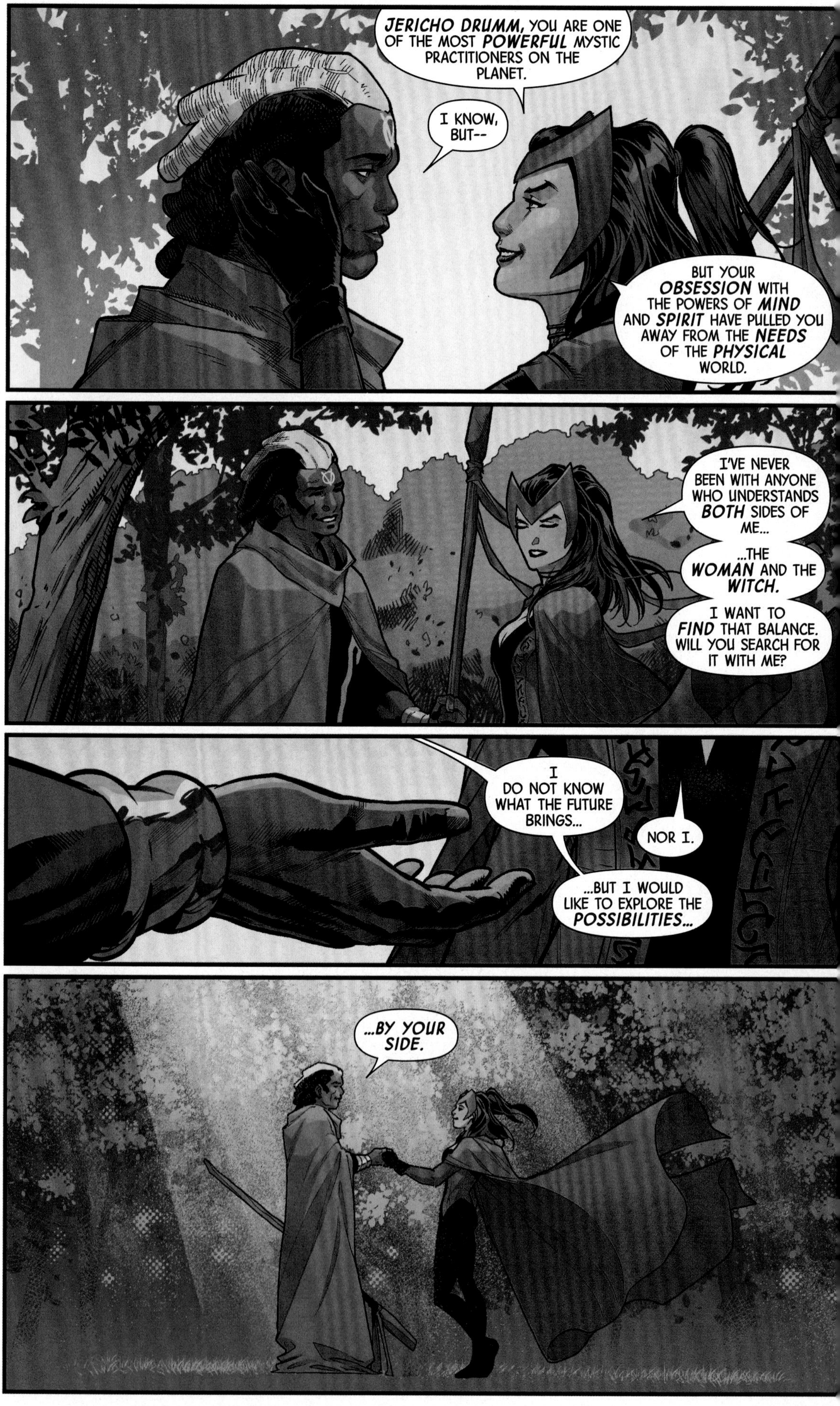

JERICHO DRUMM, YOU ARE ONE OF THE MOST POWERFUL MYSTIC PRACTITIONERS ON THE PLANET.
I KNOW, BUT--
BUT YOUR OBSESSION WITH THE POWERS OF MIND AND SPIRIT HAVE PULLED YOU AWAY FROM THE NEEDS OF THE PHYSICAL WORLD.
I'VE NEVER BEEN WITH ANYONE WHO UNDERSTANDS BOTH SIDES OF ME...
...THE WOMAN AND THE WITCH.
I WANT TO FIND THAT BALANCE. WILL YOU SEARCH FOR IT WITH ME?
I DO NOT KNOW WHAT THE FUTURE BRINGS...
NOR I.
...BUT I WOULD LIKE TO EXPLORE THE POSSIBILITIES...
...BY YOUR SIDE.

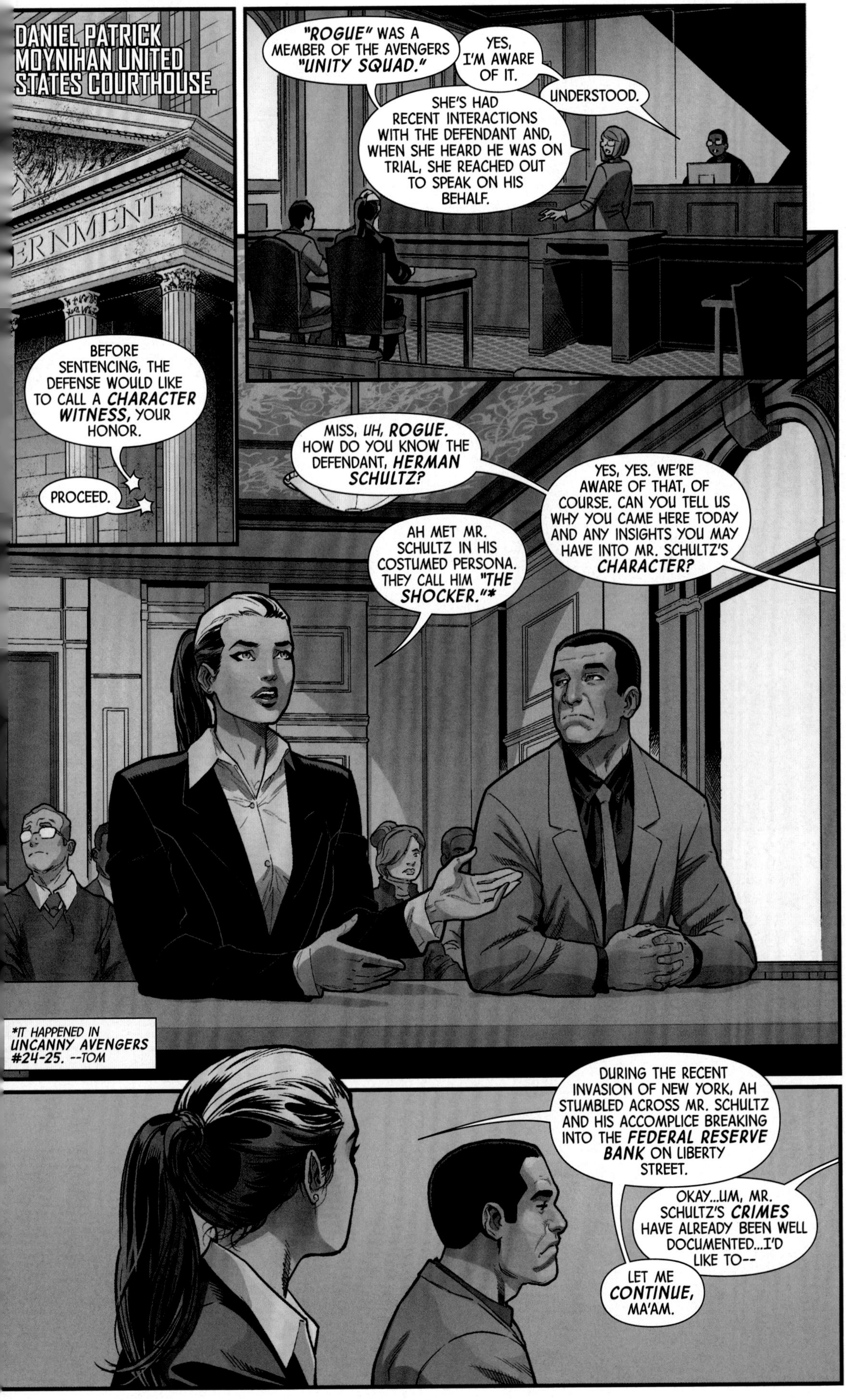

DANIEL PATRICK MOYNIHAN UNITED STATES COURTHOUSE.
ERNMENT
BEFORE SENTENCING, THE DEFENSE WOULD LIKE TO CALL A CHARACTER WITNESS, YOUR HONOR.
PROCEED.
"ROGUE" WAS A MEMBER OF THE AVENGERS "UNITY SQUAD."
SHE'S HAD RECENT INTERACTIONS WITH THE DEFENDANT AND, WHEN SHE HEARD HE WAS ON TRIAL, SHE REACHED OUT TO SPEAK ON HIS BEHALF.
YES, I'M AWARE OF IT.
UNDERSTOOD.
MISS, UH, ROGUE. HOW DO YOU KNOW THE DEFENDANT, HERMAN SCHULTZ?
AH MET MR. SCHULTZ IN HIS COSTUMED PERSONA. THEY CALL HIM "THE SHOCKER."*
YES, YES. WE'RE AWARE OF THAT, OF COURSE. CAN YOU TELL US WHY YOU CAME HERE TODAY AND ANY INSIGHTS YOU MAY HAVE INTO MR. SCHULTZ'S CHARACTER?
*IT HAPPENED IN UNCANNY AVENGERS #24-25. --TOM
DURING THE RECENT INVASION OF NEW YORK, AH STUMBLED ACROSS MR. SCHULTZ AND HIS ACCOMPLICE BREAKING INTO THE FEDERAL RESERVE BANK ON LIBERTY STREET.
OKAY...UM, MR. SCHULTZ'S CRIMES HAVE ALREADY BEEN WELL DOCUMENTED...I'D LIKE TO--
LET ME CONTINUE, MA'AM.

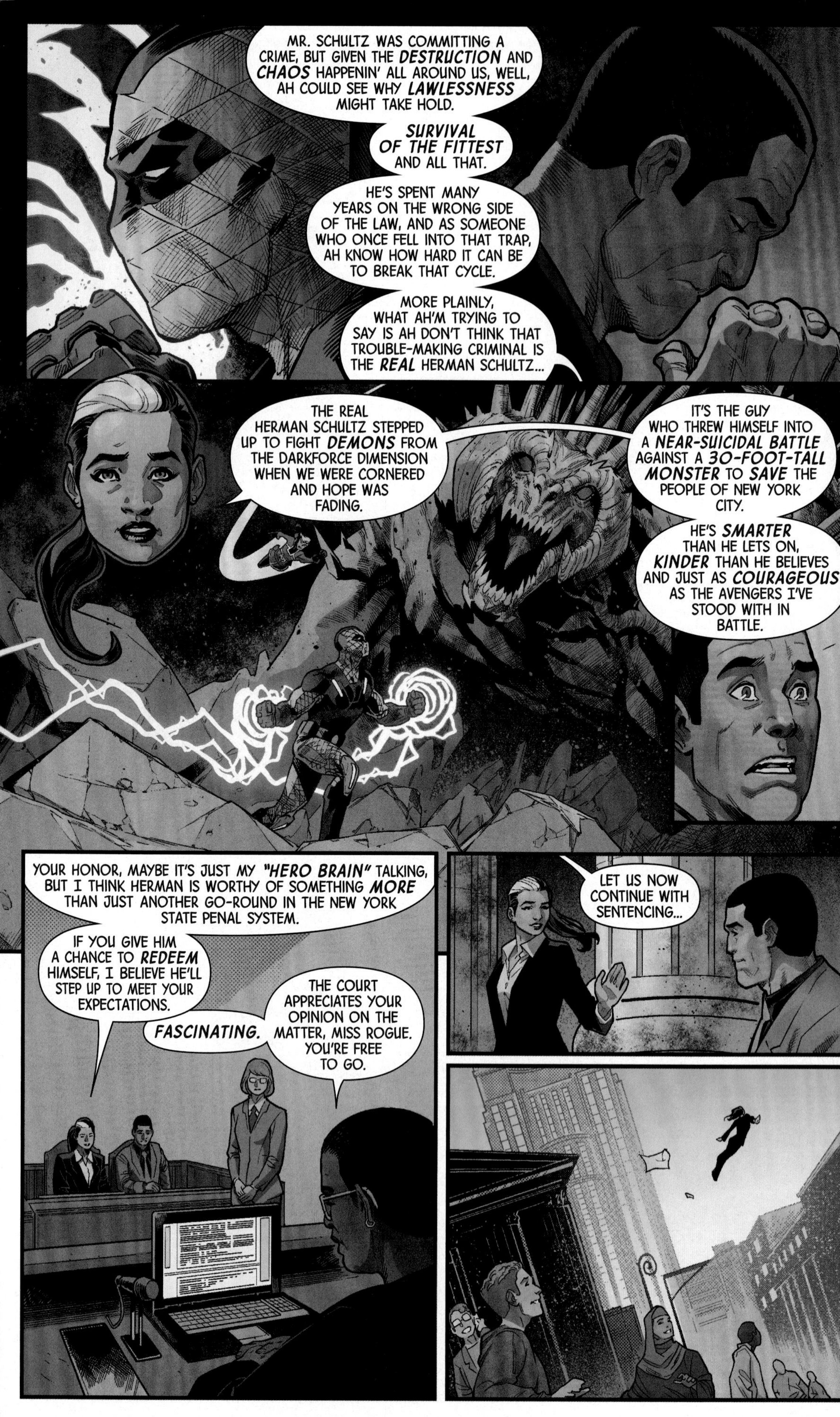

MR. SCHULTZ WAS COMMITTING A CRIME, BUT GIVEN THE DESTRUCTION AND CHAOS HAPPENIN' ALL AROUND US, WELL, AH COULD SEE WHY LAWLESSNESS MIGHT TAKE HOLD.
SURVIVAL OF THE FITTEST AND ALL THAT.
HE'S SPENT MANY YEARS ON THE WRONG SIDE OF THE LAW, AND AS SOMEONE WHO ONCE FELL INTO THAT TRAP, AH KNOW HOW HARD IT CAN BE TO BREAK THAT CYCLE.
MORE PLAINLY, WHAT AH'M TRYING TO SAY IS AH DON'T THINK THAT TROUBLE-MAKING CRIMINAL IS THE REAL HERMAN SCHULTZ...
THE REAL HERMAN SCHULTZ STEPPED UP TO FIGHT DEMONS FROM THE DARKFORCE DIMENSION WHEN WE WERE CORNERED AND HOPE WAS FADING.
IT'S THE GUY WHO THREW HIMSELF INTO A NEAR-SUICIDAL BATTLE AGAINST A 30-FOOT-TALL MONSTER TO SAVE THE PEOPLE OF NEW YORK CITY.
HE'S SMARTER THAN HE LETS ON, KINDER THAN HE BELIEVES AND JUST AS COURAGEOUS AS THE AVENGERS I'VE STOOD WITH IN BATTLE.
YOUR HONOR, MAYBE IT'S JUST MY "HERO BRAIN" TALKING, BUT I THINK HERMAN IS WORTHY OF SOMETHING MORE THAN JUST ANOTHER GO-ROUND IN THE NEW YORK STATE PENAL SYSTEM.
IF YOU GIVE HIM A CHANCE TO REDEEM HIMSELF, I BELIEVE HE'LL STEP UP TO MEET YOUR EXPECTATIONS.
FASCINATING.
THE COURT APPRECIATES YOUR OPINION ON THE MATTER, MISS ROGUE. YOU'RE FREE TO GO.
LET US NOW CONTINUE WITH SENTENCING...

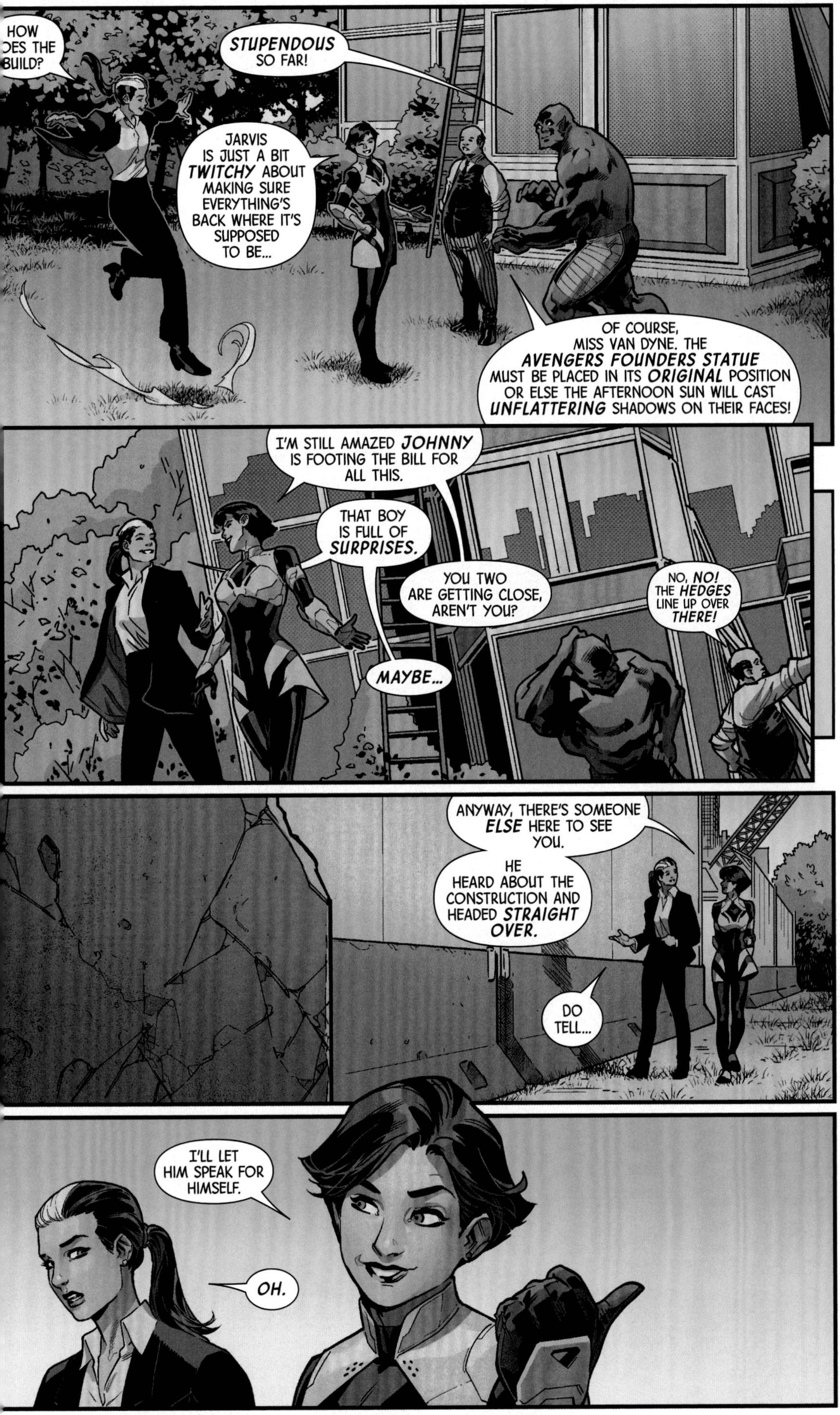

HOW
OES THE
BUILD?
STUPENDOUS SO FAR!
JARVIS IS JUST A BIT TWITCHY ABOUT MAKING SURE EVERYTHING'S BACK WHERE IT'S SUPPOSED TO BE...
OF COURSE, MISS VAN DYNE. THE AVENGERS FOUNDERS STATUE MUST BE PLACED IN ITS ORIGINAL POSITION OR ELSE THE AFTERNOON SUN WILL CAST UNFLATTERING SHADOWS ON THEIR FACES!
I'M STILL AMAZED JOHNNY IS FOOTING THE BILL FOR ALL THIS.
THAT BOY IS FULL OF SURPRISES.
YOU TWO ARE GETTING CLOSE, AREN'T YOU?
MAYBE...
NO, NO! THE HEDGES LINE UP OVER THERE!
ANYWAY, THERE'S SOMEONE ELSE HERE TO SEE YOU.
HE HEARD ABOUT THE CONSTRUCTION AND HEADED STRAIGHT OVER.
DO TELL...
I'LL LET HIM SPEAK FOR HIMSELF.
OH.

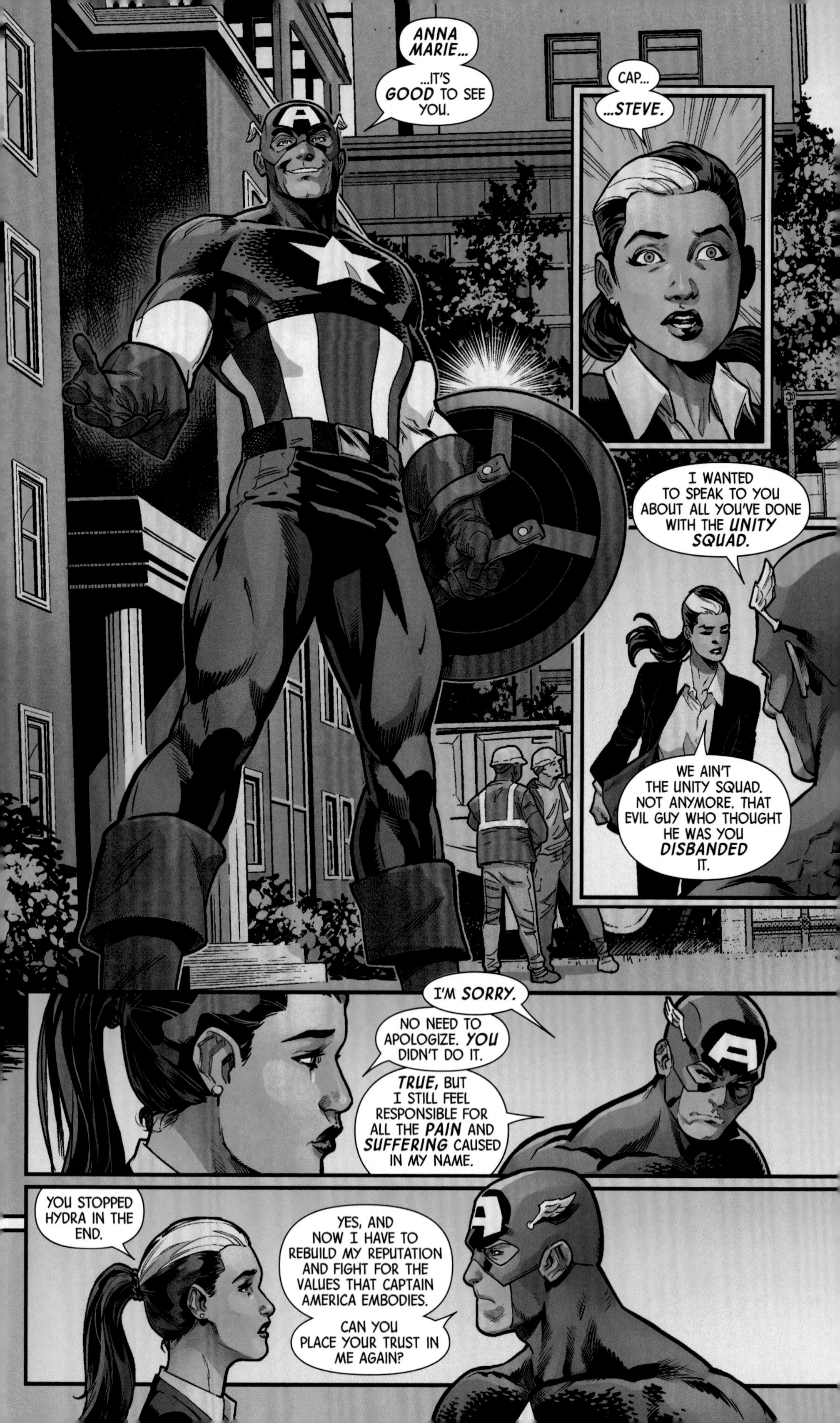
ANNA MARIE...
...IT'S GOOD TO SEE YOU.
CAP...
...STEVE.
I WANTED TO SPEAK TO YOU ABOUT ALL YOU'VE DONE WITH THE UNITY SQUAD.
WE AIN'T THE UNITY SQUAD. NOT ANYMORE. THAT EVIL GUY WHO THOUGHT HE WAS YOU DISBANDED IT.
I'M SORRY.
NO NEED TO APOLOGIZE. YOU DIDN'T DO IT.
TRUE, BUT I STILL FEEL RESPONSIBLE FOR ALL THE PAIN AND SUFFERING CAUSED IN MY NAME.
YOU STOPPED HYDRA IN THE END.
YES, AND NOW I HAVE TO REBUILD MY REPUTATION AND FIGHT FOR THE VALUES THAT CAPTAIN AMERICA EMBODIES.
CAN YOU PLACE YOUR TRUST IN ME AGAIN?

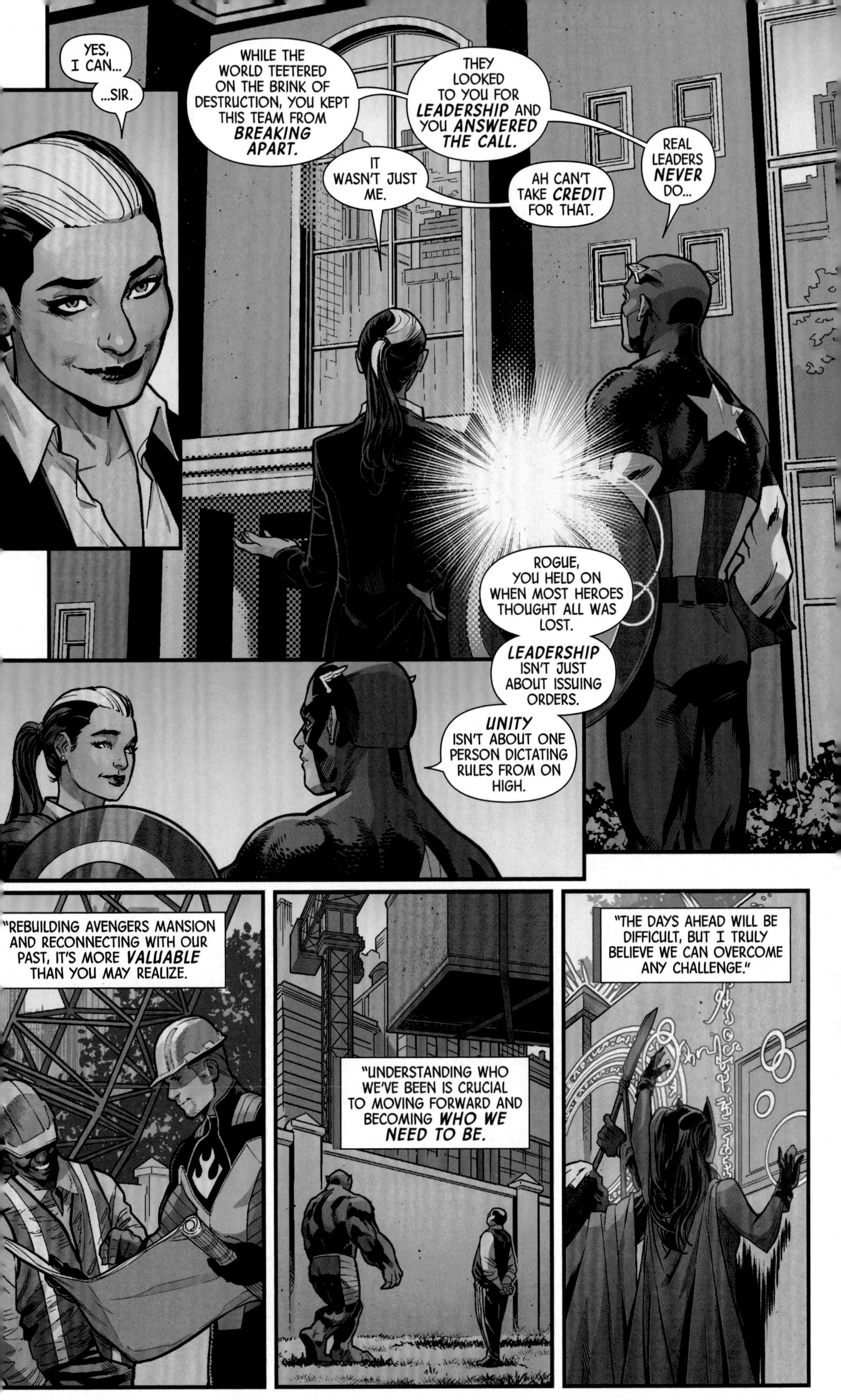

YES, I CAN...
...SIR.
WHILE THE WORLD TEETERED ON THE BRINK OF DESTRUCTION, YOU KEPT THIS TEAM FROM *BREAKING APART.*
THEY LOOKED TO YOU FOR *LEADERSHIP* AND YOU *ANSWERED THE CALL.*
IT WASN'T JUST ME.
AH CAN'T TAKE *CREDIT* FOR THAT.
REAL LEADERS *NEVER* DO...
ROGUE, YOU HELD ON WHEN MOST HEROES THOUGHT ALL WAS LOST.
LEADERSHIP ISN'T JUST ABOUT ISSUING ORDERS.
UNITY ISN'T ABOUT ONE PERSON DICTATING RULES FROM ON HIGH.
"REBUILDING AVENGERS MANSION AND RECONNECTING WITH OUR PAST, IT'S MORE *VALUABLE* THAN YOU MAY REALIZE.
"UNDERSTANDING WHO WE'VE BEEN IS CRUCIAL TO MOVING FORWARD AND BECOMING *WHO WE NEED TO BE.*
"THE DAYS AHEAD WILL BE DIFFICULT, BUT I TRULY BELIEVE WE CAN OVERCOME ANY CHALLENGE."

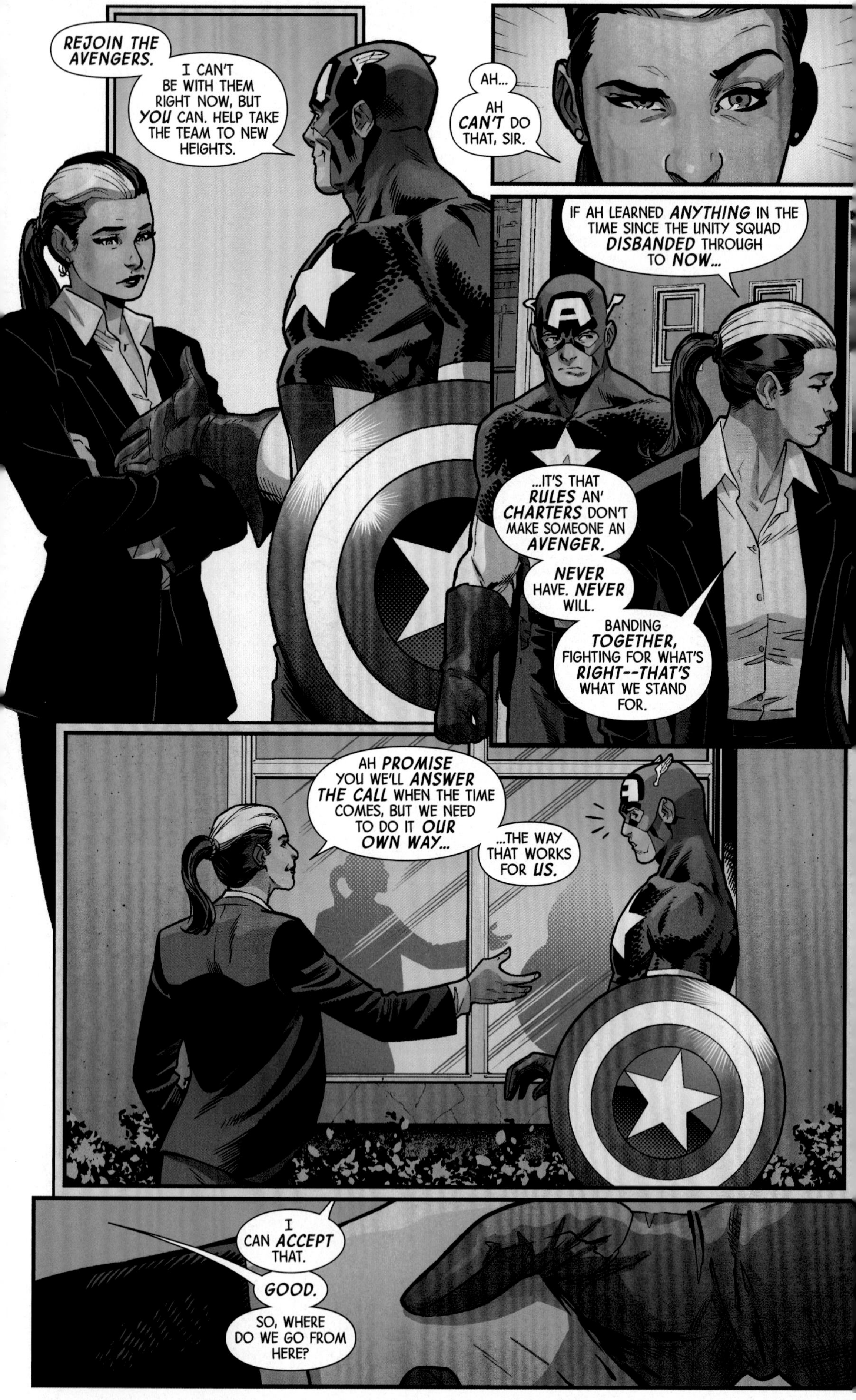
REJOIN THE AVENGERS.
I CAN'T BE WITH THEM RIGHT NOW, BUT YOU CAN. HELP TAKE THE TEAM TO NEW HEIGHTS.
AH...
AH CAN'T DO THAT, SIR.
IF AH LEARNED ANYTHING IN THE TIME SINCE THE UNITY SQUAD DISBANDED THROUGH TO NOW...
...IT'S THAT RULES AN' CHARTERS DON'T MAKE SOMEONE AN AVENGER.
NEVER HAVE. NEVER WILL.
BANDING TOGETHER, FIGHTING FOR WHAT'S RIGHT--THAT'S WHAT WE STAND FOR.
AH PROMISE YOU WE'LL ANSWER THE CALL WHEN THE TIME COMES, BUT WE NEED TO DO IT OUR OWN WAY...
...THE WAY THAT WORKS FOR US.
I CAN ACCEPT THAT.
GOOD.
SO, WHERE DO WE GO FROM HERE?

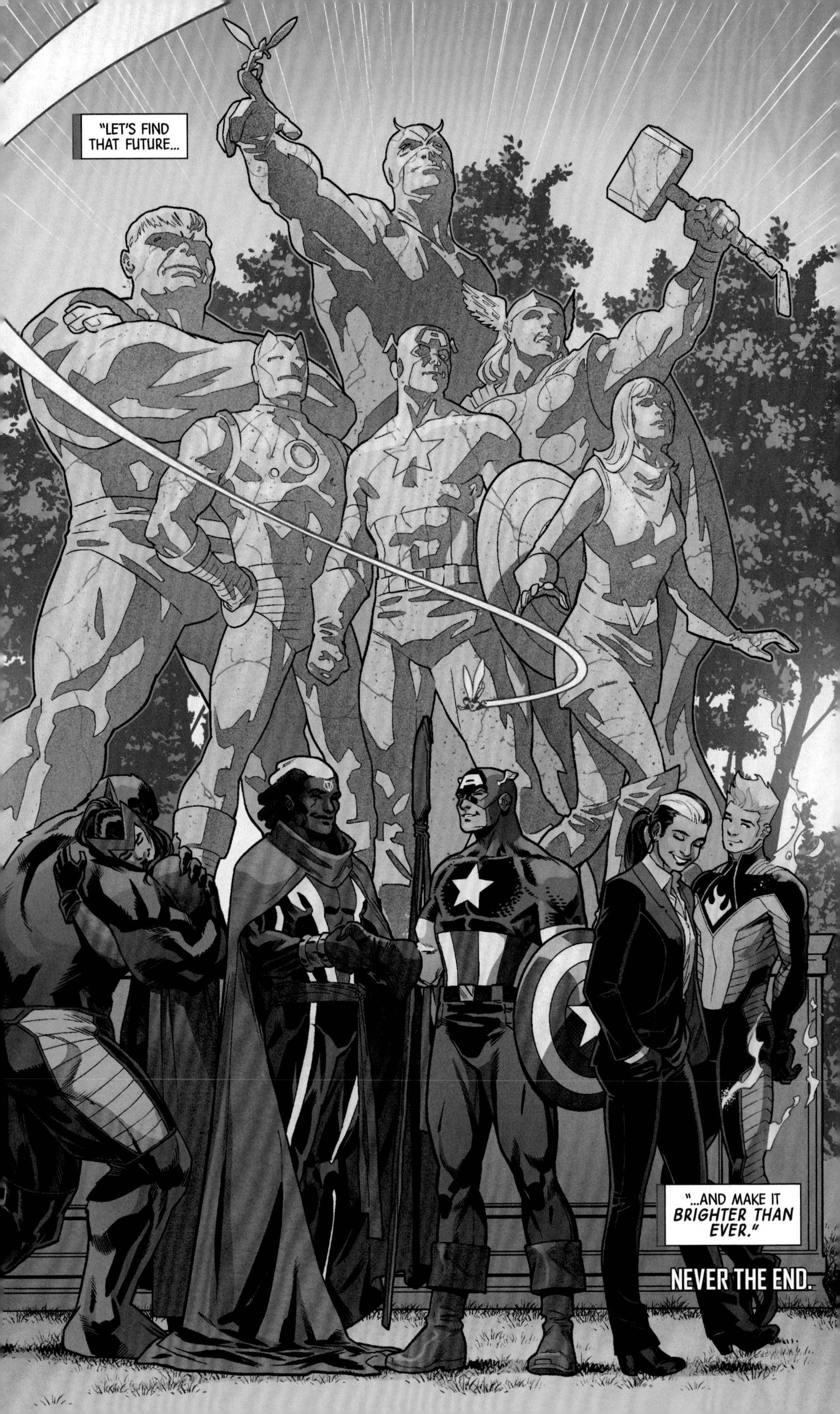
"LET'S FIND THAT FUTURE...
"...AND MAKE IT *BRIGHTER THAN EVER.*"
NEVER THE END.

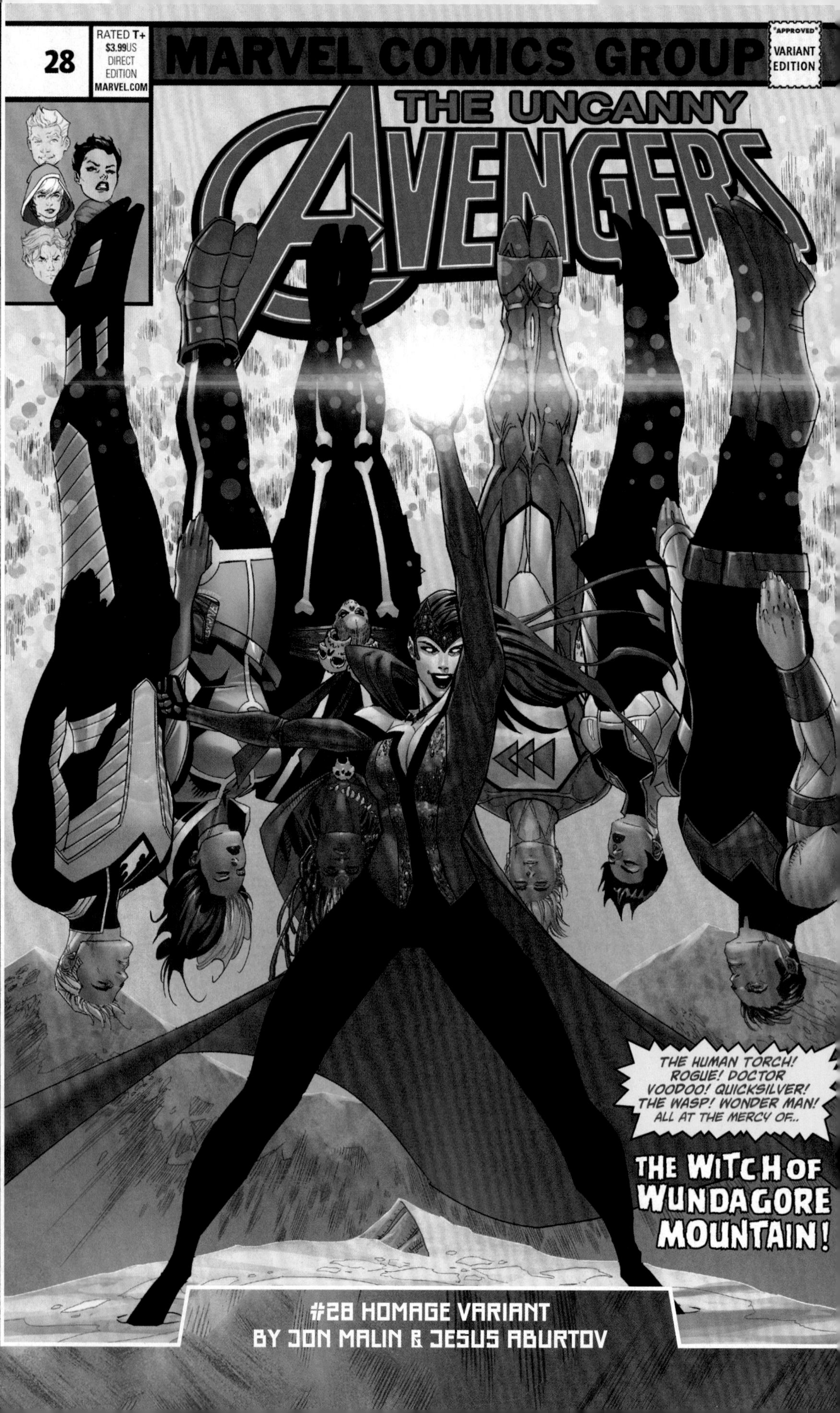
28
RATED T+
$3.99US
DIRECT
EDITION
MARVEL.COM
MARVEL COMICS GROUP
"APPROVED"
VARIANT
EDITION
THE UNCANNY
AVENGERS
THE HUMAN TORCH! ROGUE! DOCTOR VOODOO! QUICKSILVER! THE WASP! WONDER MAN! ALL AT THE MERCY OF...
THE WITCH OF WUNDAGORE MOUNTAIN!
#28 HOMAGE VARIANT
BY JON MALIN & JESUS ABURTOV

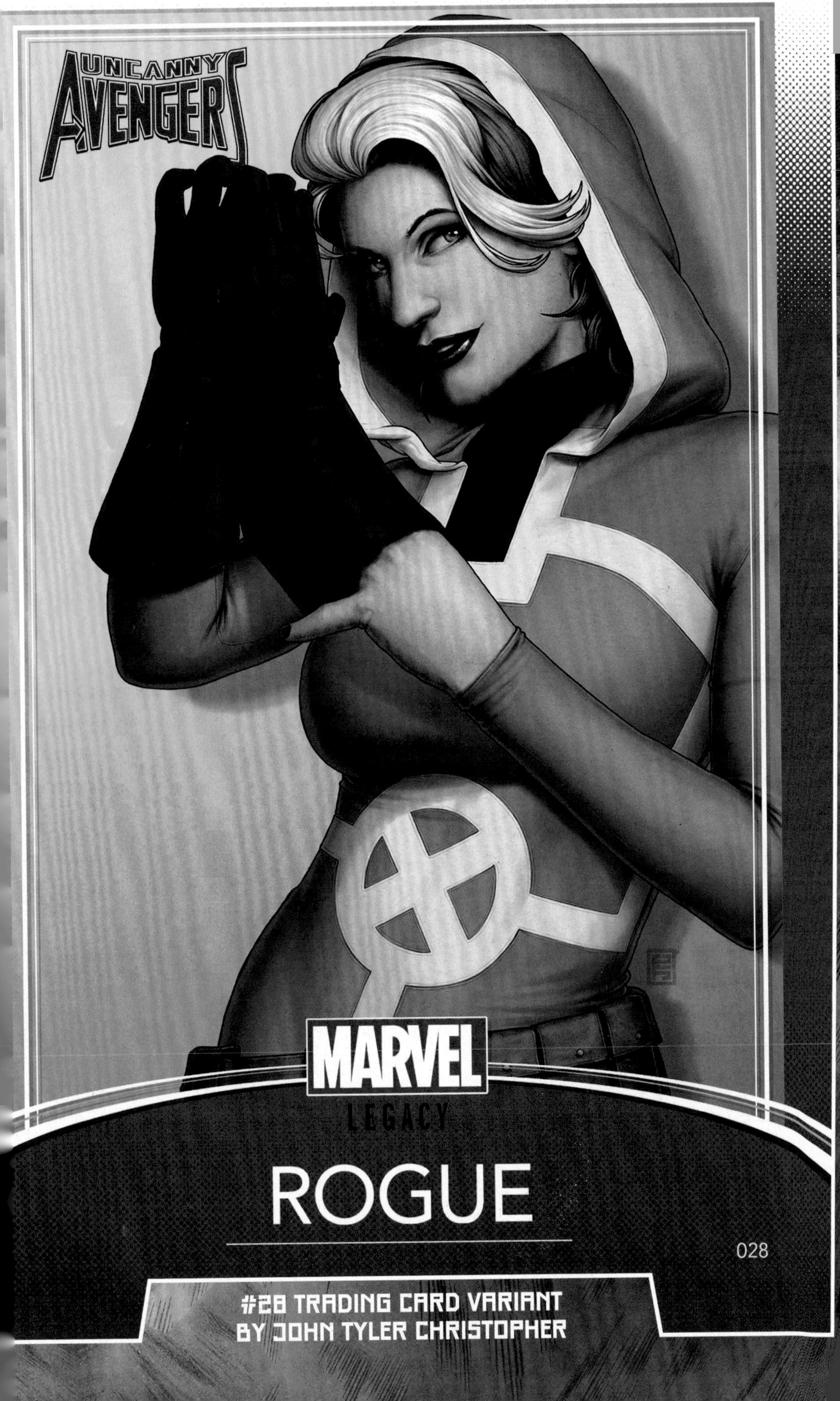
UNCANNY AVENGERS
MARVEL
LEGACY
ROGUE
028
#28 TRADING CARD VARIANT
BY JOHN TYLER CHRISTOPHER

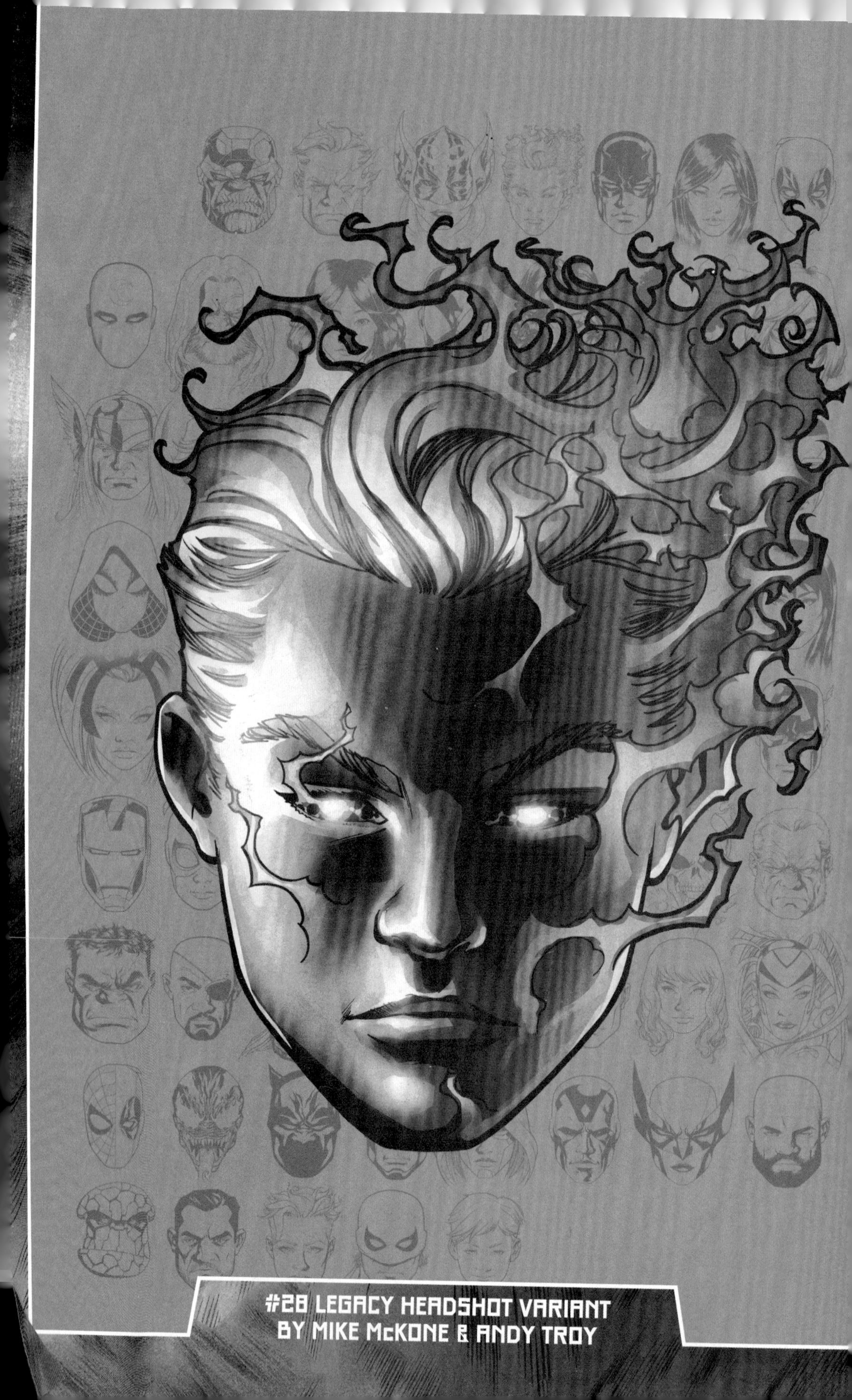

#28 LEGACY HEADSHOT VARIANT
BY MIKE McKONE & ANDY TROY